JOURNEY TO CERTAINTY

Journey to Certainty

The Quintessence of the Dzogchen View

An Exploration of Mipham's *Beacon of Certainty*

Anyen Rinpoche

Translated and edited by Allison Choying Zangmo

WISDOM PUBLICATIONS • BOSTON

Wisdom Publications
199 Elm Street
Somerville MA 02144 USA
www.wisdompubs.org

Library of Congress Cataloging-in-Publication Data
Anyen Rinpoche.
 Journey to certainty : the quintessence of the Dzogchen view : an exploration of
Mipham's Beacon of certainty / Anyen Rinpoche ; translated and edited by Allison Choy-
ing Zangmo.
    pages cm
 Includes translation from Tibetan.
 Includes index.
 ISBN 1-61429-009-1 (pbk. : alk. paper)
 1. Mi-pham-rgya-mtsho, 'Jam-mgon 'Ju, 1846–1912. Nes ses sgron me. 2. Rñin-ma-pa
(Sect)—Doctrines. 3. Rdzogs-chen. I. Graboski, Allison, 1974– translator, editor. II. Title.
 BQ7662.4.M533A68 2012
 294.3'420423—dc23

                                    2011048870

ISBN 9781614290094
eBook ISBN 9781614290179

16 15 14 13 12
 5 4 3 2 1

Cover design by Phil Pascuzzo. Interior design by Gopa&Ted2. Set in ITC Galliard Pro
10.3/14.4.

I offer this book to all of the genuine Lineage Masters, and especially to the one whose kindness is unequalled, the mighty Dharma sovereign Kyabje Tsara Dharmakirti Rinpoche.

Publisher's Acknowledgment

THE PUBLISHER gratefully acknowledges the generous help of the Hershey Family Foundation in sponsoring the publication of this book.

Table of Contents

Introducing Certainty

CHAPTER ONE

Introducing Mipham Rinpoche's
Beacon of Certainty

What Is Certainty?

T HE QUALITY CALLED "CERTAINTY" is an essential aspect of the Secret Mantrayana path, the pinnacle of which is the teachings of *Dzogchen*, or "the Great Perfection." In fact, I would go so far as to call certainty the *quintessence* of Dzogchen. The difference between an authentic yogi who abides in the perfectly pure view of the uncontrived dharmakaya and the yogi who merely *appears* to abide in that view is whether his or her practice has been preceded by and developed upon the bedrock of certainty.

As with much of the language used in the Vajrayana teachings, *certainty* is a word that is not easily defined, because the meaning of certainty changes depending on the individual practitioner. Our understanding of the word certainty, like our actual experience of certainty, will evolve and deepen as we progress along the spiritual path. Accordingly, this book is organized and presented to lead a Vajrayana practitioner into the ever-deepening and evolving experience of certainty.

In the beginning, certainty is merely an intellectual idea that is further developed through listening, contemplation, and often debate. If a practitioner is then trained by an authentic master of the Secret Mantrayana, certainty will naturally transition from an intellectual notion to an ever-deepening experience. Once we gain some experience of certainty, we develop a feeling of conviction that helps us to cut through doubts about the meaning of the profound instructions and view presented in Madhyamaka (Skt.; Middle Way) philosophy, the *Prajnaparamita* texts, and the tantras. This is irreversible certainty.

Finally, for the supreme yogi, certainty is imbued with the perfectly pure view itself. Thus we rest in certainty, and it becomes the experience of realization itself.

To perfect the ground, path, and result of Dzogchen, we must work on multiple levels—intellectual, experiential, and through resting in the view of meditation—to develop personal insight into certainty. Training in meditation cannot help us if we do not gain certainty in the experience of the perfectly pure view, including conviction as to what the view is and what it is not. We will remain mired in wildness or dullness, and overpowered by our habitual tendencies.

The great master Longchenpa said, "Until the state of duality sets into the vast expanse free of grasping, we must rely upon various methods of listening, contemplation, and meditation." This means that we should never stop refining our practice until we reach this ultimate state.

The Bridge Between Sutra and Tantra

Many Buddhists in the West are only interested in the most profound Tibetan Buddhist teachings of Mahamudra and Dzogchen. These practitioners mistakenly believe that the sutra teachings of the Causal Vehicle—the Buddha's teachings as presented in the first and second turnings of the Wheel of Dharma—are useless. They liken the study of the sutras to mere intellectualism that will not further their meditative experience. This is a mistaken way of thinking.

Many Westerners also undervalue the practice of *tonglen*, or sending and receiving; "Oh, I know that practice—that's just a breathing technique. It's a beginner's practice." This is also mistaken. These practitioners are not grounded in the teachings, nor is their energy grounded in practice. They seem to float from here to there, from one teaching to the next, and do not make much progress.

Buddhism in the West wears a very different face than the Buddhism of traditional Tibet. In Tibet, we understand the holistic, interrelated nature of the entire path, and that which comes earlier provides the foundation for what comes later. Outside of Tibet, though, much of this understanding has not penetrated deeply. As a result, we find that Western practitioners are confused about the importance of the sutras, and especially of Madhyamaka philosophy. As I see it, developing certainty is the great antidote to this problem. Traditionally, Mipham Rinpoche's *Beacon of Certainty* provides the bridge between sutra and tantra. In other words, by developing certainty from the coarsest level to the most profound conviction, we learn to bring the wisdom of the sutras to the teachings of Atiyoga Dzogchen, apply them, and to then abide in a more profound, perfect, and complete experience. This is the real meaning of Dzogchen: it is the all-inclusive, Great Perfection.

I cannot say there is no reason to study or practice at all if you do not know how to connect the wisdom of the sutras to the teachings of Atiyoga Dzogchen—but I will share with you a story that occurred when the great Indian yogi Atisha came to Tibet. At that time, all Tibetan people were practicing Dzogchen (or maybe they were just pretending to practice!), and when Atisha arrived, he discovered that the Tibetan yogis were actually practicing based on nothing more than a page or two of oral *upadesha* (Tib. *man ngag*; pith) instructions, with no other study or training as a foundation for these teachings.

Atisha advised the yogis that they should study volumes of the sutras and the more elaborate texts on Madhyamaka "as thick as the neck of a *zo*" (Tib.; hybrid cattle). We would all be wise to take Atisha's advice. We are all lucky to have the chance to develop our meditation through access to teachings by authentic lamas and studying profound texts like *The Beacon of Certainty*. Let's not waste this chance!

A Short Biography of Mipham Rinpoche

Reading the biography of a great teacher gives us a sense of trust or belief in what we are about to study. It helps us to realize that his or her teaching may hold a profound meaning for us. Mipham's biography also provides a context for his teaching style. Mipham Rinpoche often uses a debating style as he writes. In other words, he refutes the assertions of some philosophical schools while affirming others in order to make his point clear for the reader. Mipham Rinpoche's biography reveals his great respect for all four lineages of Tibetan Buddhism, his deep knowledge and understanding of their teachings, and also why he teaches from a particular point of view.

It is quite difficult to give the biography of a great bodhisattva like Mipham Rinpoche, because such a being's Dharma activity always appears in accordance with the beings that perceive it. It is like the way that the autumn moon, shining full in the sky, simultaneously appears slightly differently in different types of water, depending on the quality of the water. In this way, the lives of great masters will look different to each of us. Accordingly, here we will look at Mipham Rinpoche's biography in a way that is practical and supportive to our study.

Mipham Rinpoche was born into an extraordinary family lineage. The name of his family line is the Lineage of the Luminous Gods. His father was Gonpo Targye of the Ju Clan. Many great practitioners took birth from his father's ancestral lineage—not just lamas and scholars, but *siddhas* (accomplished yogis) and mantric healers. Mipham Rinpoche's great-grandfather was an emanation of the Medicine Buddha. His mother, Sing Chung, was of the Mukpo Clan, which descended from the great, enlightened King Gesar.

Interestingly, Mipham Rinpoche was not recognized as a *tulku*, an "emanation body" of a great lama, nor was he enthroned in a monastery when he was a child. He went through his training and education as an ordinary monk. His good qualities as a scholar soon brought him recognition in Tibet, however. This is very different than what happens today. In Tibet, children are now often recognized as tulkus when they are children; they are enthroned and treated specially. Some of these tulkus grow up to act worse than ordinary beings. But this was not the case with Mipham Rinpoche. He was recognized by others and revered simply because of his conduct, his intelligence, and his wisdom.

Mipham Rinpoche never claimed, "I am an emanation of Manjushri— I am special, I am smart." People could see his extraordinary nature anyway. They could not help but to see it. That is why I personally have such strong faith in great masters like Mipham Rinpoche.

From the time that Mipham Rinpoche was born in Kham in 1846, he displayed the qualities of a tulku: great compassion, loving-kindness, and selflessness. He did not exhibit arrogance or self-importance. He expressed his uncommon nature even while he was a small child. As an example, when Mipham Rinpoche was around age six or seven, he memorized the text *Ascertaining the Three Vows*. He began to compose teachings on scholarly texts when he was ten years old. Around age fifteen, he went to a monastery called Sang Ngak Choling, a branch of the Shechen Lineage. There, he took *getsul*, or apprentice, monastic vows. He was given the affectionate name Tsun Chung Khepa, which means "the small master."

Mipham Rinpoche's supreme *yidam* (Tib.; tutelary) deity was Manjushri. Between the ages of sixteen and seventeen, Mipham Rinpoche went to stay in a hermitage named Gyunang, and completed an eighteen-month solitary retreat on the Manjushri practice called *Jampa Malseng*. As a result of this retreat, he gained the ability to understand the meaning of the sutras and tantras merely by reading them, even without receiving empowerments, transmissions, or upadesha instructions.

Even though Mipham Rinpoche attained this extraordinary ability and did not really need to receive any more teachings, he relied on many, many masters. He received as many lineage teachings as he could to avoid the faults that can befall a practitioner who does not rely on great masters and also to keep lineages from being cut.

Mipham Rinpoche became the heart son of many great lamas, but two in particular were Patrul Rinpoche and Jamyang Khyentse Wangpo. His relationship with these lamas was such that it was like pouring the vase or the contents of one master's mind to the other; the qualities of their realization were indivisible. Mipham Rinpoche particularly relied upon the great master Jamyang Khyentse Wangpo with body, speech, and mind, doing exactly what his lama requested at any time. There is not even one account of Mipham Rinpoche failing to fulfill the request of his lama.

This is a difficult example for us to follow, but one thing we can take from this is to remember that when a lama asks us to do something, the lama is not doing it for his or her own benefit, but is pointing out something that could help us. Because Mipham Rinpoche had the wisdom and other good qualities to see this, he was able to put all of his lama's instructions into practice without questioning them.

One of the most important acknowledgments of Mipham Rinpoche's realization was his enthronement as an emanation of Manjushri. On the day of his enthronement, Jamyang Khyentse Wangpo made four enlightened declarations: that Mipham Rinpoche's realization was the same as the Buddha Maitreya's; that his knowledge and wisdom were equal to Manjushri's; that his ability in logic, debate, and philosophy was equal to Dharmakirti; and that his wisdom would penetrate all corners of the globe. At the end of the ceremony, Jamyang Khyentse Wangpo presented him with a *pandita's* hat. Mipham Rinpoche then was asked to compose texts for the benefit of all beings. In particular, he organized the teachings of the Nyingma tradition—which had been mainly a practitioner's tradition up until that point—so that they could be systematically studied.

He effortlessly and freely composed texts on topics from the *hinayana* up to the most profound teachings of Atiyoga Dzogchen. It was said that he spent all day in meditation and composed texts during his tea breaks. Along with the omniscient Longchenpa, Mipham Rinpoche is considered to be the source of the Nyingma doctrine.

Mipham Rinpoche also studied with another famous master of the Kagyu and Nyingma lineage, Jamgon Kongtrul Lodrö Thaye, from whom he received both ordinary and extraordinary teachings. With this lama, he studied not only Dharma teachings but also grammar, logic, and the arts and sciences.

Mipham Rinpoche was so brilliant that he designed many things that we see in modern technology today, such as airplanes. He developed elaborate plans for his new inventions, but after reflecting, he thought, "If a great scholar such as myself makes technology as important as Dharma practice, ordinary Tibetans will lose their faith in Dharma and they will simply start to follow after materialism." For this reason, Mipham Rinpoche destroyed all of the technological innovations that he designed. But we should know that his vast knowledge was not restricted simply to Dharma; it was all-encompassing.

Actually, I am very proud that Mipham Rinpoche is part of my heritage. Not only Western people are good at science! We Tibetans also had a technological genius among us!

The Eight Treasures of Courage

The last line of the prayer to Manjushri called "The Great Treasure of Blessings" references the attainment of the *eight treasures of cour-*

age, sometimes called the *eight treasures of liberation*. These qualities are manifested by a person who truly embodies or expresses the energy and the heart-mind of the yidam deity. It results in being able to effortlessly accomplish many activities that benefit beings. Mipham Rinpoche spent over thirteen years in retreat in meditation on his yidam deity Manjushri and attained all of these eight treasures as a result.

The first treasure is that of not forgetting words and meanings. The remaining treasures are the treasure of completely blossomed intelligence, the treasure of realizing the complete meaning of the sutras and tantras, the treasure of holding in the mind all things heard or studied, the treasure of courage to provide all beings with excellent teachings, the treasure of Dharma that enables one to protect the doctrine, the treasure of bodhichitta that is continuously inseparable from the Three Jewels, and the treasure of accomplishments that gives one the patience to forebear abiding in the unborn nature of the dharmakaya.

Mipham Rinpoche Was a Scholar of all Four Lineages

Mipham Rinpoche's study and interaction with great lamas of every Tibetan lineage demonstrates what it truly means to be "nonsectarian" (Tib. *ris med*). The idea of nonsectarian teachings is very popular these days. It is difficult to truly be free of prejudice or to avoid thinking your own way is the best. In Tibet, we say, "Claiming you are nonsectarian is really just a way to cover up your own prejudice."

There are wonderful stories about Mipham Rinpoche receiving teachings from various lamas who represented all four lineages of Tibetan Buddhism. In one story, he received a transmission of *Entering the Middle Way* from a Gelugpa *geshe* (Tib.; master scholar) named Bumsar. The Gelugpa lineage has a very beautiful tradition of testing you right after you receive a transmission. Mipham Rinpoche had only received a transmission—no commentary or teachings were given. When Bumsar Geshe asked questions, Mipham Rinpoche gave an entire commentary on the transmission he had just received. Bumsar Geshe was so surprised that in the middle of his monastery he announced that he had studied Madhyamaka and logic his entire life, but what he had learned in the past could not be compared to the knowledge that he had gained from the commentary that Mipham Rinpoche had just given him on the spot. This shows that Mipham Rinpoche was not a prejudiced scholar. He was the student of many great masters and he had no feeling that "my way is the best way."

Mipham Rinpoche not only studied with Gelug geshes but there are also stories of him becoming the student of great masters of other traditions. Once, the great Sakya master Loter Wangpo gave him a transmission of Sakya Pandita's *Treasury of Reasoning*. When he asked questions to test Mipham Rinpoche's understanding, Mipham Rinpoche composed a commentary of the text right on the spot as well. And this was not a one-time occurrence—actually, he was able to fully penetrate the meaning of any text right on the spot. I already mentioned that Mipham Rinpoche was the student of the great Kagyu-Nyingma master Kongtrul Lodrö Thaye, so we should remember that Mipham Rinpoche actively studied with masters of all four Tibetan Buddhist lineages.

We must examine the teachings of all Buddhist schools openly and honestly. It is important to realize that the ones we are drawn to study are dependent upon our own karma. It does not mean, for example, that the Nyingma teachings or the presentation of the Nyingma view is the best. But if we have a habitual tendency to practice this view, it is the best one for us. Because it is the best for us, we should study a text like *The Beacon of Certainty*, because Mipham Rinpoche's presentation is unmistaken and easy to understand. We should not think of our preferences as an absolute, however. The teachings that we connect with and choose to study are not absolutely better, they are just better for us.

When we examine the arguments of great scholars of different traditions, we make the teachings beautiful, real, and alive to us. There is no prejudice involved in this activity. It is simply a way that Buddhist scholars interact with each other. We can think of the four sects of Tibetan Buddhism as four paths to the top of a mountain; you can climb the mountain from any side. But again, you have to find the way that is right for you. When you use valid cognition to engage in a thorough examination of the path, it helps to find your way up the mountain. We'll explore the idea of "valid cognition" more in the next chapter.

Question and answer, debate and refutation, are the tools that help you find your way. In the same way that a precious stone becomes more and more beautiful with polishing, we use debate and refutation to make a particular teaching's precious qualities self-apparent. Although each of the schools of Tibetan Buddhism present the view differently, it is helpful to remember that these teachings were first given by great, realized siddhas, who experienced the view in a specific way. While their teachings were given as methods for others to follow and use, they are not necessarily the naked, direct meaning of the siddha's words. When followers took up the method, they may not have fully grasped the profound realization of the siddha's mind. So we can think of Mipham Rinpoche as clarifying or helping us to better understand the view through his text.

Mipham Rinpoche did not often speak about his skills or his experience to others. For example, when he was sixteen or seventeen, he directly saw a manifestation of Manjushri, the bodhisattva of transcendent wisdom, his yidam deity. He did not advertise this publicly, but he did tell a very few close students who later recounted it to others. In the same way, he did not brag about his own knowledge, unmistaken and flawless as it was. Instead, he often mentioned the good fortune he had to receive teachings from so many great scholars, even though he may not have had time to study, receive commentary on them, or to master them. When Mipham Rinpoche spoke of his own realization, he attributed it to his strong faith, diligent practice of the yidam deity, and putting the instructions of his lamas into practice.

Mipham Rinpoche recognized that he had developed uncommon certainty in the Dharma, but he never attributed that to his own effort alone.

The Purpose of Composing The Beacon of Certainty

To properly understand *The Beacon of Certainty*, to make the teachings meaningful and rich, we need to understand its background and the context of the times in which it was written. It is helpful to understand the philosophical arguments that Mipham Rinpoche responded to, and the general climate that surrounded him.

This particular text was composed at the request of Mipham Rinpoche's lama, Jamyang Khyentse Wangpo. At the time the request was made, there were other texts that explained the meaning of Dzogchen and the perfectly pure view. However, the specific request was to create a text that described the union and interconnection between the sutras and the tantras so that practitioners could properly listen to, contemplate, and meditate on teachings. The text was also to be written in accordance with sutra, tantra, and the upadesha instructions—the tradition of orally transmitting the pith instructions in the Secret Mantrayana— without contradicting any of these three, and to bring them all together as one.

Mipham Rinpoche had a pure motivation to fulfill his lama's request. This text was especially written for people who are good at talking about philosophy and meditation, but not quite as good at understanding how to put the teachings into practice. The topics in this text are explored by debate and an interchange of ideas. The debate does not come from a motivation of anger or contentiousness; rather, this kind of debate is used to dispel doubts and help clarify our understanding of each philosophical position. Also, we should not conclude that there is even a hair of negativity within this text despite the fact that there is a debate going on.

Mipham Rinpoche himself said that he felt no negativity toward the others he engaged in debate with while he composed his text. He also said that if a text is composed while completely free of anger, then it becomes an ornament of the teachings, a profound method to master the teachings—but anger is a corrupting force that takes away these good qualities.

We can make an analogy to scientific research, where engaging in academic debate actually improves scientific understanding over time. In this same way, a book—especially in this format—that engages in research, gathering information or ideas about other schools, and offers question and answer in debate, actually refines and makes the teachings much more profound because of the type of dialogue being engaged in.

As an example, a Gelug geshe named Geshe Losang Rabsel debated Mipham Rinpoche through a series of letters. The debate was not very friendly or kind-spirited in the beginning. There was disagreement and no real sense of mutual respect. Over time, however, the great qualities of both masters were revealed, and they became very great friends and ultimately became single-minded in their assertions about Dharma. They were not like ordinary people who get angry and fight or harbor resentments for a long time. They transcended all prejudice and partiality.

Losang Rabsel wrote the following verse in praise of Mipham Rinpoche:

> The clouds of Dharma-wealth gather in the sky,
> In the golden mandala of the place called Kham,
> [Above] the one whose fame resounds like the great drum
>   of the gods,
> I rejoice in the Dharma-king of definitive meaning!
> By the spark which ignites and burns the grass of all afflictions,
> The faults arising from them are essentially destroyed.
> Because of this, I decorate the expanse of sky
> With this stainless offering scarf of divine fabric,
> As white as the clouds, to the one whose body embraces
>   the earth.

People who have spent time around Buddhism may have heard that there are philosophical disagreements between the Nyingma and Gelug schools, and you may have even heard that Mipham Rinpoche did not speak kindly of the Gelug lineage or vice versa. That is absolutely not true; there was and is a great sense of mutual respect between masters of these lineages.

We should always examine our motivation when we want to compare the four schools of Tibetan Buddhism. We should not think that our school is superior to another, or make ourselves feel somehow special. This is a big mistake. People should not make those kinds of judgments between the schools and between teachers or Dharma groups. Be sure of the lineage you have a karmic connection with and follow that lineage seriously; take up that path with diligence—but do it all without disparaging others. Receive teachings from the other schools as a support to your main practice, following Mipham Rinpoche's example of impartiality.

Always use the path of Dharma for virtuous, good results. We should not use one path to denigrate another path—for doing so truly degrades the Dharma.

A Brief History of Khenpo Kunpal from Dzogchen Monastery

The author of the most well-known commentary on *The Beacon of Certainty*, which I have used as reference for these teachings, is a great scholar and Dzogchen master named Khenpo Kunzang Palden. Although there is disagreement as to the year of his birth, I believe he was born around 1862 because he was a close student of Patrul Rinpoche, who passed away in 1888. If he were born in the 1870s as some sources indicate, he would have been too young to receive extensive teachings from Patrul Rinpoche.

Khenpo Kunpal, as he is called, was born in Dzachukha Valley, in Kham. As a small child, he expressed great loving-kindness and deep compassion toward all beings, and was described as an ornament of bodhichitta. Based on renunciation, he took monastic vows and entered the gate of the Dharma. He relied upon the great Longchen Nyingthig master Onbo Tenzin Norbu as his first teacher at Dzogchen Monastery, receiving teachings on the sutras, tantras, and the traditional arts such as poetry. As he was very poor, without enough money for butter lamps to see by at night, he followed the moonlight throughout the night in order to continue his intensive studies. By dawn, he would discover that he had climbed to the top of a mountain peak, having followed the light of the setting moon. Many of his fellow monks teased him, saying that worldly people followed the sun to the peak of the mountain to take care of livestock during the day. However, Khenpo Kunpal and the moon went together to the top of the mountain in order to illuminate the meaning of the scriptures.

His uncommon lamas were Patrul Rinpoche, Mipham Rinpoche, the Fifth Dzogchen Rinpoche, and Jamyang Khyentse Wangbo. From these great masters, he received transmissions, empowerments, and teachings on the entirety of the *kama* and *terma*, the long lineage of teachings passed directly from the Buddha Shakyamuni and the "short" lineage of rediscovered treasures. Patrul Rinpoche was his uncommon root lama from the point of view of directly pointing out the nature of indivisible wisdom.

Khenpo Kunpal was incredibly poor. He wore tattered clothing and no shoes. During the winter, his feet became frostbitten; his skin split and bled. Seeing his bloody feet, Patrul Rinpoche blessed him, saying that because of his great diligence, one day he would have the ability to benefit many beings.

Later, Khenpo Kunpal went to the Kathok region where he became the first khenpo to give teachings and spread enlightened activity at Kathok Shedra, the monastic university in Kathok. There, he gave extensive teachings, sometimes teaching more than ten classes a day—and he never took even a single day off! His teachings always began with teachings about the importance of aspiration prayers and an uncontrived motivation of bodhichitta, and finished with a pure dedication of the merit. Khenpo Kunpal's teachings grew out of his great bodhichitta; he taught based on his own experience and realization of the teachings of Patrul Rinpoche and Mipham Rinpoche.

Khenpo Kunpal was a lama to many great masters who followed, including Pöpa Tulku, Kathok Sidu, Shechen Gyaltsab, Khyentse Chokyi Lodro, and the two Kathok Khenchens: Ngagchung and Nuden. He was also a lama to my own root lama, Kyabje Tsara Dharmakirti Rinpoche.

Khenpo Kunpal is well known for many great compositions, including his commentary to *The Beacon of Certainty* and a commentary to Shantideva's *Entering the Way of a Bodhisattva* that was composed in accordance with Patrul Rinpoche's own words. He dissolved into the *dharmadhatu* (Tib. *chos dyings*; basic space of phenomena) around age eighty-three.

CHAPTER TWO:

The Introductory Sections

Five Ways to Teach the Dharma

BEFORE BEGINNING the formal presentation of teachings on Mipham Rinpoche's great masterpiece, I want to describe the teaching style I will use. I regard this book as a companion guide to *The Beacon of Certainty*, rather than a formal commentary. It is meant to be a practical guide; a practitioner's guide to the spirit of the text.

Generally speaking, there are five ways to teach the Dharma, and we use all five in Nyingma tradition. These range in a continuum between a very detailed explanation and a more general approach.

The most detailed style is a scholarly oral explanation of a text called the *scholar's word guide*. The teaching is very subtle and quite long. Not even one word or phrase is left out when giving the teaching. On the other end of the spectrum is a very general style of transmission, usually given by someone of high status, called the *high-status coarse guide*. There may be no teaching at all given on the words; it is merely an empowerment or transmission.

A third style of teaching is called the *kusuli's condensed word guide*. A *kusuli* is a wandering yogi who carries only his realization with him. This is also a very condensed style of teaching, but the focus is on short, essential pithy phrases transmitted by an incredibly realized being. Padampa Sangye and Milarepa taught in this style.

The particular teaching style that I have chosen for this guidebook is called the *guide of experience*. In this style, the lama teaches based on his or her own experience of the meaning of the text as taught by the lineage masters, using modern language. This is in contrast to the scholarly approach, which uses philosophical terminology and may be inaccessible to practitioners without a scholarly background. The great master Gonpo Lhudrup praised this style, saying, "The understanding of the words is more important than a presentation of exact philosophical terminology."

Since I left Tibet, I have come to feel that this is the most effective way to teach modern practitioners. Without the benefit of our experience, students will not understand the meaning of the teachings. The relationship between the translator and the lama is also incredibly important. The translator has to know how to use general language to convey the lama's ideas, even if the lama is not able to do that in the English language.

Because I have focused on a *guide of experience*, the commentary will not cover every word or even every line of the text. Instead, I will present what I believe to be the most meaningful and useful ideas for modern practitioners, adding the words and ideas of other great masters where they shed light on a given topic and attempting to make this guidebook a roadmap of the path for the practitioner. In doing so, I have attempted to present the essential meaning of Mipham Rinpoche's marvelous text.

Finally, the fifth style is called the *arrogant one's obscured guide*. This happens when a person gives Dharma teachings that are not in accordance with tradition. The essential teachings of Dharma are not at all present. We should avoid listening to teachings like these at all costs!

With that in mind, let us turn to the introductory verses of *The Beacon of Certainty*.

The Title of the Text

The full name of this text is *The Precious Beacon of Certainty*. The Tibetan word for "beacon" can be translated into English in several different ways. It could be translated simply as "light" or "lantern." However, *beacon* is a better choice because a beacon from a lighthouse looks out over the ocean, guiding ships across the expansive waters and out of harm's way. This creates a beautiful Dharma metaphor, with Mipham Rinpoche's text helping us to see our way across the ocean of samsara.

What about the word *certainty?* We all have an ordinary, colloquial idea of the meaning of this word, and we may even have an idea about using the word *certainty* in the context of Dharma. We will reflect and deepen our exploration on the following two questions throughout our study of the text: What is the defining quality of certainty? What kind of certainty does a practitioner need?

We can start with a working definition: *Certainty is conviction in the essential meaning of profound great emptiness, the vast good qualities of Dharma, and the path that is difficult to generate and cannot be stolen by or undermined by anyone.*

Realization manifests, free of the darkness of doubt, through the cultivation of certainty. Doubt is likened to darkness, which obscures the aspect of appearance. As Mipham Rinpoche skillfully elaborates throughout his text, without the aspect of appearance, it is not possible to abide in the uncontrived view of Dzogchen. "Great emptiness" refers to emptiness endowed with appearance. Thus, in order to properly understand and experience the view of Dzogchen, we must be free of doubt's shadow. A final quality of certainty is that it is uncontrived; it cannot be faked or fabricated. Thus, we should begin to differentiate between authentic certainty and mere wishful thinking.

The Supports for Gaining Certainty

What brings us to a state of certainty? First, we must rely on the three-fold activity of listening to the teachings, contemplating their meaning, and putting the meaning into practice through meditation. I would say that of these three, listening or study is the most necessary. Listening to teachings, and developing faith based upon that listening, is the key to the precious treasury of certainty.

And what is the absolute necessity for any type of listening, contemplation, or meditation? The answer is, of course, bodhichitta. What is the perfectly pure motivation of bodhichitta? First, we focus on sentient beings and we think that any root of virtue that we attain through our listening and contemplation, we do for the benefit of self and others. This is called *conventional* bodhichitta.

Additionally, we should reflect that phenomena are like a dream or an illusion. If we understand this to mean the uncontrived state or, better yet, we understand it to mean the view of Dzogchen, we should rest in that understanding. This is *ultimate* bodhichitta. We should always strive to practice twofold bodhichitta in both our worldly life as well as the Dharma.

We need other supports to dispel the darkness of doubt. First, we need the support of clear intelligence, so that we can engage in personal examination. We need the opportunity to receive teachings, and we also need a spiritual friend, a lama. Without the benefit of a spiritual friend, even having clear intelligence is not particularly helpful. Not just any spiritual friend will do, however. We need to develop an uncommon relationship with a spiritual friend whom we continuously rely upon. In a sense, the relationship with the lama becomes like the support for research or study. We learn how the lama acts, we learn about the lama's conduct, we learn how the lama engages in Dharma—how he or she interacts skillfully with the world. In Tibet we say, "Whoever relies upon a mountain of gold will experience the whole world as gold." This metaphor perfectly describes the personal fruition we might experience if our practice relies upon a spiritual friend—who is as valuable to us as gold.

If we want to gain certainty in the perfectly pure view of Dzogchen, we need a very close relationship with a spiritual friend. We should not be lazy about developing such a relationship, or be fickle in our choice once it's undertaken—it is not like changing boyfriends or girlfriends!

Praise to Manjushri

Mipham Rinpoche begins with an offering of praise to Manjushri to create good dependent arising, or auspicious conditions, for the composition of the text. Stating that ordinary beings are always trapped in the net of doubt, he likens Manjushri to a light that, when placed in the vicinity of the heart and mind, dispels darkness completely. Khenpo Kunpal says, "[The lamp of Manjushri] successfully draws out perfectly pure certainty that cannot be stolen, and which is free of two-mindedness, exaggeration, and degeneration." Mipham Rinpoche advises us that offering prayers to Manjushri will help clear our own confusion.

The Two Eyes of Valid Cognition

The next idea presented in the introductory section is that of the two types, or two "eyes," of valid cognition. We will talk about valid cognition at length as we work through the text. At this point, a simple working definition will be adequate: *Valid cognition is using the intellect to correctly understand phenomena.* This definition generally refers to how we perceive ordinary phenomena.

In this case, the two types of valid cognition are the valid cognition of the conventional and the valid cognition of the ultimate; the two eyes are our understanding of conventional and ultimate reality.

It is a lovely metaphor to think of these two as being our eyes. If we were a person who had only one eye, we would be able to perceive *something*. While that perception would be ordinary to us, we would never see what somebody who has two good eyes could see. Even though we might not know the difference, our sight would always be incomplete. Similarly, when the two eyes of valid cognition are isolated from each other, we become unbalanced; we do not see properly. Without an understanding of both the conventional and the ultimate, it is impossible to gain unmistaken conviction in the unborn, uncontrived nature. We will talk about this much more in later sections.

When Mipham Rinpoche says that we need the two eyes of valid cognition to blaze the beacon of certainty, he is not talking from the point of view of the sutra, but from the point of view of the Secret Mantrayana—of being introduced to and abiding in the nature of mind.

Generally, the Dzogchen teachings include three distinct series of teachings, or styles of direct introduction. In Tibetan, these are the *semde* (Tib.; mind series), *longde* (Tib.; expanse series), and *mengnagde* (Tib.; pith series). For example, the *semde* is the series of mind transmissions in which all phenomena are recognized as the union of the conventional and ultimate truths or, synonomously, the union of method and wisdom. Without certainty, however, we lose the chance to receive these direct transmissions. Without the two eyes of valid cognition, we would be lost in the presence of a great master who says, "Abide in the union of emptiness and appearance." What will we do? How will we relate to those words? A Tibetan proverb says, "When the fog is thick, a fox cannot even find its own den." That is what your mind will be like—even though you are fortunate enough to hear the words of a master, you will feel confused and disoriented.

When we say that this text creates a bridge between sutra and tantra, this means that it creates a connection between ourselves and profound teachings that we would have a very hard time connecting with and relating to on an ordinary level. We can generally say that certainty gives us the potential to understand and recognize the uncontrived view of Dzogchen. *The Beacon of Certainty* presents this uncontrived view through the use of logic. Guidance from a master then enables us to transform that logical understanding into experience. For one who studies and practices in this way, there is great benefit in terms of actualizing the nature of mind.

Instantaneous recognition of the nature of mind, free from doubt, is quite rare without serious listening and contemplation as a foundation. It could only occur in a karmically endowed student such as Longchenpa. In contrast, as ordinary beings, our entire experience of the teachings can best be described as vague. The experience may seem clear in the beginning, but clarity wears off with time and we are left unsure of what we thought we knew. In other words, we lack certainty. When we do not have certainty about what the words of the teachings really point to, then all we have is confusion.

In summary, Mipham Rinpoche tells us that we need to rely upon the two eyes of valid cognition, that the fault of not having these two eyes is that we will not be liberated from samsara and we will be unable to understand the pith instructions or experience the nature of mind. Most importantly for us as practitioners, the two eyes of valid cognition will allow us to tell the difference between the mistaken and the perfectly pure path.

The Perfectly Pure Path

Mipham Rinpoche defines the perfectly pure path for us. All teachings in the sutra and tantra can be condensed into the ground, the path, and the result. The ground is defined as the indivisibility of the two truths, or the two eyes of valid cognition. The path is defined as the two accumulations, or method and wisdom. The result is defined as the manifestation of the two *kayas* (Skt.; enlightened body). It is important that we see that all of these contain a piece of the others. We can never separate the ground, the path, and the result.

The ground, path, and result are approached quite differently in the teachings of the so-called Causal Vehicles as opposed to the Resultant Vehicle, of which the Secret Mantryana teachings are a part. In the Causal Vehicle, the ground and path are taught to be the cause, and realization is taught to be the result. This can be aligned to the Four Noble Truths, where the truths of suffering, the origin of suffering, and the path are taught to be the cause, and the truth of cessation is taught to be the result. In the Resultant Vehicle, however, the ground, path, and result are all of an equal nature, since the nature of the phenomenal world is that of great purity and equality. Thus, the Resultant Vehicle is so-called because a practitioner takes up the result of primordial wisdom as the path and then actualizes that experience as realization. The dichotomy of cause and effect does not describe the relationship between sentient beings and buddhas, the way it does in the Causal Vehicle.

Over the course of our study of this text, when we hear teachings about the perfectly pure path, we might think to ourselves, "Mipham Rinpoche called this the perfectly pure path and I *probably* agree." This is not the meaning of certainty. As practitioners, we should achieve personal understanding and experience. We should not simply accept what is being taught at face value—but we should verify and validate it for ourselves. This too is part of the meaning of "certainty."

Buddha Nature

Another reason why *The Beacon of Certainty* acts as a bridge between the sutra and tantra teachings can be understood in relation to the perfectly pure path. It has to do with the idea of buddha nature. The sutras give us general ideas of the mind's basic nature or ground. These ideas are further developed in the tantras by presenting the idea of buddha nature, the basis for self-arisen intrinsic awareness or *rigpa*. These ideas make more sense when they are developed one upon the other in the same way that the ground, the path, and the result make sense when they are not separated.

We need to gain personal understanding of and experience in rigpa. The experience of rigpa is a crucial part of the Dzogchen teachings, especially when we talk about *indivisible rigpa* and emptiness—or abiding in the perfectly pure, uncontrived view. When we have gained some understanding of the meaning and experience of rigpa, buddha nature, and the ground, then when the lama introduces us to the nature of mind, it is like seeing an old friend.

Our practice and study can be compared to walking to the top of a long hill. As we walk, we gain experience and notice all of the dangers and details of what is happening around us. We get to know where we are very intimately. On the other hand, if we were simply dropped onto the top of the mountain peak, while we would be at the same place as if we had walked there, we would lack personal certainty about what is below us or how to get up again. This is like the difference between working with both the sutra and tantra, and jumping in without any reference point.

The Mistaken Path

The mistaken path can be described as the path of a practitioner with little or no experience who receives many teachings and "sort of" practices. Some people also like to use the phrase "on and off" to describe their practice. This is the mere appearance of a Dharma practitioner. Another way the mistaken path manifests is that we may feel extremely passionate about the Dharma for about a year—we burn like fire, we are thoroughly diligent in our practice, and receive an ocean of teachings and empowerments—then, one day, we just stop. This happens because we lack certainty in many aspects of the path. We lack certainty in the truth of suffering and in the potential of the path to lead us to manifest wisdom. We lack certainty and conviction in the benefits of life-long Dharma practice.

Being passionate can sometimes be a good quality, but in terms of

Dharma practice, having a tempered passion is a much better quality. When our energy gets too high, we lose our enthusiasm. It is better to be moderate and to temper our enthusiasm so that we do not run out of energy.

Valid Cognition, Examination, and Certainty

Each of us needs to use our own intelligence as we progress along the Buddhist path. We can describe what happens if we don't do this by using the analogy of what happens when a dog sees a deer. As soon as the dog sees the deer, it begins to chase it. The dog engages in no examination; it does not stop to think about whether it should follow the deer or not. It just runs. We must not approach the Dharma like that.

Specifically, we need to use valid cognition to examine both the lama and the path. First, we need to examine the lama's qualities as a teacher, and ensure that the lama holds an authentic lineage. The most important thing is to find a lama who truly embodies bodhichitta. When we become free of doubt about the lama's good qualities, then we should work at becoming skilled at relying on the lama. We should also work on developing trust and a personal relationship with the lama. When we achieve this kind of certainty, the lama-student relationship has a sense of ease about it because there is no mental or emotional struggle.

Before we go any further, we can also relate valid cognition to certainty. One of the really big problems we can have when we get into the realm of examination is that our neuroses take over. We never really get to the point where we are done examining and ready to move on. We become cynics and skeptics. We never want to accept anything, so we just keep examining.

Remember that certainty is our beacon. We should examine the lama and the path, but once we find certainty in what we have been examining, we should put it into practice. This style of examination complements meditation, but it does not replace meditation. Basically, we meditate to gain experience in what we are examining. Then based on that experience, we are able to examine more deeply. Over time, this transforms our meditation. As we progress through this profound wish-fulfilling jewel, remember to bring examination together with meditation in order to work toward certainty.

Setting the Stage for the Teaching

Mipham Rinpoche begins with praise for the truly great sages Chandrakirti and Dharmakirti, who attained the "sky-like ultimate nature" and clearly see the nature of conventional phenomena. He then describes an encounter between a wandering mendicant and a great, honest-minded sage who has used valid cognition to engage in thorough examination as a support for practice and realization. The mendicant has doubts that must be cleared away before he can accept the philosophy of the Dharma.

Who are the sage and the wanderer? They are not identified in the text, but I think that both the sage and the wanderer are Mipham Rinpoche. This is a poetic encounter; it is a mental encounter between Mipham Rinpoche's own valid cognition, which is engaging in honest examination, and the sage who will answer and clarify any doubts.

Khenpo Kunpal's commentary says that the wanderer is trying to "analyze that which is hard to realize." What is it that is hard to realize? There are two things. The first is profound emptiness. The second is the vast qualities that come to fruition on the *bhumis* (Skt.; levels of realization) and paths. In the *Beacon*, there are seven key questions posed by the mendicant, and each question is related to understanding and realizing the meaning of emptiness, as well as the ever-deepening experience of realization itself. We'll explore the seven questions in more detail starting in the next chapter.

The root text goes on to say that these questions are extremely difficult to answer. These questions have been asked of the scholars of all four schools of Tibetan Buddhism many times. Mipham Rinpoche mentions that he has read their answers, but he cannot just follow the words of others. A person who just follows the words of others cannot be given the name "scholar" and does not deserve the praise of a scholar.

When we just follow another's words, our understanding and our practice has no real substance. Again, this is a result of a lack of certainty. You may study with or have the fortune to meet a lama who has directly seen the face of Manjushri. But sometimes students of this lama will start to say, "I have seen Manjushri, too," even though that is not true. This is really what Mipham Rinpoche is talking about. He tells us directly that we should use our own valid cognition and intellect to cultivate certainty and experience realization for ourselves—and not to puff ourselves up and claim we are realized when we are not.

The commentary says, "Unlike the scholar who just follows after the words of others, you should perfectly and completely examine for yourself the subjects that are hard to realize, and relax, in order that you can make a subtle examination." This comment emphasizes abiding in honesty. We should use our own intelligence to examine the profound Madhyamaka and make our examination free of prejudice or cunning. We are relaxed because there is no deception or game-playing going on in the mind. As Dharma practitioners, honesty is incredibly important. Our meditation should be perfectly pure; it should be free of self-deception. We should be clear about what we know and what we do not know. We should be okay with both knowing and not knowing, because both are a basis to work from. We should know if something is or something is not. And if we are not sure, we should focus on working toward getting to a point where we are sure.

Mipham Rinpoche says that an answer given while abiding in honesty will create "proof through speech." He means that the answer, in itself, can constitute proof because an honest answer has the ring of truth; we recognize it as being true. The great master Patrul Rinpoche is such an example; he always abided in honesty when he answered questions and gave teachings. As a result, his teachings are not only melodious and eloquent to listen to, but they are easy to access; their honesty rings true to us and we can relate to them for that reason.

The commentary describes the topics in this text as vast, expansive, and extremely difficult to realize. The answers are like a great, deep ocean of profound Dharma. As a result, there is a danger that we could be brazen or mercenary, wanting to use the Dharma for fame, for attaining recognition from others, without regard to the meaning of the profound sutra and tantra. Mipham Rinpoche warns us of this danger; it will cause us to accumulate negative karma, and in the end, to abandon the Dharma. He gives the example of a man from a poor family who dares to have an affair with the king's wife and is suddenly in danger of losing his life.

This is a very, very good message for us. Right now, we can see all kinds of spiritual teachers in the West, we can read all kinds of Buddhist books in the West, and we can listen to all kinds of teachings, even on the Internet or YouTube. We should always try to cultivate pure perception and not use the Dharma for selfish purposes.

Regarding our own limited experience with the Dharma, always keep in mind the famous Tibetan story of the frog in the well, who thinks he knows the meaning of the word "ocean" from inside his small space—his small mind. One day, when he truly encounters the vastness of the ocean, he faints. We should know that we are all frogs. We have never been to the ocean.

CHAPTER THREE:

Introducing the Seven Questions

A METAPHOR OF POLISHING a precious stone is often used to describe scholarly debate and discussion. To make the Dharma teachings more beautiful and eliminate what is unnecessary, we polish the teachings using scriptural quotations and logic. Mipham Rinpoche takes this ordinary Dharma activity to another level in *The Beacon of Certainty*, which is why this text accomplishes the incredible feat of bringing sutra and tantra together. As I said earlier, he not only wants to polish the teachings from the point of view of the scriptural quotations and logic in the sutras and tantras, but also from the point of view of the upadesha, the pith instructions. Because it is difficult to unify these three, he uses the exercise of asking and then answering seven questions to accomplish it. As such, based on our own exploration of these seven questions, we should each come to a place where we too can unify the sutras and the tantras in our own minds.

What follows is simply a short introduction to each of the seven questions.

THE FIRST QUESTION: *Many scholars who teach on the ultimate view teach that it is a nonaffirming negative; some teach it as an affirming negative. Which one of these is the ultimate view that is not in contradiction with scripture, logic, and the upadeshas? Which one of them really is in accord with the meaning of the unborn, ultimate nature?*

Mipham Rinpoche assumes we have studied basic Madhyamaka logic, including establishing the uncontrived view through cutting through the four extremes of existence, nonexistence, both, and neither. If we have not studied these teachings, we may want to review basic Madhyamaka logic as presented in Nagarjuna's *Root of Wisdom* and the other texts in his Madhyamaka collection, Khenpo Bodhisattva's *Ornament of the Middle Way* with commentary by Mipham Rinpoche, and Chandrakirti's *Entering the Middle Way.*

Building on our understanding of basic Madhyamaka logic and cutting through the four extremes, a few definitions will help us begin to understand this question. A "nonaffirming negative" negates a position without establishing a new position in its place. In other words, it negates another's position while also saying that "My own position is not established."

An "affirming negative," on the other hand, negates the position and then goes on to make a positive statement like, "Therefore, the opposite must be true." For example, saying, "It's not dark outside," implies that it is light. The affirming negative is like a coin with two sides. When you say, "It is not this side," you imply that it is the other one. However, the nonaffirming negative is like a coin with only one side. When you say, "It is not this side," there is no other side to implicate.

Taking the position of the nonaffirming negative as the view puts us in danger of falling into the extreme of nihilism. Similarly, taking the affirming negative as the view puts us in danger of falling into the extreme of permanence. However, when we talk about the perfectly pure view, it must be free of both of these extremes of nihilism and permanence; we call it the *uncontrived view of Dzogchen.* So Mipham Rinpoche's response to this question will be quite useful to help us to properly understand the uncontrived view.

We may be tempted to think that we understand these ideas well when we actually have only a shallow understanding, that once we know what an affirming and a nonaffirming negative are, there is no reason to go beyond that. We should understand that when we truly study and understand these ideas, they help us to avoid falling into extremes when we actually sit down on the cushion to meditate. For that reason, it is worth our time and energy to master these ideas, rather than just learn a little bit about them.

THE SECOND QUESTION: *Do shravaka and pratyeka arhats realize both the selflessness of phenomena and the selflessness of the individual? If they do realize both, is this contrary to logic, scripture, and the upadeshas? If they do not realize both, is this contrary to logic, scripture, and the upadeshas?*

The shravaka and pratyeka arhats are highly realized beings who have attained the pinnacle of the Hinayana vehicle: liberation from samsara. They are not on the Mahayana path of the bodhisattva. Because their path is different, their realization is different from a Mahayana master's. Through this question, we will explore the idea that complete realization must consist of two different kinds of selflessness: the selflessness of the individual and of phenomena.

The selflessness of the individual means that a person and the ego do not truly exist, that there is no real "me." The selflessness of phenomena expands this realization to all phenomena. There is no phenomenon that is permanent, solid, or existent.

THE THIRD QUESTION: *When abiding in the unborn, ultimate nature, is conceptual grasping present or not?*

When we practice meditation, we generally divide it into the actual meditation session, a period of time when we sit down to meditate, and then the period that comes after. This question has to do with the actual meditation period. A more detailed version of this question is: *When we abide in meditation, if conceptual grasping is present, does that embody the true meaning of the unborn nature? If there is no conceptual grasping, does that embody the true meaning of the unborn nature?*

Perhaps the answer to this question, which we will cover in detail later, depends on our current experience as meditation practitioners. For example, beginning practitioners will find that grasping is present during "meditation" practice. There is analysis. There are concepts. And, at this point, those concepts are necessary.

A meditator who has received upadesha instructions, however, should understand that meditation is completely free of grasping and analysis. So we are actually using the same word *meditation*, but we define it differently based on our own experience as practitioners.

THE FOURTH QUESTION: *When one meditates, should one use analytical meditation or should meditation be done with no analysis at all?*

There is a good reason for us to reflect on this question. It is possible that a lama or other teacher of meditation could teach that meditation is simply an experience of a lack of concepts, examination, or thinking. In fact, many people have told me that they have heard that meditation is "stopping the mind," or "being free of thoughts." This question gets at what we actually do when we sit down to practice.

For beginning practitioners, if analysis does not precede meditation, then what do we actually meditate on? Analysis is critically important in the beginning. Analysis creates the potential for gaining certainty in what meditation is, so that we can go beyond analysis. We can then say that the supreme yogi transforms all concepts into the experience of meditation and, at that point, meditation is completely free of analysis.

THE FIFTH QUESTION: *Of the two truths, is the conventional or the ultimate more important?*

The short answer to this question is that the conventional and the ultimate are equally important. But if we do not know conventional truth, we cannot know the ultimate. We can also describe these by saying that the conventional is "method" and the ultimate is "that which arises from method": in other words, wisdom.

THE SIXTH QUESTION: *The six types of beings see phenomena according to the way things appear to them, but are common objects the basis for perception?*

This is an important topic because it has to do with how stubborn and egotistical we are. We are extremely set in our ways. We think that we are right and we do not want to hear the ideas of others. It is very hard to understand that the interpretation of conventional reality that we perceive as being perfect and true is not perfect and true from another person's point of view. This topic explores how our perceptions might not be correct or even understandable for another person. From the point of view of the six types of beings, even the element of water appears differently to those beings because of their karma, their personalities, habitual tendencies, and sense faculties.

It is impossible to tell other people how they should perceive things. Through asking this question, Mipham Rinpoche tells us not to be too consumed by our own way of thinking. When we hear another person's perspective or ideas, we should reflect upon and examine them. We should check them against our own ideas; we should eradicate any faults that we find in our own perspective and refine and polish our understanding. This is very different from the act of judging or saying that another person's perspective is wrong.

THE SEVENTH QUESTION: *In our own tradition of Madhyamaka, is there any position taken? If so, is that contrary to scripture, logic, and the upadeshas?*

The answer to this question will bring together the meaning of the entire text. Mipham Rinpoche skillfully weaves together teachings from all of the preceding topics into one comprehensive section that presents the authentic meaning of Prasangika Madhyamaka philosophy.

After presenting his seven questions, the wanderer says to the sage, "Please answer the question without contradicting the meaning of scripture, logic, and the upadeshas, using factual reasoning, and give an answer that is true and unmistaken."

The Flow of the Commentary

Mipham Rinpoche follows a general pattern when he teaches each topic. If we understand and anticipate this, it will enhance our understanding of the text and also of his insights into the seven questions.

First, he presents the question. Then, he begins his argument by presenting a position he calls the "other position"; one that he does not find perfectly logical. He reveals the logical flaws in that argument. Then, he teaches on what he calls "our own tradition," or a position that he finds to be the proper understanding, usually in several stages of detail. By using this methodology, it becomes easy to see the difference between the two positions and why Mipham Rinpoche puts forth the understanding that he does. Mipham Rinpoche and Khenpo Kunpal also invoke the words of other great masters in the root and commentary, namely the omniscient Longchenpa, as authoritative voices on realization.

Mipham Rinpoche notes that these questions have been asked of many skilled and famous scholars, but that no scholar has been able to answer them without contradicting scripture and logic.

Mipham Rinpoche's sage ends these introductory verses by saying that he has the confidence to answer the seven questions posed by the wanderer based on the blessing of Manjushri. Thus, this dialogue between the sage and the wanderer becomes an expression of humility. It allows Mipham Rinpoche to avoid taking any credit for composing this text or for claiming to have any transcendental knowledge whatsoever. This shows the contrast between ordinary scholars who are relying on analytical intelligence and the answers in this text, which come purely from the blessings of wisdom.

Three Things to Keep in Mind with Debate

There are three things to keep in mind every time we start to read and analyze a philosophical argument. You should clarify these for yourself in each of the seven topics.

First, what assertion is being made? This is like the target. If we shoot an arrow, we have to know where the arrow is going. We have to know how much distance there is between the target and ourselves or we will not understand the ideas we are trying to work with. So, we need to know the assertion being made by our "opponent."

Second, what is the refutation? Why does the author believe the assertion is flawed? If we cannot understand the refutation, we will not understand the purpose of the argument.

Third, what is the position of the author? Authors have a goal to teach something, and will use assertions and refutations to make their point clear. What does the author wish to convey?

EXPLORING CERTAINTY
THROUGH THE SEVEN QUESTIONS

❧ ·❧

CHAPTER FOUR

The First Question

*—Do you explain the view according to an affirming
negative or a nonaffirming negative?*

THIS SECTION PROVIDES an introduction to Buddhist philosophies that assert the ultimate view as the nonaffirming negative,
the affirming negative, and the uncontrived state, free of all extremes.

Rangtong and Shentong

Although the words of this question seem difficult to understand, the
underlying meaning is simple. As Mahayana Buddhists, we all agree
that beings and phenomena are empty. But what are they empty of?
Are they empty of themselves or empty of something else?

In Buddhist philosophy, these descriptions of emptiness have formal
names. For example, *Rangtong* (Tib.; empty of self) is the common
term for a philosophy that asserts that beings and phenomena are empty
of themselves. Another way to describe this is by saying that they are
intrinsically empty, meaning empty from the inside. On the other hand,
Shentong (Tib.; empty of other) is the name given to a philosophy that
asserts that phenomena are empty of something outside themselves.
Therefore, the philosophy designates objects and beings as *extrinsically
empty*, meaning empty from the outside.

Before we go any further, I would like to give a working definition of
emptiness. *Emptiness* means that phenomena do not have a truly established nature. *Truly established* is another way of saying permanent and
unchanging. The logical implications of whether a philosophical school
is Rangtong or Shentong will become clear as we explore Mipham
Rinpoche's presentation of this first topic.

Done properly, the tradition of reading and studying philosophy supports a style of analytical meditation. Reflecting on philosophical ideas becomes a contemplative practice. When we read and contemplate the ideas of others, it not only makes our intelligence sharper, but we also begin to cultivate a sense of intellectual certainty. As we observe the play of ideas, we see them more clearly; a deeper understanding comes to us. For example, emptiness may seem one-dimensional, but when you study it this way, it comes alive. We begin to develop a personal relationship with it.

The Benefit of Understanding the Different Presentations

Comparing these two presentations of emptiness and discussing different presentations of the view helps us become familiar with each presentation's strengths and weaknesses, whether it is the Rangtong view assertion of the Later Scholars (and in this context I mean those who are followers of Je Tsongkhapa), the view of Shentong, or the Nyingma presentation of the Rangtong view. Then we can be very sure of the meaning of the words and ideas of a philosophy. Once we reflect on the teachings of different lineages and understand them in context, we become free of doubts. In other words, we begin to gain certainty.

When we do not actually study this topic, what happens when we hear teachings is that based on our own interpretation of the teachings on emptiness, we create our own meditation techniques. These self-created techniques will never match those presented by the great masters. The perfect result of realizing emptiness can never ripen and we will not be able to actualize the meaning of the Secret Mantrayana. Our goal in this chapter, therefore, is to engage in an unmistaken examination of what the teachings on emptiness mean and begin to develop our understanding of the uncontrived view based on that understanding.

The Assertion of the Later Scholars

The position asserted by the Later Scholars is that phenomena are intrinsically empty, or that they are empty of themselves. I refer to this as the Later Scholars' assertion of Rangtong—it is the Rangtong view asserted in the style of the Later Scholars. That phenomena are empty of themselves is a logical idea. However, Mipham Rinpoche will examine whether the Later Scholars truly assert intrinsic emptiness, or whether the logical implications of their position cause them to fall into extrinsic emptiness.

We will begin by examining the Later Scholars' reason for asserting the intrinsic emptiness of phenomena. This may be difficult to follow at first, especially if you are new to the tradition of philosophical debate, but if you practice patience, it will become clearer as you read and reflect on it—this is not a topic that one understands on the first reading! Also, of the seven topics, topic one is by far the most difficult to understand intellectually.

We will begin by examining the starting assertion of the Later Scholars, which gives the reason for asserting intrinsic emptiness: "If the essence of the self, the buddha nature of the *tathagathas*, were not empty, then the self would be permanent. It would be no different than the permanent self taught by non-Buddhists." In this case, if the self were permanent, then the three gates of liberation, or the mind's empty nature, clear essence, and omnipresent compassion, could not arise. Additionally, if buddha nature were not empty of itself, then clear light wisdom as described in the tantras would also be impossible.

Mipham Rinpoche adds that failing to assert the intrinsic emptiness of phenomena would contradict the scriptures of definitive meaning given in the second and third turnings of the Wheel of Dharma, where the nature of mind is asserted to be of an empty essence and clear nature. It would also contradict assertions made in scriptures composed by the Regent Maitreya, for example, in the *Ornament of Clear Realization* and the *Uttaratantra*, and Nagarjuna's *Six Collections of Madhyamaka Logic*, among others.

The Later Scholars have carefully crafted their philosophical presentation. Their school is part of a Madhyamaka tradition known as the "Madhyamikas who follow after worldly opinions." In other words, they are deeply concerned with preserving the conventional way that ordinary people communicate about and understand the ordinary world, so as not to frighten or confuse them. They avoid asserting the nonexistence of conventional phenomena, because they worry that this goes against what ordinary people believe about the world. In philosophical terms, we say they want to avoid deprecating conventional reality.

For this reason, the way the Later Scholars assert intrinsic emptiness can seem counterintuitive. Let's take the example of a cup. We have said that the Later Scholars do not want to suggest in any way that the cup does not exist, because all people agree that the cup is an object that exists. So, when they assert intrinsic emptiness, they do so by distinguishing between the essence of the cup (its "cupness") and its truly established nature. They say, "The cup is not empty of its own essence, but it is empty of having a truly established nature." The use of the word *essence* here is merely a reference to the physical presence and seeming solidity of the cup as experienced by ordinary people.

Recall that "empty" means empty or free of a truly established nature. We can also say that *emptiness* means being free of true characteristics, established characteristics, or conceptual characteristics. To say it yet another way, if phenomena can be truly established through their own characteristic natures, then they are not empty.

What about the phrase "truly established nature"? Something that is truly established is permanent and unchanging. This is the meaning of the word "exists." When we engage in a period of examination using valid cognition and Madhyamaka logic, we say that a truly established phenomenon "can withstand analysis." In other words, it cannot be broken down into parts and pieces, and therefore, it is not based on the coming together of causes and conditions. If a phenomenon cannot withstand analysis, this means that we can take it apart piece by piece until its empty nature becomes self-apparent. For example, this book cannot withstand logical analysis because it is made of paper, ink, and words. The paper and ink are made up of atoms, electrons, and so forth. As we break it down, it no longer resembles a "book." That is an example of what it means to say that a phenomenon's empty nature becomes self-apparent.

We can also contrast the way something appears with the way it abides. A pen appears conventionally in a way that everybody agrees on. We know its size and its function and its characteristics. This pen also has a way that it abides ultimately—it is empty, it is impermanent, and it lacks true establishment.

In philosophical texts, the classic example used to exemplify the Later Scholars' position is a pillar. A typical way to present the assertion is: "The pillar is not empty of the essence of the pillar. The pillar is empty of inherent existence."

Now we can see why the Later Scholars' position of emptiness is a nonaffirming negative. Recall that a nonaffirming negative is a negation that does not imply or implicitly establish any other position. From the Later Scholars' point of view, once the pillar's truly established nature is cut through, the essence of the pillar remains, but this does not imply or establish any position (existence, for example) about the nature of that appearance. Thus, the ultimate view is asserted as a nonaffirming negative. At this point, we should have a basic understanding of the first half of Mipham Rinpoche's question: *Is it correct to understand ultimate reality as a nonaffirming negative?*

Empty of Its Own Essence

Many questions probably came up after reading the Later Scholars' basic assertion. What does it mean to say that the pillar is not empty of its own essence and that we are only cutting through the existence of a truly established nature of the pillar? This is a difficult question, but we will come to understand it if we are patient. A further exploration of the Later Scholars' understanding of Rangtong will help us develop a better basis for our own overall understanding.

Regarding the Later Scholars' basic assertion of the emptiness of phenomena, I already mentioned that the reference to a phenomenon's "essence" is a reference to the conventional appearance of phenomenon. No essence can exist in the sphere of ultimate reality. Additionally, from the Later Scholars' point of view, if you assert that the conventional essence of the cup is empty, then the cup itself will cease to exist in conventional reality. But a cup appears; we see it, we can use it! The Later Scholars do not want to contradict this appearance; they abstain from making any assertions about conventional reality at all.

Similarly, when we talk about cutting through the truly established nature of the cup, we are also talking about the conventional sphere. If a reference to establishment is present at all, it could only be in the context of the conventional.

Actually, this begins to make sense once we introduce another idea from Later Scholars' philosophy. The Later Scholars also assert that once you refute the four extremes of existence, nonexistence, both existence and nonexistence, and neither existence nor nonexistence, as we do in Madhyamaka philosophy, that the refutations become never-ending. For example, when you refute the extreme of existence, the refutation of the extreme of existence also has to be refuted using the four extremes. And then for each of those four extremes you refute, there are another four extremes. The refutation of the four extremes goes on infinitely.

Therefore, the Later Scholars decided to qualify their refutation of the four extremes as being made only from the point of view of ultimate reality. So, ultimately, we would say that there is no existence, ultimately there is no nonexistence, and ultimately there are not both existence and nonexistence, ultimately there are not neither existence nor non-existence. They do not address conventional reality at all. They leave conventional reality exactly as it appears, without analysis.

Thus, if we are a Later Scholar, we do not want to say that the pillar is empty of the pillar because that statement deals with conventional reality. The real object of refutation is the truly established nature of that pillar; it is the conceptual idea of that pillar. Their refutations only occur in the sphere of ultimate reality. For all of these reasons, the Later Scholars posit the nonaffirming negative to be the ultimate view. *In sum, the Later Scholars wish to cut through the truly established nature of all phenomena while not establishing any other position.*

Here is another way to think about it: It is as though, stuck on the side of every single conventional object, there is a label called "true establishment." The Later Scholars want to cut through that label of true establishment and remove it from the side of those objects. They argue that by doing so, this establishes intrinsic emptiness. It seems that by doing this, the Later Scholars are putting some space between conventional and ultimate reality. When they attach the label of true establishment to the object and refute that, the consequence is that they can establish emptiness ultimately without even touching conventional reality.

As a result, the appearance of an entity and its truly established nature become two different things, because one is refuted and found to be empty, but not the other. Actually, they must be separated for this philosophy to be consistent; otherwise to refute one *would be* to refute the other.

The Later Scholars have a good reason and motivation for putting space between conventional and ultimate reality. Beings have very strong attachment toward ordinary reality, and refuting conventional reality may cause some people to become frightened and unable to engage in the Buddhist path. This presentation actually benefits such beings.

Let me say directly that this is a very difficult subject to understand. Students often have a strong reaction when beginning to think about emptiness in this way. They might wonder, "Why are we talking about this? It is very difficult." Actually, it *is* hard to understand, because we have never used our minds in this way before. As Buddhists, we may have spoken of or read the word "emptiness" hundreds or thousands of times, but we have never really tried to grapple with its meaning. Continued study and reflection allows us to clarify our understanding of emptiness. This is the real point of Mipham Rinpoche's first question and answer.

I have already said that topic one is about developing a personal relationship with emptiness. Personal experience is the basis for certainty. and intellectual certainty is the only place we can start. By intellectually engaging with the idea of emptiness, we take steps toward a direct experience of the uncontrived view of Dzogchen.

One effective way to engage with the view of emptiness is through repeated reflection. The more we reflect on the fact that objects or any phenomena lack a permanent, lasting, unchanging nature, the more conviction we develop and we begin to feel less attachment toward outer objects. Even though it is an analytical understanding, it slowly transforms the way that we perceive and interact with the world. Over time, this transformation will become authentic and complete.

Extrinsic Emptiness

The other proposed ultimate view is extrinsic emptiness, a school of thought traditionally expounded by the Jonangpas and some Kagyu scholars. The most commonly used example relates to the buddha nature. The starting assertion goes like this: "If the qualities of a buddha were not already present and complete within the mindstream of a sentient being, then they would have to be created." Logically this is a problem, because if the qualities of a buddha can be created, they would also be subject to destruction, which would make them impermanent. Therefore, those qualities, or the buddha nature, must already be fully present in the mindstream of the sentient beings. When you strip away all the obscurations that are covering the qualities of a buddha, they are able to manifest. Thus, buddha nature itself is steady, everlasting, and unchanging. This is an example of extrinsic emptiness because buddha nature is empty of what is external to it—the impure conventional phenomena that obscure the mind. Thus, the view as posited using extrinsic emptiness is that ultimate reality is empty of all dualistic phenomena. Ultimate reality is therefore empty of other, with that "other" being conventional phenomena.

We can now reintroduce the term "affirming negative." Because this approach defines ultimate reality by saying that it is empty of conventional phenomena, it illustrates an affirming negative. Implicitly, ultimate nature becomes its own kind of limit or position, from which we are to understand emptiness. Now we can understand the second half of Mipham Rinpoche's question: *Can we correctly understand ultimate reality as being an affirming negative?*

Philosophers of the Shentong School talk about the nature of ultimate reality from the point of view of the unchanging nature of suchness. Because they assert this position, they say that ultimate reality is empty of conventional or dualistic phenomena. That helps them to establish their philosophical goal. If we describe buddha nature as being primordial, unchanging, and permanent, then the only explanation for us not seeing it is that it is being obscured. We must assert that the buddha nature is empty of these obscurations, and that they can be stripped away, or else realization is impossible. Actually, this idea sounds quite logical.

In summary, proponents of the Shentong view wish to explain how suchness can be an unchanging state of wisdom that is always present, yet sentient beings still experience conventional ignorance and lack realization.

The Words of the Buddha Maitreya

The Buddha Maitreya said:

> Here, there is nothing to clear away;
> There is not even a little bit of establishment.
> Perfect purity itself is the perfectly pure view.
> Perfectly pure vision is complete liberation.

I have noticed that when Mipham Rinpoche chooses a quotation or metaphor, he can actually use the same quotation to refute both the Shentong assertion and the Later Scholars' assertion of Rangtong at the same time! First, Maitreya's verse refutes the Shentong view by saying, "There is nothing to clear away." This contradicts the Shentong idea that ultimate reality is empty of conventional phenomena. Since "there isn't even a little bit of establishment," what need is there to abandon or empty the ultimate of conventional phenomena?

The quotation also refutes the Rangtong position presented by the Later Scholars. Based on the Later Scholars' assertion of intrinsic emptiness, we must clear away the truly established nature that is stuck on the side of the object. But, again, this quotation says, "there is nothing to clear away."

Next, the quotation says, "There isn't even a little bit of establishment." Again, from the Later Scholars' point of view, we clear away the object's truly established nature but then we leave the leftover conventional object unanalyzed. It still has a conventional existence, even though this quotation says that it is not even a little bit established, even conventionally.

The Buddha Maitreya's words state the correct understanding of the view. When we abide in the perfectly pure view, there cannot be anything to clear away or any position to take in the face of that view.

This is consistent in all four schools of Tibetan Buddhism, whether it is the view of Dzogchen (the ultimate view of the Nyingma School), or Mahamudra (the ultimate view of the Kagyu School), the Union of Samsara and Nirvana (the ultimate view of the Sakya School), or the Great Madhyamaka (the ultimate view of the Gelug School).

Introducing Mipham Rinpoche's Own Tradition

Mipham Rinpoche now gives the Nyingma presentation of the view of Rangtong, saying that ultimate nature, or ultimate reality, is completely uncontrived. It is of the nature of indivisible appearance and emptiness, free of any separation. This is referred to as the uncontrived view of Dzogchen.

Because of the way that Mipham Rinpoche defines the view, we cannot say that there is any leftover appearance or object of refutation, in the way that the Later Scholars posit Rangtong, nor is it similar to the view of extrinsic emptiness posited by Shentong philosophers. Mipham Rinpoche defines ultimate reality as being beyond any object of refutation, beyond any kind of affirmation, and beyond any other kind of philosophical position.

Because the ultimate, uncontrived view is free of positions, Mipham Rinpoche does not accept either the affirming negative or the non-affirming negative as the ultimate view. He believes that both of these views assert a position. From the point of view of the nonaffirming negative, there is some grasping at negation. Although the extreme of existence is refuted, there is still grasping at the other extremes. From the point of view of Shentong, a distinction is made between the conventional and the ultimate; they are separate rather than indivisible because one is empty of the other. Thus, the view is laden with both grasping and abandonment toward both samsara and nirvana.

Mipham Rinpoche's position is very logical. It makes sense that if there is any abandoning or grasping then it is not the ultimate view. Reflect on Tilopa's words to his student Naropa, "Appearances do not bind. Grasping binds. Cut through all grasping." Even if we are grasping at ultimate reality, we are still grasping. It is still a position. From the point of view of its ability to bind, a golden shackle is equal to one made of rope.

We may wonder, "Why don't the Later Scholars cut through all grasping when they posit the ultimate view, as Tilopa suggests?" Well, if we recall the details of their philosophy and its goals, they actually assert that grasping is necessary. In order to preserve the existence of conventional reality as ordinary people do, we need to have a certain kind of grasping. Also, we need strong grasping at negation in order for the Later Scholars' assertion of Rangtong to be logically consistent, since one grasps at the ultimate lack of a truly established nature, the nonaffirming negative, as the view.

The Nonaffirming Negative Is Good for Beginners

Even though it contains a mode of grasping, Mipham Rinpoche says that the nonaffirming negative is good for beginning practitioners. When beginners first encounter the idea of emptiness, they need to grasp at the idea of negation. They have no other way to understand emptiness.

Often when we try to reflect on emptiness, or when we sit down to practice, we have no basis to know what emptiness really means. We go with our idea, what our sense of emptiness might be; this is what is meant by the words "grasping at emptiness" or "grasping at negation." It makes perfect sense. This is a good quality of the Later Scholars' view of Rangtong, because it gives beginning practitioners a way to work with emptiness. In general, the Gelug philosophy, the philosophical school that was formed based on the teachings of Je Tsongkapa, is very supportive of beginning practitioners. It is designed that way.

There is a proverb that says, "When a cat tries to compete with a tiger, the cat will hit its butt on a rock." We could say that the Later Scholars' presentation keeps us from hitting our butts on a rock, because it gives us something to work with. It helps us build a foundation. On the other hand, the weakness in this philosophy is that the nonaffirming negative is not a correct assertion of the uncontrived view. But we can still understand the presentation of the nonaffirming negative as adding necessary support to the practice of meditation for all of us.

The weakness in the Nyingma philosophy is that many beginners on the path want to jump into abiding in the view and they do hit their butts on rocks. This is because they just want to reach the peak. They do not want to walk, they do not want to work, and they do not want to build a foundation. We Nyingmapas say, "The view is nondual, it is free of grasping," and we think that is enough and we do not need to do anything else to actually *experience* that view. We cannot actually ride a tiger, but we try anyway. Many of us do get thrown off and we either stop practicing or become arrogant or confused and practice incorrectly. The good quality of the Nyingma philosophy is that it gives a logical and correct presentation of the uncontrived view.

When Nyingma or Kagyu teachers give public Mahamudra and Dzogchen teachings, all levels of students come to receive those teachings. Some people have a foundation and have faith in Dzogchen and Mahamudra teachings, but many do not. Those without a proper foundation may leave and say things like, "My whole life is meditation. I don't need to practice formally."

This is the biggest weakness in Nyingmapa and Kagyupa practitioners. These practitioners should work on foundational practice. Be careful not to think that ordinary samsara is actually nirvana. Samsara is samsara until we *realize* that it is not—only then is samsara nirvana. Actually, there is so much respect for the existence of samsara in the Later Scholars' presentation that it actually does not let you fall into the mindset of "Everything is practice. This is all nirvana." Having a sense that samsara is real, even if we do not have a lot of attachment to that idea, helps us think of samsara as something formidable that we actually have to deal with instead of trying to mentally get rid of it.

Which View Is More Useful?

Then, Mipham Rinpoche asks himself a question: *When a practitioner examines the empty nature of all phenomena, which one is more useful? Is it the affirming negative or the nonaffirming negative?*

He answers that the nonaffirming negative is the most useful for practitioners who are beginning their examination of emptiness. He bases this on the words of the great masters Chandrakirti, Longchenpa, and Rongzom Pandita. The minds of these three great scholars are like one tree with different branches.

Logically, we should understand that when we examine the primordially pure view without the support of the nonaffirming negative, how could realization of the view be possible? While this is a practical and useful idea that has its place, we should not practice it our whole life. We should not forget to move on when we are able to, when it makes sense for us to go beyond it. We can think of the nonaffirming negative as a good support for analysis and practice. It is like an easy flight of stairs that takes you part way up the great mountain of realization.

Where Do We Place Dualistic Existence?

Here is something to reflect on that can deepen our understanding: When we talk about dualistic perception, or how things "exist," does phenomena's dualistic nature fall within the sphere of the perceiver or does it fall within the sphere of the object?

When I hear the Later Scholars' assertion, it seems that the object of refutation is being placed on the object, since one cuts through only the object's truly established nature. However, in actuality, true establishment does not really go with the object; true establishment can only be defined based on the mind's grasping. One of the consequences of refuting only an object's truly established nature is that there is something left over after you refute it. This is clear if you recall the actual logic being stated: *The pillar is not empty of the pillar; it is empty of the pillar's true establishment.* This implies that the pillar—how it appears conventionally—is somehow its own individual entity that is separate and distinct from its appearance.

Actually, I do not believe that Je Tsongkhapa himself asserted the ultimate view as the nonaffirming negative. In the *Three Principal Aspects of the Path*, Tsongkapa said:

> For as long as the meaning of these two—
> Infallible dependently arisen appearances
>   and emptiness free of assertions—
> Seem to be isolated,
> One has not yet realized the Buddha's wisdom.

One day, without alternating, they will appear as a singular
[expression].
After merely seeing infallible interdependent origination
Certainly, all modes of grasping at objects will perish.
Then, analysis of the view has been perfected.

Sometimes, this final line is also given as "This is called seeing the view of the dharmadhatu."

The followers of Je Tsongkhapa have asserted that the nonaffirming negative is the ultimate view, however. From their point of view, this type of grasping at nonexistence is necessary to preserve the character of conventional reality.

Actually, many individuals who hear teachings on Dzogchen may fall into nihilism as a result. When they hear that everything is refuted, they may think, "There is no karma, there are no teachings, there is no practice, there is not anything." The Later Scholars' presentation may help some of these practitioners to avoid falling into that wrong view.

None of us should ever start to cultivate the wrong idea that the Gelug school does not have perfectly pure ideas and a perfectly pure view. Changkya Rolpa'i Dorje was a great siddha of the Gelug tradition who composed vajra songs, or songs of realization. He was not only a scholar but also a realized yogi who became inseparable with the yidam deity.

The Elaborate Explanation

The next section of the text is called the elaborate explanation. In this elaborate explanation, we will revisit the Later Scholars' assertion of Rangtong and also briefly revisit Shentong. Mipham Rinpoche plays a little transformation game with us in this section. He takes the Later Scholars' view of intrinsic emptiness and transforms it into extrinsic emptiness. It is a little bit complicated, but it is very beautiful once you get a sense of it.

The Later Scholars Say that the Nonaffirming Negative Is Uncontrived

Mipham Rinpoche sets up his target by discussing the way that the Later Scholars assert the uncontrived view. The uncontrived view is usually described as having two indivisible qualities: an empty essence and a clear nature. The Later Scholars say that from the point of view of the empty essence, the nonaffirming negative is completely uncontrived. From the point of view of the clear nature, it is the expression of the indivisible, enlightened body or inseparable, indestructible wisdom. It is uncompounded, naturally expressed, spontaneously present, and has all of the good qualities of the buddhas. This is how we always hear the uncontrived nature described. Except you may have noticed that, in this explanation, the nonaffirming negative is what is said to be uncontrived. That is the one distinction from Mipham Rinpoche's presentation.

The Svatantrika Madhyamaka—which is just below the most profound school in the Madhyamaka philosophy, the Prasangika Madhyamaka—uses a term called *nominal ultimate reality*. A working definition of the word "nominal" is "in name only," as in something that is just merely labeled as ultimate reality, without examination. Mipham Rinpoche says that the nonaffirming negative is really nominal ultimate reality, since it does not rise to the level of true uncontrivance.

Perhaps equating the nonaffirming negative to nominal ultimate reality does not quite give enough respect to the philosophy. The nonaffirming negative enables us to cut through one of the four extremes: the extreme of existence. This is a big thing to cut through. However, we should understand that we are not able to cut through all four extremes. So when we compare the nonaffirming negative, which cuts through the first of the four extremes, and actual ultimate reality or the uncontrived view, which cuts through all four of the extremes, we see that there is quite a difference between them.

Three Logical Flaws

Mipham Rinpoche says that the ultimate view cannot be the non-affirming negative. If this were so, three logical flaws would arise and contradict the words of the great Madhyamaka master Chandrakirti.

First, conventional phenomena could withstand analysis. When we say that "a pillar is not empty of being a pillar; it is empty of its truly established nature," then conventional phenomena are able to withstand logical analysis. This means that conventional truth is not empty. Remember that if phenomena can withstand analysis, this means that, conventionally, the nature of phenomena is existent, unchanging, and permanent.

Second, birth is not refuted in the sphere of ultimate reality. If the cup has a truly established nature and is not empty of the cup's own essence, then ultimately we cannot refute how the cup came to be. The object of refutation must be the cup's own essence in order for it to ultimately have a primordially unborn nature. Cutting through only the cup's truly established nature does not achieve this.

This becomes more absurd if we try to apply it to an actual being. Take the example of David. "David is not empty of David; David is empty of David's truly established nature." Notice that the object of refutation is not self-grasping itself (i.e., David's own grasping at himself). The object of refutation is only the truly established nature of his self-grasping. Thus, David's actual self-grasping is untouched by the refutation and realization could not possibly be the result.

Third, the wisdom of the noble ones' equipoise would be the cause for the destruction of entities. If appearance and emptiness are inseparable, then their nature is thoroughly mixed. There is no possibility, as the Later Scholars posit, of putting space between them so that one of the two truths is empty while the other is not. Because the Later Scholars assert that phenomena are ultimately empty of truly established nature, this actually destroys conventional entities, which are asserted to exist conventionally.

We will revisit these three flaws and their implications in the seventh question and answer in more detail.

What If Appearance and Emptiness Were Distinct?

We have seen how, logically speaking, emptiness has become separated from conventional appearance when the nonaffirming negative is posited as the view. So what happens if appearance and emptiness become distinct rather than inseparable?

If the pillar is not empty of the pillar, but is empty of the pillar's truly established nature, then the emptiness is not that of the pillar itself. The emptiness is just the emptiness of the pillar's true existence. So actually, emptiness is never able to refute the pillar at all. Emptiness is not an expression of the pillar's nature.

For that reason, in *The Wish-Fulfilling Treasury,* the great master Longchenpa said that it is impossible for appearance separated from emptiness to be a valid expression of the two truths. For this reason, it is unsuitable as an object of realization. For example, if we feel anger toward an enemy, knowing that the sky is empty will not help us realize the emptiness of our enemy. Having attachment to the appearance of an entity and knowing that emptiness is sitting just beside it will not help us. This is the crux of Mipham Rinpoche's argument. We know that Nagarjuna posits the ultimate view as being indivisible dependent arising and emptiness. In order for this to be possible, appearance and emptiness must be in union. It does not work if they are separate. Conventional phenomena must be dependently arisen and ultimately empty.

The *King of Meditative Absorption Sutra* states that when a man perceives a beautiful woman, he will experience desire. Desire is experienced based on the direct perception of outer objects. We do not develop desire based on the truly existent nature that is stuck on the side of the object. It develops based on the actual object itself. On the other hand, if dualistic perception becomes completely undone, there is no need for attachment to develop. Thus, when we do not grasp at conventional phenomena, we are naturally liberated from the experience of grasping. Grasping is based on a misapprehension, a misunderstanding of the actual nature of phenomena. Then grasping becomes confusion.

This is beneficial for practitioners who know anything about Dzogchen practice. In the Dzogchen teachings, we often talk about the experience of self-liberation. Self-liberation implies that the essence of phenomena liberates itself. However, the Gelugpa style of cutting through an object's truly existent nature cannot be superimposed onto the practice of Dzogchen. We would be putting a concept on top of a style of meditation that is not conducive to conceptualization of any kind.

Indivisible Appearance and Emptiness Are Like Fire and Warmth

According to Mipham Rinpoche's presentation of Rangtong, the nature of phenomena must be indivisible appearance and emptiness. Two metaphors illustrate the meaning of indivisible nature: "fire and warmth" and "water and wetness." They are suitable to exemplify indivisibility because, without one, the other cannot be expressed.

At this point in the text, Mipham Rinpoche points out that when we refute the pillar's truly existent nature and its truly existent nature becomes empty, it leaves behind an unrefuted leftover appearance. If we have a cup and refute its truly existent nature so that it is empty, we still have the leftover appearance of the cup. The empty nature and the leftover appearance are unsuitable to express the indivisibility of "fire and warmth." They actually become separate entities altogether.

We have heard the idea that the union of appearance and emptiness is great wisdom. How is this like fire and warmth? Are fire and warmth of one essence? I think that everyone would agree that, from a conventional point of view, they must be of one essence. But they are also distinct. At this point, we can describe them as two aspects of one essence, although *even this* conceptual idea will be refuted later, in the seventh question and answer.

In this way, we can also understand the indivisible nature of conventional and ultimate reality. Conventional reality appears. It appears in such a way that all of us can agree upon it and we can talk about it. It has functions that we can rely upon, and that are useful to us. However, this very same nature is thoroughly unestablished. They are like two aspects of one essence. Similarly, we also say that samsara and nirvana are like two aspects of one essence.

Mipham Rinpoche points out that the situation of the leftover unanalyzed appearance and the emptiness of true establishment is different from "two aspects of one essence." Instead of being indivisible, they are like strands of black and white thread being twisted together. There are two distinct essences that will always remain separate. So, his metaphor of the black and white thread twisting together is in contrast to the metaphor of "one essence and two aspects," which is exemplified by fire and warmth.

These contrasting metaphors are extremely helpful for our contemplation and practice. When we ordinary beings think about the world around us, we see appearances. We naturally see them as being contradictory to emptiness. So to us, appearance and emptiness appear to be fire and water. When Mipham Rinpoche compares appearance-emptiness to fire and warmth and then contrasts with the two-colored thread, he gives us an antidote, or a mental method, to work through this problem.

When we sit down to practice, mental discursiveness arises and our minds are distracted by the appearance of thoughts, memories, and hopes. This does not necessarily mean we see objective appearances with our eyes, but we do see all kinds of things through the mind's eye. We should recognize that the main problem that we have in mastering meditation is that when those appearances arise, we are unable to abide in them as empty appearances. Instead, we always try to refute or destroy the appearances, which exhausts us. On the other hand, if we truly experience inseparable appearance and emptiness as one, we will not be exhausted at all by whatever appears to our minds because we will see the emptiness of such appearances at the same moment they appear.

The Elaborate Explanation on Shentong

We have talked at length about why the view of the followers of Tsongkhapa is not suitable, but what about the view of Shentong? Why is this view not an example of indivisibility, or the nature of fire and warmth?

Actually, the view of Shentong sounds logical when you use the example of buddha nature and the need to strip away defilements in order for wisdom to shine through. But, let's consider a more ordinary example, since every single phenomenon has an aspect of suchness to it. We can again take the example of a cup. The ultimate nature, or *dharmata*, of the cup is empty of the conventional cup. That implies that there is a dharmata of the cup that is separate from the appearance of the cup that we see. Again, they are like two essences rather than two aspects of one essence.

Is Buddha Nature Permanent?

From the point of view of Shentong as taught by Jonang Taranatha, buddha nature is permanent. If the buddha nature can change, then how could it be the buddha nature?

The Nyingmapas do not describe buddha nature as being permanent. Rather, they describe it as "great uncompounded," because it cannot be broken down into parts. Although it is uncompounded, it is still capable of being naturally expressed as the three *kayas*, or enlightened embodiments and primordial wisdom. Thus, it is "great." For that reason, it is possible for all of us to have, inherent within us, the good qualities of the buddha nature, and also for it to express as the three kayas. Once our minds and karma are sufficiently purified, the three kayas express spontaneously. According to philosophy, the idea of expression is contradictory to the idea of permanence. One way to define permanence is the inability to take action. It is, by definition, the inability to express.

If buddha nature were permanent, all the results of the buddha nature, meaning complete buddhahood, would have to be here right now. Additionally, since buddha nature is the cause for realization, the result would have to be within the cause, which is illogical. Conventionally, we know that causes lead to results. We logically cannot posit a situation where the result is found within the cause.

Two Schools of Shentong

Mipham Rinpoche distinguishes between the presentation of extrinsic emptiness that is designated by words and extrinsic emptiness that is inherently extrinsic by meaning. He says that one school of philosophy identifies itself as Shentong, but additionally, the Later Scholars' presentation of Rangtong is actually Shentong. The reason is that neither of these philosophies is suitable to express the union of appearance and emptiness.

As a side note, the master Kongtrul Lodrö Thaye instructed Mipham Rinpoche to compose a text taking the position of extrinsic emptiness. He did write that text, which is called *The Lion's Roar Asserting Shentong*. In that text, Mipham Rinpoche takes extrinsic emptiness as his own philosophy. It is a testament to Mipham Rinpoche's brilliance that he was able to write two different texts while taking each distinct philosophy as his own.

The Affirming Negative and Nonaffirming Negative Both Express Extrinsic Emptiness

Next, Mipham Rinpoche discusses why the nonaffirming negative and affirming negative are contrary to the inseparable view from the point of view of scripture, logic, and philosophical assertions. As an aside, Mipham Rinpoche assumes that he has already refuted the Later Scholars' presentation of Rangtong and that it has been transformed to Shentong.

First, he refutes both Shentong views using the words of the same scripture. If the pillar (which represents the Later Scholars' Shentong view) and the dharmata (which represents the Jonangpa Shentong view) are not both empty of their own essences but are only empty of either their truly established nature (which represents the Later Scholars' Shentong view) or conventional reality (which represents the Jonangpa Shentong view), then there is always an unrefuted basis that is left over. Therefore, this leftover basis must be truly established. This is contradictory to the short, middle, and long versions of the *Prajnaparamita* texts. Also, Mipham Rinpoche quotes the Heart Sutra, saying, "Form is emptiness and emptiness is form." Any other way of understanding appearance, or form, and emptiness is contrary to this scripture.

Next, he refutes both Shentong schools using logic. He asks, "Are the essences of the pillar and the pillar's truly established nature one or distinct?" He analyzes both cases. First, if they are one, then by refuting the truly established nature of the pillar, we also refute the pillar itself, similar to the way that when we put out a fire, there is no heat. If the essences are distinct, when we refute the pillar's truly established nature, then nothing happens to the pillar itself. It is not empty; it can withstand analysis. Either way that we try to reason it, there is a flaw in the logic.

Finally, Mipham Rinpoche refutes the Shentong schools using the Later Scholars' own assertions. If we say that pillars or other objects are not each empty of their own essences, then their essences will seem to exist. If the truly established nature is the object of refutation, it becomes an "other." For example, a vase becomes empty of the other, which is its truly established nature. Mipham Rinpoche makes a play on words when he says that by using the word *other*, "You claim to reject extrinsic emptiness, but really what you are asserting is the emptiness of this thing's other." This is contradictory to the idea of intrinsic emptiness.

Mipham Rinpoche says that we do not need to fear speaking so directly about the emptiness of an object. Even the Buddha Shakyamuni himself said directly, "Form is emptiness, emptiness is form." We do not need to fear the consequences of saying that something is empty.

Why Shentong Is Unsuitable to Express Inseparability

We have talked about the fact that all philosophical schools describe the nature of wisdom as indivisible wisdom, or a state of equality. Why cannot either style of Shentong be described as a state of equality?

From the point of view of those who assert Shentong, nirvana is not empty of its own essence, but it *is* empty of samsara. Likewise, from the point of view of the Later Scholars' presentation of Shentong, the pillar or any other phenomena is not empty of itself; it is empty of its truly established nature. Mipham Rinpoche asserts that this does not qualify as Great Emptiness, meaning emptiness that is not separate from appearance, because it cannot express the quality of inseparability. In order for this to be possible, phenomena must be empty of their own essence.

The reason why Shentong is unsuitable to express inseparability is that samsara and nirvana are treated as two separate things when one is empty of the other. This is contrary to the descriptions that we read about the indivisible nature of samsara and nirvana. For example, the tantras describe samsara and nirvana as being in a state of equality. If they are in an equal state, they cannot be separate. The tantras also say that the perception of either samsara or nirvana, based on the same set of circumstances, depends wholly on one's realization. So again, when we separate them, they are not in direct relationship to one another. This logically contradicts the tantras' description of the nature of samsara and nirvana.

Again, let's use the real-world example of the cup. The cup is a conventional phenomenon that does appear. Then we have the dharmata or suchness of the cup, which is the cup's ultimate nature. Are these of one essence or they are distinct?

From the Shentong perspective, they must be distinct, because one is empty of the other. In actuality, however, it is impossible to separate the cup from the cup's dharmata. Thus, one weakness of the Shentong philosophy is that it is very hard to experience the view properly because the Shentong understanding of the view does not give a proper example to point out the nature of inseparability.

The second weakness with this philosophy is that when we say that nirvana is not empty of itself but is empty of samsara, then the ultimate nature seems to have a real, lasting, and definitive quality. We grasp at it as the extreme of existence, a kind of position. We have already talked about the fact that if any concepts or grasping are present, this obstructs our recognition of the uncontrived view.

We can summarize the logical problem with Shentong by saying that appearance and emptiness cannot be a singular expression. The appearance of the cup and the emptiness of the cup become separate. This is described through Mipham Rinpoche's metaphor of a horse and a cow. The root text says that a horse is empty of a cow. This much is obvious. But, here, Mipham Rinpoche means to point out that there is no relationship between a horse and the cow. For that reason, if we put the emptiness of the cow on top of the horse, it does not benefit us at all. We are talking about emptiness that is something different than the horse altogether!

An Explanation from the Point of View of Dependent Arising

We know that the definition of dependent arising is that conventional appearances appear dependent on causes and conditions. From this point of view, appearance and emptiness are like a form and its shadow. If we say that the cup arises through interdependent causes and conditions, then emptiness naturally arises along with it, because anything that is dependently arisen is, by nature, empty. Dependently arisen phenomena have no inherent characteristics. Another way that we say this in regard to samsara and nirvana is that one naturally arises, or coemerges, along with the other. If one is not a natural expression of the other, then we cannot say that they are inseparable. It has to be possible for both wisdom and conventional appearances to express simultaneously.

The Water Moon as Metaphor for Why Extrinsic Emptiness Is Unsuitable

Mipham Rinpoche gives a second metaphor to illustrate the flaw of Shentong reasoning. All beings know that the moon in the sky—the actual moon—is not the same as the reflection of the moon in water. To say that the water moon is empty of the moon in the sky is not the proper way to understand indivisible appearance and emptiness. One thing that is illustrative about this metaphor is that the two moons look the same because one is the reflection of the other. But in reality, the comparison points out how even a reflection of the moon must be empty of its own essence; it cannot simply be empty of the moon in the sky.

If the statement "The reflection of the moon is empty of the moon in the sky" were the expression of the ultimate state, it would not be amazing at all. After all, even mere cowherders know this, not to mention great scholars!

On the other hand, if we understand dependent arising properly, we know that as things appear, they are also empty; from the moment that things are empty, they also appear. That is truly marvelous!

We Need Certainty in the Indivisible Nature of Appearance and Emptiness

Without strong conviction in the indivisible nature of appearance and emptiness, we will have difficulty when we meditate. For example, often we have trouble opening our eyes when we meditate. We have trouble meditating in loud places. This is because of our lack of certainty in the nature of indivisible wisdom.

If we had certainty in indivisible emptiness and appearance, then appearances would not bother us in the way that they do. When we hear a sound, if we had certainty in the fact that sound and emptiness are indivisible, we would simply think that, "The proper thing to do is abide in that sound." We would do it naturally. That would come from our conviction that conventional phenomena are in a state of equality with the uncontrived nature.

If we think back to examples of great siddhas, they did not always practice in the wilderness alone, undistracted. They practiced in the middle of cities. They practiced in the midst of vast numbers of people. They had certainty in the indivisible nature of appearance and emptiness, the indivisible nature of sound and emptiness, the indivisible nature of concepts and wisdom. This led them to be able to experience the expression of indivisible wisdom under conditions that normal people cannot.

Mipham Rinpoche's Own Tradition

Mipham Rinpoche begins his elaborate explanation of his own tradition by using the same example of the water moon. Here, Mipham Rinpoche says that if we experience the water moon itself, and we examine it in outer, inner, and secret ways, we find that the essence of the water moon itself has not even a little bit of an established nature. All phenomena without exception are completely empty of their own essence.

Mipham Rinpoche goes on to say that even though the essence of the water moon has an unestablished, uncontrived nature, it is still not con-tradictory that the water moon appears as an expression of dependent arising. This is exactly the meaning of the metaphor "fire and warmth." It is different from the presentation of the horse being empty of the cow, in which the two essences of the horse and cow are separate.

As ordinary beings, it seems contradictory that phenomenal appearances are natural expressions of emptiness. We counteract that ordinary way of thinking through studying Madhyamaka, through studying texts such as *The Beacon of Certainty*, and finally through receiving teachings on Secret Mantrayana. Through contemplating these texts and gaining certainty, indivisible appearance and emptiness become free of contradiction. When inseparable appearance and emptiness become free of contradiction, this is more marvelous than any ordinary marvel!

Mipham Rinpoche goes on to say that any being that develops certainty in the union of appearance and emptiness is worthy of all the buddhas' praise. These ideas are so beautiful that we feel overjoyed simply by recalling them.

From the point of view of the empty essence, all phenomena in samsara and nirvana are the nature of uncontrived emptiness, and yet they appear. While phenomena appear, the basis of their emptiness is not lost. Because the basis of emptiness is not lost, appearance is possible; appearances express. As things appear, the basis of appearance is not lost simply because phenomena are empty.

The basic nature of something is "that thing, just as it is." So when we say, "the appearance's basic nature," we are saying "the appearance, whatever or however it is." We are not trying to overlay or superimpose anything upon it. The basic nature of all empty phenomena is the same; from this point of view, they are equal.

If we are practicing generation stage or visualization, or perfection stage, we tend to generate attachment to what we think are good experiences and we want to keep experiencing them. If something arises in our mind that we think is bad, we want to abandon and reject it. Mipham Rinpoche is pointing out that, whether it is concepts, appearances, or sound, we are unable to recognize the equal, basic nature of those concepts, appearances, or sounds. We judge them and say that they are good or they are bad; we do not recognize the appearance as being an empty appearance.

If we contemplate the idea, "No matter how things appear, they are empty; no matter how things are empty, they appear," we begin to gain certainty in phenomena's indivisible nature. This enables us to have no obstacle to recognizing indivisible appearance and emptiness when we practice. When done properly, this is called "abiding in the uncontrived view."

Milarepa said, "Examine the mind, day and night, until you recognize that there is nothing to see, nothing lasting or permanent. Abide in that. This is the view of Mahamudra."

After reading and contemplating this first chapter of *The Beacon of Certainty*, if you were to face a great master who asked you to explain the nature of appearance and emptiness, you should be able to do that. You should have confidence that you could do this by simply using the example of a cup or any object in front of you. You could say, "This cup appears and the basic nature of appearance is not lost, yet it is empty. Although it is empty and the basic nature of emptiness is not lost, it appears." There is no contradiction between appearance and emptiness. It is completely logical and it is easy to understand. This is the real basis for intellectual certainty.

CHAPTER FIVE:

The Second Question

*—Do shravaka and pratyeka arhats realize both the selflessness
of phenomena and the selflessness of the individual?*

THE SECOND QUESTION posed by the wanderer leads to another
philosophical exploration that helps us to develop intellectual certainty. As we examined the first question and answer, we began to
develop a personal relationship with emptiness. In this topic, we will
further our exploration of emptiness, looking at important ideas like
dependently imputed emptiness and *mere emptiness*, the two "selves" of
the individual and phenomena, as well as when a practitioner attains
liberation from samsara.

The intellectual understanding of emptiness we are developing will
be incredibly important as the text progresses, as Mipham Rinpoche
explains the uncontrived view of Dzogchen based on this initial understanding. In other words, we are poised on the bridge between sutra
and tantra and are about to take a step toward tantra. We should not
discount the value of intellectual certainty as we develop our understanding of the Secret Mantrayana.

Are the Three Vehicles Equal?

Let's begin our explanation of this topic with a question. Regarding the
three vehicles—the shravaka vehicle, the pratyekabuddha vehicle, and
the Mahayana vehicle—are the view, path, and result, or realization,
the same or are they distinct? Logically speaking, if the view is different,
then the path must be different. And if the path is different, then the
result must be different.

To introduce the topic, we will assume that the view of the different vehicles, as well as the path and result, is different. We will come to understand these differences as we further explore Mipham Rinpoche's teachings on this topic.

The Realization of All Schools Is Profound

Quite directly speaking, some Buddhists think that the Hinayana teachings are lesser or somehow inferior to those of the Mahayana. Although this topic discusses the differences between the Hinayana and Mahayana vehicles, the purpose is *not* to develop judgment or prejudice. We should acknowledge that it is difficult to attain the realization of an arhat based on the Hinayana teaching, even for Mahayana practitioners. Arhats attain complete liberation from samsara, although as we will see, this is not exactly the same as the attainment of complete buddhahood that results from the Mahayana path. Nonetheless, liberation from samsara is very profound realization. We should be humbled by the realization of the arhats, rather than thinking ourselves superior to them, especially when we are mired in samsara ourselves!

From our mouths, we often advertise the kind of practitioners we think we are, by saying things like, "I am a Dzogchen yogi." This is just an expression of pride. When we recognize that the realization of the arhats is profound, it helps remind us of our arrogance and not to think that we know so much more.

We should know something about the practices and philosophies of each school in the Buddhist tradition. What are each school's good qualities? What are their weaknesses? We should respectfully explore this topic, just as we explored the differences in the Tibetan traditions in the last topic.

Refuting the Scholars of Old

This topic begins with a refutation of the "Scholars of Old," which include some Nyingma scholars. These scholars taught many years before Mipham Rinpoche. These scholars assert that the shravaka and pratyekabuddha practitioners—two paths within the Hinayana school—realize the selflessness of the individual. In other words, they realize that the self is nonexistent. They have no realization whatsoever of the selflessness of outer phenomena, however.

The selflessness of phenomena includes all outer and inner phenomena, not just the personal self. When we realize the emptiness of all phenomena, we are also able to refute the four extremes of existence, nonexistence, both, and neither. Thus, we are directly able to experience the unborn nature of phenomena.

Mipham Rinpoche says that the assertion of the Scholars of Old is contrary to logic and scripture. He posits that shravakas and pratyekabuddhas also realize something called the *dependently imputed emptiness* of outer phenomena.

Let's give a working definition of dependently imputed emptiness. Because the shravakas and pratyekabuddhas realize emptiness of the self, they must impute (meaning to mentally imply or designate) that outer phenonema are also empty. It is called dependently imputed emptiness because this knowledge or mental designation arises only in dependence on their own realization of the emptiness of self, rather than as direct realization.

Mipham Rinpoche is trying to convey his belief that without at least some realization of the emptiness of outer phenomena, liberation from samsara is not possible. In other words, liberation from samsara is not simply the realization of the emptiness of our personal selves. It also has to do with the imputation that outer phenomena are empty.

Dependently imputed emptiness describes the realization of mere emptiness rather than "unqualified emptiness," or emptiness that is not limited or qualified in any way. Mere emptiness is a shallower or less pervasive realization of emptiness; this idea will be further developed in coming chapters, so it is good to keep this term in mind.

The Dependently Imputed "I"

Shravakas and pratyekabuddhas realize the emptiness of what Mipham Rinpoche calls the *dependently imputed "I."* He uses this terminology to linguistically convey that the self is not real. It is just something that is being named or designated based on the causes and conditions of the five aggregates. It is the "I" that appears and is labeled by the dualistic mind.

Mipham Rinpoche goes on to say that when we cognize the lack of true existence of the self, we are at least partially realizing dependently imputed emptiness of outer phenomena. Thus, if we recognize the selflessness of the dependently imputed "I," then we have understood, at least partially, the basis of emptiness of all phenomena.

The first thing that we should know as Vajrayana practitioners is that arhats have realized the emptiness of the dependently imputed "I." This allows them to realize the selflessness of the individual person. Again, this is a profound state of realization. Self-attachment is extremely hard to cut through.

We should ask ourselves what kind of certainty do we actually have in the fact that the self is merely dependently imputed? Do we ever really think, "I'm just labeling myself" on a deep level? If we reflect on the concept of the dependently imputed "I," our own self-attachment and arrogance will lessen.

As we contemplate this topic, we should try to gain certainty in the meaning of dependently imputed emptiness. We should not just work for intellectual understanding; we need a gut-level experience. In other words, we need to deeply reflect on the fact that all of the phenomena that we see around us are simply being labeled and named by the dualistic mind. This will make the selflessness of phenomena much easier to realize.

A Single Mode of Emptiness

Mipham Rinpoche goes on to explain that although the self and outer phenomena appear differently to us, their way, or mode, of being empty is the same. We distinguish between these phenomena as being different on a conventional level, however. He asserts that of the two selves of the individual and phenomena, one is general and one is specific, like trees and junipers. But which of the two selves is general, and which is specific? The individual is like the juniper, and phenomena are like the general phenomena of trees. Applying this metaphor to the topic of emptiness, the emptiness of all phenomena is general. An individual is a subset or class of all general phenomena. Thus, the realization of the emptiness of the individual self is a specific realization of emptiness. If you can understand this, the entire chapter will be much easier to understand.

In the Mahayana school, of which Vajrayana Buddhism is a part, our goal is to attain complete and perfect realization of the emptiness of the individual self as well as of all outer phenomena. What we have just learned is that realization according to the Hinayana Buddhist teachings is specific realization, rather than a general one. Since the results are different, the view and path of the two vehicles must also be different.

The Prajnaparamita *Was Taught to Four Kinds of Sons*

The *Prajnaparamita*, the Buddha's teachings on transcendental wisdom, is the like the mother who teaches four kinds of sons. These four sons are the practitioners on the shravaka path, the pratyekabuddha path, the Mahayana path, and the noble buddhas. This metaphor refers to the fact that a mother can have many kinds of sons and daughters. They will have different capacities and different strengths. It seems natural that the teachings can be given in different ways, depending on the type of being that gravitates toward each path.

When we hear the words "the perfection of wisdom," or wisdom *paramita*, some of us think that these are only contained within the Mahayana teachings. Actually, aspects of the paramita of wisdom are included in the Hinayana teachings as well. Because of this, we know that Hinayana practitioners must have some realization of the emptiness of phenomena. If not, the teachings on the *Prajnaparamita* would be contradicted. We would be saying that only certain kinds of Buddhists realize the nature of wisdom.

We should know that a practitioner who does not rely upon the paramita of wisdom teachings will not attain liberation from samsara. That is the very meaning of paramita—it's Sanskrit for "the far shore"; the paramitas carry you from samsara to the far shore of nirvana.

Let's reflect on the importance of actually studying the *Prajna-paramita* teachings. We could say that it is possible to decrease our attachment to self and our coarse afflictive emotions based on a worldly path alone. Many spiritual practices or techniques enable us to cut through some of our afflictive emotions and self-attachment. But generally, we describe something that enables us to *completely* cut through as a transcendental teaching. This is a very nice way to translate the word paramita: it is a transcendental cutting through.

If we only cut through the coarse aspect of attachment and the coarse afflictive emotions, our latent, subtle habitual tendencies will surface again. The same old habits will manifest. We start to grasp at the self, which leads us to express afflictive emotions and take rebirth in samsara again. So we can think that only when the wisdom paramita is taught is it possible to abandon the subtle afflictive emotions as well as cut through the root of the afflictive emotions entirely.

An interesting thing has just happened—Mipham Rinpoche has just refuted some of the scholars of his own lineage! He believes these scholars have made a mistake by not understanding that the Hinayana teachings do incorporate the *Prajnaparamita*. This is a great example of how we cannot necessarily conclude that this text is prejudiced or in favor of any particular school. Mipham Rinpoche did not follow the teachings of his own lineage blindly. Rather, he worked on examining, composing texts, and debating in order to purify the meaning of his own lineage teachings.

At this point, it is probably helpful to summarize Mipham Rinpoche's own position. If there is not some—although incomplete—realization of dependently imputed emptiness, then it is impossible to abandon the afflictive emotions and transcend samsara. In fact, we cannot even cut through the subtle afflictive emotions, let alone their root.

What Is the Difference Between the Two Hinayana Schools?

The two Hinayana schools of the shravakas and pratyekabuddhas differ in the subtlety of their understanding of emptiness. The shravaka school examines both particles of matter and particles of consciousness to determine whether such particles are thoroughly impermanent. By breaking phenomena into particles of matter, they see impermanence at a coarse level. However, when they get to a very subtle level, they have no way to logically establish unqualified emptiness or what we Madhyamikas call the *uncontrived nature* that is free of all extremes. At a certain point, they assert that there are indivisible particles of matter that cannot be broken down any further. Thus, the particles of matter that make up outer phenomena are, at a certain level, truly existent. This is one reason we say that Hinayana practitioners realize only *mere emptiness;* they do not see the impermanence of phenomena at the deepest level.

The same problem occurs regarding particles of consciousness. When they examine consciousness, they see that it is mostly impermanent. But when they get to a very subtle level, they believe that there are indivisible moments of consciousness that are truly existent and cannot be broken down. So in terms of both matter and consciousness, they cannot fully realize emptiness.

The difference between the shravakas and the pratyekabuddhas is that the pratyekabuddhas realize that matter can be fully broken down. They do not believe that there are indivisible particles of matter. However, they do believe that indivisible moments of consciousness truly exist. In summary, the pratyekabuddhas believe that the mind has a subtle, truly existent element to it, even though they fully understand that outer phenomena are completely empty.

There are also differences in terms of the path they practice. Shravakas practice in a community and they rely upon a living master. Pratyekabuddhas live completely alone. They rely on written teachings, so it is possible for pratyekabuddhas to exist even at a time when there are no living masters. The pratyekabuddhas also have teachings on the twelve links of dependent arising and know how to work with the links from ignorance to death and also in reverse from death to ignorance.

What Is the Root of Samsara?

Mipham Rinpoche has finished refuting the Scholars of Old. He will now refute the view held by the Later Scholars, specifically those who follow Je Tsongkapa. In order to understand his refutation, we need to understand what comprises the root of samsara. All of us will probably answer "ignorance" in response to that question. But, more specifically, is it ignorance that is based on the attachment to the individual self or the ignorance that is based on attachment to outer phenomena?

As we have already stated, Mipham Rinpoche says that liberation from samsara entails realizing the emptiness of self and a little bit of the emptiness of phenomena. The Nyingma and Sakya schools say that ignorance based on attachment to self is the root of samsara. The Gelug school asserts something different, however. They say that grasping at outer phenomena as truly existent is the root of samsara. This is defined as the obscuration of the afflictive emotions, and it is this obscuration that causes one to take birth in samsara. Mipham Rinpoche asserts that this statement contradicts the meaning of some important scriptures. For example, Nagarjuna and his spiritual son Aryadeva said:

> As long as grasping at the body exists, self-attachment exists. If [self-attachment] exists, by the power of karma and afflictive emotions, one will take birth in samsara. After the object [of the individual] is seen as selfless, the seed of existence is abandoned and it is said that liberation is attained.

This scripture states that it is based on attachment to the individual self, rather than to phenomena in general, that one takes birth in samsara.

All Three Vehicles Are Equal on the Path of Seeing

Next, Mipham Rinpoche examines the assertion made by some later scholars, "The objects of abandonment and realization on the path of seeing of all three vehicles are equal."

Let's start with a working definition of the path of seeing. The path of realization can be broken down into five paths, or stages. Those five paths are: the path of accumulation, the path of preparation, the path of seeing, the path of meditation, and the path of no further learning. The path of seeing is generally where philosophers place the direct experience of emptiness; thus we call it the path where we *see* emptiness.

With that in mind, let's examine this question: Is the abandonment and realization on the path of seeing equal for the shravakas, pratyekabuddhas, and Mahayana Buddhist practitioners?

Mipham Rinpoche says that this is illogical. Let's just think about it from an ordinary point of view. Each of the five paths is distinct. To move from one path to the next, we have to abandon certain things and realize certain things, or we cannot be said to have attained the qualities of the next path. On the third path, the path of seeing, all the coarse afflictive emotions are abandoned. The realization attained is called the "wisdom of the path of seeing" and it enables us to abandon the root of samsara. However, a number of faults or logical contradictions will arise if we assert that this happens for all the schools in the same way while on this path.

First, Mipham Rinpoche begins by giving a scriptural presentation. The *Prajnaparamita*, the teachings of the Secret Mantrayana, and the sutras and the tantras all say there are differences in the abandonment and realization of the paths of the three vehicles. So the assertion is contradictory to these texts on its face.

One reason that Mipham Rinpoche states this is because we describe the teachings of the first turning of the wheel of Dharma as interpretable, or requiring explanation. In other words, they are conventional teachings. The second and third turnings of the wheel of Dharma contain what are called definitive teachings. These are the teachings on ultimate reality. We call these *self-apparent teachings*, as their meaning does not need interpretation.

Mipham Rinpoche says that if the assertion of the Later Scholars were true, we would have to reclassify the definitive teachings of the *Prajnaparamita*, the Vajrayana, and even the Mahayana sutras as interpretable teachings. This is because all of these present the realization on the various paths of seeing as being in distinct levels. Thus, to interpret them as being the same would be to treat them as interpretable rather than definitive teachings.

Mipham Rinpoche goes on to reason that the assertion of the Later Scholars creates another complication. These teachings generally state that once the shravakas and pratyekabuddhas attain liberation from samsara, which is the result of their path, they then have to enter the Mahayana path from the beginning in order to attain the complete result of buddhahood. But if they have already attained the result of the path of seeing—liberation from samsara—and the realization of the Hinayana path is the same as the Mahayana path of seeing, there is no need for them to enter the Mahayana path from the beginning. They would start at the fourth of the Mahayana paths because they have already finished the first three while practicing the Hinayana vehicle.

Based on this logic, we might wonder, "I know that practitioners on the Hinayana path have abandoned their attachment to self, so why can't they just start purifying the cognitive obscurations right where they are? Why do they have to start the Mahayana path from the beginning?"

But this possibility is complicated by the way that Tsongkhapa and his followers teach the path. Tsongkhapa asserts that there are seven impure bhumis, and that a practitioner starts to abandon the cognitive obscurations when they reach the eighth bhumi. The logical flaw is that if the three vehicles are equal in realization at the path of seeing, then there is nothing to abandon at all on the first seven bhumis of the Mahayana path, because it was already abandoned on the Hinayana path. Then, finally, on the eighth bhumi, an arhat will start abandoning the cognitive obscurations.

The Dull Ones Become Sharp

Another interesting result is, if you accept the position of the Later Scholars, "the ones with dull faculties become sharp, and the ones with sharp faculties become dull." Mipham Rinpoche explains this logical consequence by saying that the shravakas and pratyekabuddhas are said to attain the realization of their path in seven lifetimes once they enter the path of accumulation, after which they will attain the state of an arhat. That means in about seven lifetimes, they will attain the level of the path of seeing on the Mahayana path. In the Mahayana path, it is taught that it takes endless *kalpas*—aeons—to attain this same state. So if you accept this position, then the path of the shravakas and pratyeka-buddhas becomes the quick path, and the Mahayana path becomes the long path.

Je Tsongkhapa answers these critiques by saying that the arhats have not perfected all of the necessary qualities in the first to the seventh bhumis. For example, they have not accumulated enough merit, they do not have the proper kind of compassion, they do not have Mahayana bodhichitta, and they have not habituated themselves to the Mahayana teachings on the *Prajnaparamita.*

Mipham Rinpoche makes a joke at the end of this section in the root text. He says, "When the sun is shining brightly, isn't it incredible that you still need a candle to dispel the darkness?" This has to do with the Later Scholars' assertion that arhats already possess the antidote of wisdom on the seventh bhumi, but are unable to use it to abandon the cognitive obscurations. Mipham Rinpoche is really saying, sort of increduously, "You already have wisdom, but you still need to develop compassion and bodhichitta, accumulate merit, and habituate to the *Prajnaparamita?*" Khenpo Kunpal also says in the commentary, "When the sun appears perfectly free of clouds, it is laughable that it would be necessary to rely on a candle to dispel the body of darkness."

The Refutation of the Sakya Position

The great Sakya scholar, Gorampa, splits the aggregates into two types. One is the continuum of the corporeal body and the other is of outer phenomena. Then, he says that shravakas and pratyekabuddhas realize the emptiness of the aggregates of their own continuum, but they do not realize the aggregates of outer phenomena. Is this a logical position?

To answer this question, let's think in terms of all possible objects of knowledge; all possible things that could be cognized. There are two types: things that are compounded and things that are uncompounded. Here is a working definition of compounded: that which can be broken down into pieces; that which is an expression of dependent arising.

Next, we should ask if there are any compounded phenomena that are not part of the five aggregates that make up the physical continuum of the corporeal body. It seems obvious that all composite phenomena condense into the five aggregates that are also part of our very own bodies.

Mipham Rinpoche's challenge to Gorampa's logic, then, is that if one has realized the emptiness of the five aggregates of the body, then they must have realized the emptiness of all composite phenomena. If all composite phenomena condense into those five aggregates, then the only thing left to realize is uncomposite phenomena, an example of which is space.

Of this, Mipham Rinpoche says, "Space is like the son of a barren woman. It cannot even be established conventionally. There is no need to talk about it ultimately. Logicians do not even have to describe uncomposite phenomena. They are easily realized as being empty." Thus, if the only thing left to realize is uncomposite phenomena, we need not talk about it because its emptiness is self-apparent.

Gorampa might answer that the way we relate to our own aggregates is different than how we relate to the aggregates of all outer cognizable objects. For example, we feel our physical body, our limbs, and our flesh from the inside, while we do not personally feel or relate to outer phenomena in the same way. We know our own thoughts and feelings, while we do not similarly know the minds of others. Thus, the statement that it is possible to realize the emptiness of our own aggregates even while not realizing the emptiness of the outside aggregates is logical. We should remember that Gorampa, like Tsongkhapa, is teaching to his own audience.

The Importance of Bringing the Teachings into Experience

When we study philosophy, we have to come back to the question: what is the benefit of knowing the logic of a particular philosophy? I believe that dependently imputed emptiness is very beneficial for us to reflect on. As practitioners of the Mahayana school, we all say that phenomena are dependently imputed, or that they are expressions of dependent arising. But in truth, we lack certainty in this idea.

If we had real certainty, then no matter what happiness or suffering came to us in this life, we would have conviction in impermanence. For this reason, mental unhappiness and strong afflictive emotions would not have the hold on us as they do now. Without this certainty, we can talk about dependent imputation and dependently arisen conventional appearances, but our words are like those spoken by a parrot.

Through the kindness of my own root lama, I feel I am able to give commentary on any text. I am confident that, even if my commentary is not perfect—because I am not a buddha—I can give a good commentary on it. But at the same time, mere knowledge does not make us realized. Knowledge simply leads us to gain experience and to develop certainty in the meaning of these words and ideas.

It is good for us to know the philosophy of the shravakas and pratyekabuddhas, but it is even better for us to bring it into the Mahayana path with us and to gain experience in the meaning of the teachings. The great scholar Sakya Pandita said, "When the mind holds the aspiration of bodhichitta, even a ritual practice of the shravaka or pratyekabuddha tradition becomes of the Mahayana tradition." As practitioners of the Mahayana, we can learn the logic of the shravakas and pratyekabuddhas and we can use it to enrich our own understanding of the path.

There are many more Buddhists now around the globe today than there were thousands of years ago. But if we think about the qualities of those Buddhists now as opposed to then, today's Buddhists cannot compare with the good qualities of the practitioners of old. When I think about some of the lamas or professors who are now teaching, I realize that Buddhist philosophy has become just a subject to lecture upon. Many are not keeping the essence of the teachings in their heart as they teach. So we could say that these days, more and more people have knowledge, but fewer and fewer people have the essence of the teachings, or even intellectual certainty in the ideas contained within them.

One way that we can contrast the difference between knowledge based on experience versus knowledge based on books is in the way that one answers questions. A teacher who is extremely experienced can answer any question. No matter how many questions you follow up with, he or she will continually find a skillful way to answer a question. When a teacher teaches based on knowledge from books, he or she often cannot answer questions skillfully. The teacher will think, "I will have to look that up." Knowledge from experience is different. It is an inner knowing that arises from certainty.

Once when I was in Tibet, I went to see a lama who I had heard was a good scholar. I listened to him give teachings, and when he finished I offered him a *khata*, a traditional offering scarf. I said, "Can I ask you some questions?"

He said, "Sure!" so I asked him a few questions. He answered. His answers brought me more questions. So I asked more questions, and he answered. Those answers brought me more questions. I finally asked a question he could not answer, and he got upset. I was a little bit sad as a result of that experience. He could have been honest. He could have said, "I'm sorry, I cannot answer that." My feeling is that he was a very good scholar, but he did not know the essence of the teachings through experience. If he understood the essence of the teaching, everything would be there and he would be able to answer perfectly!

Mipham Rinpoche's Own View

Mipham Rinpoche will explain his own view in three parts. First, Mipham Rinpoche establishes his point of view based on the teachings of the glorious Chandrakirti, a great Prasangika Madhyamaka scholar. Second, he relies on the teachings of the great master Longchenpa. Then, he raises doubts and clarifies them.

The Assertions of Chandrakirti

First, Mipham Rinpoche relies on the autocommentary of Chandrakirti's *Entering the Middle Way*, a great Madhyamaka text. In this text, Chandrakirti describes and classifies emptiness so that beings can be completely liberated from the two kinds of self-grasping. According to Chandrakirti, the realization of emptiness of shravakas, pratyekabuddhas, and Mahayana practitioners are all classified differently.

He goes on to say that practitioners of each school were taught specific methods in order to gain the realization that is particular to that school. The shravakas and pratyekabuddhas were taught the method for realizing the selflessness of the individual. Those on the Mahayana path were taught the method to purify the cognitive obscurations and realize the two kinds of selflessness. Thus, the shravakas and pratyekabuddhas are given the method to attain liberation from samsara, whereas Mahayana practitioners are given the method to realize complete omniscience. By presenting this particular part of Chandrakirti's text, Mipham Rinpoche says that there is a need to classify emptiness and to assert that realization occurs in different ways and to different depths.

He goes on to point out that the goal of the shravaka and pratyeka-buddha paths is to dispel the obstacles to realizing the selflessness of the individual. Therefore, the methods that they use dispel the afflictive emotions. On the other hand, they do not strive toward realizing the impermanence of the two partless types of particles; partless material particles and partless moments of consciousness. For that reason, it does not make sense that they would realize complete omniscience.

The View of Longchenpa

Mipham Rinpoche then presents an assertion made in one of Longchen-pa's seven great treasuries, *The Wish-Fulfilling Treasury*, where he said that the Scholars of Old debated this very question. He then answers the question by saying that since shravakas and pratyekabuddhas real-ize the dependently imputed selflessness of the individual, they real-ize an aspect of the selflessness of phenomena. If this were not true, it would be impossible that they could have completely abandoned grasping at "I," and as a result, liberation from samsara would be impossible.

The crux of Longchenpa's assertion is that if one does not realize dependently imputed emptiness, the state of an arhat cannot be attained. Going through this argument logically, it is said that the shravakas and pratyekabuddhas cannot realize the emptiness of all phenomena because they accept the existence of subtle partless particles. We could ask whether or not those partless particles are included in the definition of all phenomena. The answer is that they are objects of knowledge that can be apprehended by the mind. For that reason, they must be phenomena.

Moreover, there is no philosophy or text that asserts that the shravakas and pratyekabuddhas have realized the emptiness of partless particles. For that reason, it is impossible that they realize the emptiness, or unborn empty nature, of all phenomena. This would be in contradiction to scripture. For that reason, Longchenpa asserts that they must realize dependently imputed emptiness but they do not realize the emptiness of all phenomena.

In summary, Mipham Rinpoche's position is that arhats realize a little bit of the emptiness of phenomena, but the *size* of this realization is like the space inside a sesame seed; it is very small. Mipham Rinpoche also says that they have tasted the ocean of unqualified emptiness. However, drinking a cupful of the ocean is not the same as drinking the whole thing, even though we can say that we have "drunk the ocean" in both cases. Thus, their realization is said to be of mere emptiness.

Conventional and Ultimate Reality

Shravakas and pratyekabuddhas examine phenomena on a very coarse level and see its impermanence. However, they eventually reach a certain level and decide that particles can no longer be broken down (thus, they are "partless"). If you reflect on how conventional and ultimate reality are viewed in the Vajrayana, I think you will find the contradiction in this idea.

From the Hinayana point of view, conventional reality becomes the coarse level and ultimate reality becomes the subtle level of phenomenal existence. Therefore, conventional and ultimate reality are on the same side—a cup has both a conventional and an ultimate nature from the shravaka and pratyekabuddha point of view, because it is both coarse and subtle.

This is very different from the idea of indivisible appearance and emptiness. If we are to realize the unborn nature of a phenomenon, there cannot be any substantial existence from its own point of view. However, from the point of view of the shravakas and pratyekabuddhas, ultimate reality itself is substantial existence, and this contradiction makes realization impossible. Realization of the emptiness of this cup's subtle, ultimate nature is impossible, because it is composed of particles that substantially exist.

The Explanation on the Necessity and the Way to Certainly Realize the Nature of Ultimate Phenomena

This section begins with a question. First, I will give the basis for the question. If we realize the dependently imputed emptiness of one thing—for example, if we know that a pillar is empty by dependent imputation—then isn't it easy to realize the dependently imputed emptiness of other phenomena as well? Thus, Mipham Rinpoche asks, "If you see the empty inside of a sugarcane stalk, isn't this the same as seeing the emptiness of all others?"

The answer to this question, Mipham Rinpoche tells us, has to do with the goal of practitioners who reach the arhat state. Their goal is very focused—their goal is to attain liberation from samsara, specifically to abandon the afflictive emotions and to cut through the ego, which is the root of samsara. They make their efforts for this very narrow purpose. They do not have the goal, or even the idea, that they should realize the emptiness or unborn, uncontrived nature of all phenomena. They have no scriptures that give teachings on this. They have no methods that teach how to do this, nor do they have upadesha instructions that are passed down through a lineage that would enable them to gain insight into how to do this. If, on the other hand, an arhat did have this aspiration, and they relied upon such teachings and such a method, of course they would attain complete realization.

Mipham Rinpoche goes on to say that even some philosophies within the Mahayana schools also have limitations. For example, the *Chitta-matra* (Skt.; Mind Only) school recognizes the emptiness of all outer phenomena, but yet there is a subtle type of grasping toward the mind's true existence. So Mipham Rinpoche again asks, "If they can realize the emptiness of outer phenomena, then why are they not able to realize the inner emptiness of the mind?" Yet, they do not.

Mipham Rinpoche's goal in bringing this up is that no philosophy can go beyond what it sets out to establish, whether it be a philosophy of the Hinayana or of the Mahayana. It has no scriptural basis for going beyond it, it teaches no methods for going beyond it, nor does it have any type of secret or oral tradition that points out how to go beyond it.

The Inner and Outer Lamas

Mipham Rinpoche says that two conditions must come together in order for us to realize the unborn nature of all phenomena: the inner and outer lama. One reason the shravakas and pratyekabuddhas cannot realize the unborn nature of all phenomena is that they only rely upon an outer lama. In the case of the pratyekabuddhas, it is more like a mere lama because he or she may not even be a living person.

The inner lama is a teaching specific to the Secret Mantrayana. When we build a proper foundation and follow an outer lama with devotion, it becomes possible to catch a glimpse of inner wisdom. This inner wisdom becomes a guide for us as well, and it is called the inner lama.

In our individualistic Western culture, most people really like the idea of the inner lama. It is important to remember that Mipham Rinpoche teaches reliance on the outer and inner lamas *together*. He says that reliance on the outer lama is necessary to even catch a glimpse of the inner lama. We do not enter the path and then just follow our own intrinsic wisdom, which will likely turn out to be egoic. We should remember that this is one of the ideas that Mipham Rinpoche refutes throughout this text.

Mipham Rinpoche also says there are differences in faculties between the practitioners of the Hinayana and of the Mahayana. He character-izes this difference by saying that some practitioners can rely upon their own strength, while practitioners with duller faculties must rely upon the strength of another. *Relying on your own strength* does not mean that you are not relying upon a teacher. Rather, it means that your faculties are sharp and that you naturally have the disposition to enter the path of the Mahayana, even without getting distracted or going elsewhere first.

To arrive on this path undistracted—what a cause for rejoicing! We should all reflect on the fact that we have entered the Mahayana path. We have met with the conditions of the outer lama, which will also bring us to meet the inner lama. After reflecting on the fact that we have good conditions that many others have not obtained, we should resolve not to lose this chance to practice during this lifetime.

Mipham Rinpoche points out some other differences between the Hinayana and the Mahayana. The paramitas, which are taught as num-bering either six or ten in the Mahayana, are not taught in exactly the same way in the Hinayana school. For that reason, it is hard to say that they could lead to the same type of realization.

Mipham Rinpoche concludes this section by saying that based on the conditions of the outer and inner lama, it is possible for the realization of the indivisible unborn nature of phenomena to be realized. Based on the practice of Dzogchen, this realization is quickly attained. Yet Mipham Rinpoche tells us in this text that without the outer and inner lama, even the practices of Dzogchen will not lead us to realization quickly.

Cut Through the Body in Its Entirety

The last section of this chapter contains several quotations by Nagarjuna from *The Precious Garland*. At this particular point in the text, Mipham Rinpoche gives commentary on Nagarjuna's text using the words of Longchenpa. By applying Longchenpa's teachings to Nagarjuna's basic scriptural quotations, the meaning is clarified and unmistaken.

We will start with the same idea that we started with in the last section, which is that the shravakas and pratyekabuddhas realize the selflessness of phenomena a little bit, but their realization is incomplete. Mipham Rinpoche then says that if they were to perfectly realize the selflessness of phenomena, this would contradict the meaning of Nagarjuna's scriptures.

The idea being proposed here is that merely knowing or merely understanding that the dependently imputed body is empty does not reverse or cut through grasping at the self. Khenpo Kunpal says, "mere knowing is different from realizing." In other words, we may have an understanding that the physical body is empty and that we should not grasp at it, but yet this does not reverse or cut through the instinctual tendency that we have to grasp.

We might wonder if there is any benefit at all to having an intellectual knowledge that the dependently imputed body is empty. We cannot really say that it is meaningless because it does help us to abandon our basic conceptual idea of the body. But it cannot cut through self-grasping at the instinctual level.

For example, even though we know that there is no inherently existent "I," if we are talking and someone interrupts us or is not paying attention to us, this makes us unhappy. Why is that? Simply speaking, it is because self-grasping is innate.

Mipham Rinpoche says that innate self-grasping results from grasping at the body in its entirety. When we think about the body, it is not just our physical form. We have feelings and energy, and we are habituated to reacting to so many different things. We treat our bodies as expressions of our egos. By mindfully recognizing when we are reacting strongly to a situation, we start to break down our grasping at the body in its entirety.

In the history of the teaching on the nine vehicles, there is a story told about a garden where there was a thorny, poisonous tree. Different people came up with ideas of how to protect themselves against the thorns. Someone suggested cutting each thorn from the branches one by one, and another suggested cutting off all the branches, and still others suggested cutting down the tree. These are all methods that could be used to benefit beings, but the smartest yogi would dig the tree out by the roots. When we remove the roots, nothing new can grow. So we can think that our grasping at the body in its entirety is like the root of that thorny tree. If we are able to cut through that, the three poisons could not arise even if we wanted them to. In the Vajrayana, specifically the Secret Mantrayana, we take this metaphor one step further. Rather than dig the tree up by the roots, we transform the tree's poisonous properties into medicinal nectar.

The *Precious Garland* says for as long as grasping at the body exists, then grasping at "I" exists. If grasping at "I" exists, then karma accumulates. Based on karma, then birth occurs. Mipham Rinpoche tells us if we have the aspiration to take birth in samsara again based on karma and afflictive emotions, then we should forget about examining our self-grasping. If we really want to fundamentally alter or transform our minds, then we need to work at cutting through this concept of the body in its entirety.

Nagarjuna is not the only scholar who states this. Mipham Rinpoche also relies upon the words of Chandrakirti's *Entering the Middle Way*. Chandrakirti says, "The fault of the afflictive emotion arises, without exception, from the view of the transitory collections. After understanding the object of this 'I,' a yogi negates the ego."

Why does Mipham Rinpoche call the body a transitory collection? This just refers to the fact that the body has no essence. It is a way to linguistically describe the body as being a collection of impermanent phenomena with no lasting essence. So after a yogi understands that the "I" is really just this transitory collection, then a real practitioner negates or cuts through the ego.

After Seeing the Nature of Suchness, Establishing All Vehicles as One

The idea of establishing all vehicles as one is related to the statement, "The buddhas are of a singular intention." This is a specific idea of the Nyingma school; that the knowledge gained in the lower schools ultimately has to be a subset or part of the peak vehicle, which is to say, the Dzogchen teachings. Furthermore, to be completely realized, beings must realize indivisible wisdom as pointed out in the Dzogchen teachings. This is also quoted in the tantras, so it is a general tantric idea as well.

In the *Treasury of the Dharmadhatu*, Longchenpa says that upon reaching the top, the highest peak, one can simultaneously see in all directions. Just so, this analogy applies to the different vehicles. When one reaches the highest peak, all vehicles become one because we can simultaneously see them all. They are completely indivisible from the point of view of the unborn, ultimate nature.

One scripture says, "All is indivisible in the dharmadhatu." What does it mean for a realized yogi to say that all is indivisible? This means that the object (the expanse of the dharmadhatu) and the perceiver (wisdom) are completely indistinguishable.

If Hinayana practitioners had already realized the selflessness of phenomenon, then it is illogical to try to establish all vehicles as singular. From the beginning they would have all been the same, there would have been no difference between any of them.

The Singular Thought of Nagarjuna and Maitreya

In conclusion, Mipham Rinpoche asserts that by using Longchenpa's reasoning—that Hinayana practitioners realize a little bit but not all of the selflessness of phenomena—it is possible to read the Buddha's definitive teachings, the commentaries of Nagarjuna and his followers, and Maitreya's *Prajnaparamita* in a way that is not only not contradictory but is in harmony. We have thoroughly explored how this is possible as we studied this topic. Based on Longchenpa's style of reasoning, we see that it is like pouring molasses into honey. There is no need to adopt any of their points of view while excluding the others.

CHAPTER SIX:

The Third Question

—When abiding in the unborn, ultimate nature,
is conceptual grasping present or not?

THIS TOPIC BUILDS on the intellectual certainty in emptiness that we have been cultivating so far. It presents what the view is by clearly explaining what certainty is not. Through Mipham Rinpoche's brilliant presentation, we can now begin to relate to the uncontrived view of Dzogchen by coming to a clear understanding of what mistakes we might make in understanding the view properly.

The topic starts by discussing emptiness and nonconceptuality in terms of the uncontrived view. To begin with, is the uncontrived view of Dzogchen synonymous with emptiness, is it a mere nonconceptual state, or is it distinct from these? We will then explore what is needed to transform our intellectual certainty into actual experience, in order to begin to catch a glimpse of what is meant by the phrase *actual meditation*.

When we receive teachings on the view, resting may seem easy. Perhaps this is only deceptively so. One reason it may seem easy is that there are so many places where we can make a mistake *without even knowing it*. This third question and its answer were specifically composed to help us avoid the most common mistakes we make as practitioners of the Secret Mantrayana.

Teachings on Dzogchen may also seem easy to understand. However, if we subtly examine our experience, it is actually difficult for us to bring together our intellectual understanding with our meditative experience, so that we are sure that what we experience is realization. Our intellectual understanding colors our experience when we are sitting on the cushion, and experience gives rise to realization. However, if there is a problem in our intellectual understanding of the teachings, then when we sit, our experience will not be of the perfectly pure uncontrived view. How could we experience the view when we have misunderstood the teachings? As a result, realization cannot ripen. The meditation practice of Secret Mantryana practitioners often fails to improve for this very reason.

We should now know with confidence that a precise, intellectual understanding of the view is essential. As in previous chapters, the examinations and discussions of this chapter facilitate our understanding, as these are the means for personally engaging the teachings. As our intellectual understanding becomes ever more subtle and clear, our experience of meditation will become even more stable when we sit down to practice.

Perhaps this is why Mipham Rinpoche says it is so important to bring together the meaning of the scriptures, our own logical analyses, and the meaning of the upadesha instructions completely, without contradiction. *We must be able to reconcile the meaning of the teachings on many different levels in order to understand them in a perfect and unmistaken way.*

In the spirit of personal engagement, I will give you ideas to contemplate during this chapter. I will not answer each and every question. If I were to simply give you the answers to these questions, you would not fully engage with the questions and come to a personal understanding. The purpose of my questions to you is not for you to come up with the right answers. Rather, through deep reflection on these questions, you will be able to improve your understanding of any teachings you receive. I also hope that this will help you to see the value of developing a close and personal relationship with an authentic lama, as these types of questions are generally answered based on direct interaction and instruction from a close lama.

To introduce Mipham Rinpoche's response to the third question, we should know that the path can be condensed into three parts. The first part is our preparation for practice, the second is actual abiding or actual meditation, and the third is the period that comes after practice, or post-equipoise. This chapter focuses on the second stage, actual meditation itself. For this reason, I have chosen to give an upadesha style of commentary on this topic rather than a philosophical presentation. In other words, my explanation of this topic focuses on developing experience in meditation.

Begin with Personal Examination

Many of us began practicing Buddhism and entered the Vajrayana path years ago, while others are new to the path. It is equally important for everyone to engage in regular self-examination, no matter how long they have been on the path. We should reflect on the strength of our afflictive emotions and investigate whether we have correctly understood the meaning of the teachings and applied them to our practice perfectly. One way to assess our meditation practice is to notice how easily the mind becomes overpowered by afflictive emotions. If we find that we that are still easily overpowered in spite of our efforts to practice, we should make an even greater effort to work on taming our own emotions—especially very strong emotions like jealousy or anger.

We can see the signs of internalized practice through both the quality of a practitioner's personality and through the expression of his or her meditation in daily activities. The practitioner's personality is described as subdued, or tamed. This means that a yogi acts in accordance with the teachings in a very precise way and also acts in the way that worldly people expect. The signs of meditation are easy to see, because this simply relates to whether we are expressing coarse afflictive emotions. We can actually just look at each other, or at ourselves, to see what our own personality and actions say about the strength of our practice.

Based on this explanation, we can see that the way we understand and take up the view and the way that we practice meditation directly benefits us. Simply speaking, meditation protects us from acting on our afflictive emotions. But we should not fool ourselves about this; we should not pretend that we are not bothered by our emotions. We need to make an honest effort to notice what is happening in our own minds and make an effort to practice as much as we can.

One of the strongest tendencies in Western culture is blaming others for our thoughts, feelings, and actions. As a lama, I have seen that sometimes students even blame me for their own shortcomings! If you want to understand these teachings and you practice diligently, it is also your responsibility to examine yourself and try to see your own faults clearly. If you notice that your afflictive emotions are strong, then you should take this as a sign that you do not precisely understand the view. This should not make you feel bad about yourself or become a source of depression. Rather, it should motivate you to think, "It is my responsibility as a practitioner to bring together the meaning of the teachings, my own logical analysis, and my experience. This is something I really want, and I resolve to do it."

Many of us have received teachings on Atiyoga Dzogchen, but we still must examine our minds. It is not enough to just receive teachings. By relying on Mipham Rinpoche's text, we will gain new tools that allow us to examine ourselves and to understand our own progress on the path. Remember that water that is not clean at the source will run dirty downstream. We should apply this metaphor to ourselves!

What Does Not Grasping at Anything *Mean?*

The idea of *not grasping at anything* is a very popular contemporary idea. Many people think that this is the complete and perfect definition of meditation. In this section of the text, Mipham Rinpoche will discuss whether the phrase *not grasping at anything* is synonymous with the perfectly pure uncontrived view.

Not grasping at anything is a popular idea, especially among Kagyu and Nyingma practitioners. There are even Kagyu and Nyingma lamas who teach this as the perfectly pure view of meditation. However, a practitioner who understands this to be the correct view can never really embody or express the uncontrived view. I believe that Mipham Rinpoche's goal in this chapter is to correct the ideas of this type of practitioner.

Mipham Rinpoche begins his discussion with a question, "Does the phrase *not grasping at anything* accurately describe the actual experience of meditation?" The answer is: not necessarily. The words *seem* right, but as we know, even something that sounds right may not be exactly right.

Not Grasping at Anything *as the Perfectly Pure View*

Mipham Rinpoche says that the phrase *not grasping at anything* could describe either wrong view or the perfectly pure view, depending on the level of skill and experience of the practitioner.

First, he gives a definition of *not grasping at anything* as an expression of the perfectly pure view. As we will see, Mipham Rinpoche adds many qualifications to this definition. He says a practitioner must engage in listening and cut through his or her doubts, develop certainty based on finding personal meaning in the teachings, gain meditative experience through dedicated practice, and catch glimpses of the view as a way to further develop on the path. Our personal experience in practice and uncommon certainty in the uncontrived view of meditation, in addition to our deep connection with an authentic lama who directly introduces us to the mind's nature, enables us to see the indivisible, primordial nature of wisdom, free of the four extremes. When we abide in this experience, it is called *not grasping at anything*, which *is* an expression of the perfectly pure view.

We have reflected on the nature of emptiness during the first two topics. Now, we will use our understanding of emptiness as we reflect upon the uncontrived view.

Khenpo Kunpal's commentary reads, "The dharmadhatu is free of all modes of grasping, such as existence and nonexistence. Like pouring water into water, the self dissolves into it." In the Dzogchen teachings, we often talk about the idea of *not grasping at anything* by saying that any mode of grasping dissolves into the dharmadhatu "like pouring water into water." I could try to tell you exactly what this phrase means, but it is best that each practitioner personally reflect on the meaning of this metaphor for him or herself.

The phrase "the self dissolves into it" refers to the experience of meditation—the actual experience of abiding rather than mere preparation. Again, contemplate the meaning of this phrase for yourself. Why does Khenpo Kunpal use the word *dissolve?* And how does dissolution occur?

We usually want to give simple answers to these types of questions, such as "This is pointing out the experience of nonduality." Such a generic, pat answer is not very helpful for your practice, however. Our own experience is not general but specific; it has a unique flavor that we recognize and remember. It is important for us to go beyond such generalizations when we personally contemplate the teachings.

We are very good at using our intelligence by this point, but not many of us have much experience abiding in actual meditation. For this reason, we cannot directly understand what Mipham Rinpoche is saying. Personal experience is very important. Even if we are not quite able to digest the meaning of these phrases just yet, we should feel confident that we can if we keep working with them.

The Importance of Bringing the Teaching into Experience

Not grasping at anything and being completely free of concepts are distinct phrases that have the same meaning. But you must remember that concepts are not just intellectual ideas, they are also emotions. Afflictive emotions arise at almost every instant, especially when we practice, whether they take the form of attachment, jealousy, pride, anger, or bewilderment. Even when we sit down, intending to practice, thoughts and feelings constantly arise.

If we do not know how to be free of all modes of grasping and dissolve our afflictive emotions into the dharmadhatu like pouring water into water, then we are unable to apply the meaning of this teaching to the perfectly pure view. Whenever we receive advice that points out the experience of meditation, it is essential to apply it to our own minds and afflictive emotions. Through mindfulness, we must recognize when an afflictive emotion has arisen and we also need to know the proper way to allow the emotion to dissolve into the experience of meditation.

What Is Needed for a Nonconceptual State to Be the Perfectly Pure View?

Patrul Rinpoche and other Longchen Nyingthig masters have also asked the question, "What is needed for a nonconceptual state to equal the perfectly pure view?" When the ordinary mind meets with the condition of an outer object, an afflictive emotion will arise. If, when the afflictive emotion arises, we rest effortlessly free of concepts *on top of its arising*, this *could* be perfect purity, but it is not necessarily so. However, if effort is made on top of the emotion's arising, conceptuality is definitely present. We should examine the phrase *on top of that arising*. This is an important phrase to understand. However, its meaning is experiential rather than intellectual.

Note that I said that even upon the arising of afflictive emotions, if the mind remains effortlessly free of concepts, that mere effortlessness does not *guarantee* abiding in the perfectly pure view. This is a very subtle distinction. Why did Patrul Rinpoche and his followers point this out? What is missing from the mere nonconceptual experience that does not allow it to rise to the level of resting in the uncontrived view?

Transforming an Afflictive Emotion into Wisdom

To answer this question, reflect on this example: Imagine there is a beautiful man or woman in your doorway. When you see that person, your mind immediately generates attachment. Then, because you have diligently trained in mindfulness, you recognize that you have generated attachment and effortlessly, the attachment dissolves.

Many people may think that the experience I have just described is the uncontrived view of Dzogchen. But in the Nyingma tradition, the view requires more than this. It is not just dissolution; we must actually transform the afflictive emotion into wisdom. Thus, we need to understand that merely dissolving an afflictive emotion does not ensure that it has been transformed into wisdom. They are two different things. In the example, there is no certainty at all that desire has been transformed to wisdom.

The Expression of Rigpa

When an afflictive emotion or concept dissolves, what obstructs it from becoming the perfectly pure view? If the expression of the energy of *rigpa* (Tib.; the mind's primordially present, self-cognizant wisdom awareness) is obstructed, the experience of meditation *is* nonconceptual, but it is not the perfectly pure view. In other words, the absence of the energy of rigpa prevents the affliction from transforming into wisdom. So the defining characteristic of whether that experience is mere non-conceptuality or the perfectly pure view is whether or not the expression of the mind's primordial awareness, or rigpa, is obstructed in that moment.

Let's talk about the word *expression* (Tib. *rtsal*). Generally speaking, there is *potential*, which then expresses. What is this potential? I will say a few things about it now, but we will revisit this discussion again in the fifth question and answer. In short, if there were no potential to express wisdom, the transformation of concepts to wisdom would be impossible. That is the idea behind the word "potential."

The Play of Wisdom

Let's also introduce the word *play* (Tib. *rol pa*). Most Secret Mantrayana practitioners have probably encountered the phrase *play of wisdom*. From the Tibetan point of view, the word *play* is very similar to the word *expression*, but it is a distinct word. *Play* has a sense of being a result while *expression* relates more to a potential.

Now we have three words to work with as we explore this topic: *rigpa*, *expression*, and *play*, which all relate to whether the expression of rigpa is obstructed or unobstructed. We have said that if the expression of rigpa is obstructed, then *not grasping at anything* cannot be the perfectly pure view. Alternatively, if the expression of rigpa is *unobstructed*, then *not grasping at anything* becomes the perfectly pure view. In this case, *play* can be recognized or experienced as wisdom itself and one can abide in a nonconceptual moment of perfect purity, or the uncontrived view.

Take the example of shooting a bow and arrow. In this metaphor, the arm's strength is like the energy or presence of rigpa. The distance that the arrow will fly is in proportion to the arm's strength. However, when the energy that carries the arrow exhausts itself, the arrow will naturally fall to the ground. It is not that the nonconceptual experience ceases at this point; but it is no longer perfectly pure.

I want to add one more thing about the way of abiding, again using the example of desire upon seeing the beautiful man or woman. When, on top of the condition of perceiving this object, we recognize the arising of an afflictive emotion, this is mindfulness endowed with rigpa, and we can abide effortlessly. At first, our experience of desire is very strong, but based on the presence of mindfulness endowed with rigpa, the experience of the afflictive emotion weakens while the experience of wisdom becomes stronger and stronger. In this way, the afflictive emotion is like a wave, which dissolves into the ocean of rigpa as it gets weaker and weaker. This is what it means to pour water into water.

Unobstructed Rigpa

The great master Karma Lingpa said, "Nonconceptual nonmeditation is the nature of suchness." I would explain this to mean that nonconceptual effortless abiding that is endowed with the unobstructed energy of rigpa is actual meditation, or the nature of mind itself.

In the moment we experience any of the five poisons, namely desire, anger, jealousy, pride, or ignorance, when the experience of the afflictive emotion rests in its own place and, at the same time, the energy of rigpa is not obstructed, then the essence of wisdom is present. If the energy of rigpa is missing, we abide in a hazy void, somewhere between being asleep and awake—we are not sure what state it is. We have a tendency to get lost there.

As soon as we notice that our meditation is not endowed with rigpa, we have to "wake up" our meditation. This is just like when a car runs out of gas. It eventually stops, and new energy has to be put into the car for it to move again. The only thing that can refresh our meditation is mindfulness—the recognition that the energy or glow of rigpa is no longer present.

There are two things that indicate when unobstructed rigpa is present. The first is that experience is colored by rigpa. The second is a feeling that the energy of rigpa is present. The presence of rigpa's energy is like when heat radiates off of a piece of red-hot steel. That radiation is like an energetic presence. The color of rigpa is like when you stare at something for a long time and then close your eyes, and the presence of color is still in front of your eyes.

The Power of Effort

In this degenerate time, Vajrayana practitioners usually lack the profound preparation of the yogis of old. For example, our *ngöndro* (Tib.; foundational) practice, our *shamatha* practice, and our training in the practice of *yantra* yoga (Skt.; wisdom channels, vital energies, and vital essences) are very shallow by comparison. If we had the same training and experience as the yogis of old, we would not find it difficult to abide in the actual experience of meditation, but we lack their mastery of these essential skills. Also, afflictive emotions tend to be extremely strong in the modern Western world. Therefore, we need to train over and over to recognize when an afflictive emotion arises, leaving the afflictive emotion in its own place, and we also have to notice whether unobstructed rigpa is present or not. We should know that this recognition or noticing is synonymous with the word *mindfulness.*

Effort is the only foundation that we modern practitioners have to rely on. Because we do not have the profound foundation of the yogis of old, we have to make up for it with the amount of effort that we put into our practice. *Our effort is most usefully focused on mindfulness training, because it is mindfulness that enables us to recognize and abide in the uncontrived view of Dzogchen.*

The Five Piths to Develop Actual Meditation

Dzogchen Pema Benzar gave advice to help practitioners experience actual meditation in the form of five pith instructions. These five are:

- *Increasing our faith and devotion.* It is important to remember that faith and devotion are necessary even for shamatha practice, not to mention trying to abide in the perfectly pure view. Faith and devotion are two of the keys to meditation.
- *Cultivating renunciation.* Without renunciation, we will not feel like making any effort at all. Renunciation is like the feet of our meditation. It carries us along the path.
- *The eyes of meditation are the view.* Our meditation must be endowed with the view, or it does not rise to the level of actual abiding.

- *Meditation must have life-force.* The life-force of meditation is the quality of remembrance, or mindfulness.
- *Meditation must have heart.* Bodhichitta is the heart of meditation. Bodhicitta means conventional bodhichitta and also ultimate bodhichitta, which is the nature of mind itself.

When all five of these qualities are present in our meditation, it is possible for us to *functionally abide.* This is to say that even though we do not nakedly abide in the same way as a bodhisattva on the first bhumi, we can approach that experience. When we reflect on these five qualities, we will notice that we are stronger in some qualities and weaker in others. We should work to bring all five qualities into balance.

"Not Grasping at Anything" as Wrong View

In contrast to his presentation on the perfectly pure view, Mipham Rinpoche presents *not grasping at anything* as the wrong view. Mipham Rinpoche teaches on this because a type of meditation called Hashang once spread throughout China. The Hashang teachings presented meditation as grasping at nothing at all as the correct view of meditation, with no further qualifications. Vigorous debate resulted as the Hashang teachings spread, because many people claimed that the Nyingma view was the same as the Hashang view. This particular part of the text especially applies to Western practitioners, because many meditation teachings being given in the West are much like the Hashang teachings.

We can understand that the experience of mere nonconceptuality does not equal the perfectly pure, uncontrived view in several ways. First, the Hashang or similar teachings do not mention the qualities of the view, for example its empty essence and clear nature. Additionally, there is no oral tradition of teachings that a practitioner can rely on to develop and check his or her experience, nor is there a tradition of contemplation. Practitioners are simply told to meditate, and each relies on his or her own idea of what that means.

A similar phenomenon has occurred in the West. Because the Buddhist tradition is so new here, we do not know many things that come naturally to people born into a Buddhist culture. For example, we do not know that we need to study, or what we need to study. If we fail to rely upon a lama who makes sure that we really understand the path, we could think that meditation is whatever we think it is, or whatever we want it to be. Or, as we talked about in the last section, we might think the view is mere nonconceptuality.

Mipham Rinpoche distinguishes between the *not grasping at anything* that is part of the Dzogchen tradition and ordinary, worldly meditation by saying that even practitioners in the formless realms on the worldly path may abide in a nongrasping meditative absorption, yet they have not realized the nature of wisdom. Thus, the difference between the traditions of Dzogchen and worldly meditation is like the difference between the earth and the sky.

I have heard of teachings being given in the West by teachers who say that no preparatory practice is necessary, that Dzogchen is for everyone, and that students need no prior qualifications to receive teachings. These practitioners have no experience in listening or contemplation. They are simply told to abide in a state of nonconceptual nongrasping. What Mipham Rinpoche says here is completely the opposite. He says that even a foolish person with no prior training or experience can come to us and say, "There is nothing equal to my realization! I'll introduce you to the nature of mind." Then, they tell us to "Relax in the mind, free of grasping."

From beginningless time, we have been so relaxed about everything. Do we really need anyone to tell us to relax? Mipham Rinpoche says being told to relax without striving to develop certainty by understanding scripture, logical reasoning, and the upadeshas will merely be the cause for circling again and again in the three realms of samsara. This is an uncharacteristically stern comment from Mipham Rinpoche; he feels that this is a very important point!

The Empty Void

A beginning practitioner who has little meditation experience may have an experience that seems nonconceptual, but is in fact merely fuzzy or ambiguous. There is really no clarity or awareness in this state. We may feel "spaced out" or like we are losing time while we abide. It is just like being in an empty void. We should know that this is one embodiment of *not grasping at anything.*

When we first start practicing and do not have any other experience, it seems like the empty void is exactly what meditation is supposed to be. It is especially seductive, since it seems nonconceptual and the mind seems relaxed as compared to our normal state. It is easy to get attached to it and not take our examination or practice any further. I consider the empty void to be the biggest obstacle for Dzogchen practitioners, as many practitioners completely misunderstand the view and fixate on the empty void instead.

Does the Mind Have Form or Color?

Mipham Rinpoche points out another way we could be mistaken as we try to understand the nature of mind. When we are introduced to the nature of mind in the Secret Mantrayana tradition, we are often asked questions like, "Does the mind have color? Does the mind have form?" Most of us would easily answer, "No." But why do you give this answer? It is difficult to pinpoint. Regarding the question on whether mind has form, you might answer, "Because you cannot locate it." But does a mere lack of location define the characteristic of *form?*

Why does Mipham Rinpoche point this out? One reason is that we think we already know the answers to these questions. We know intellectually that the mind has no color or form. But if you were to ask scholars or cowherders if the mind has color or form, both could answer this question correctly. It is not special knowledge. But many Vajrayana practitioners never go past this superficial exploration.

In our tradition, we are taught to examine whether a phenomenon has an origin, whether it abides or passes away. This gives rise to the idea that the phenomenon is formless and also free of other material characteristics. But I have read Western Dzogchen books written in English that present what are presumably *pointing-out instructions* that read, "Abide in that which you do not see," meaning that we are to abide in this simple lack of form and color that we have deduced intellectually. Mipham Rinpoche disagrees with giving this as an instruction to point out the view. He puts this section in his text because we are in danger of thinking that the view is the mind's mere formlessness, lack of color or other characteristics.

"Where the mind arises, where it abides, and where it passes" are difficult questions to answer. Yet our intellectual knowledge of the answers does not rise to the level of certainty. It does not give us new experience or insight into practice on its own. Mipham Rinpoche points out that intellectual understanding is quite distinct from direct experience. Conviction in our own experience is what rises to the level of certainty. Thus, repeated reflection, practice, and experience are the basis for developing deeper certainty.

The view can be described by the metaphor of a hundred streams that travel over land and converge into a single river that finally flows beneath a bridge. This is to say that we can abide in the view no matter what afflictive emotion or type of outer condition comes up. The view is like the bridge that can unify and transcend all of the streams at once.

Clear Awareness

Mipham Rinpoche defines ordinary mind by saying it has two qualities: clear nature and awareness. We combine these two when we say that the ordinary mind's nature is clear awareness. When I say clear awareness, I do not mean awareness in the sense of rigpa. I mean ordinary awareness in the sense of being able to cognize, recognize, or understand. Also notice that the word "clear" is distinct from the aspect of the nature of mind called "clarity." Additionally, ordinary mind is described as a clear, knowing mind of myriad expressions that is constantly in motion.

Three Common Mistakes About the Qualities of Mind

Three mistakes are commonly made about the mind's qualities, according to Mipham Rinpoche.

The belief that recognizing clear awareness is enough. I have heard modern lamas say that recognizing the clear awareness of the ordinary mind is sufficient to gain an understanding of the mind's nature.

Thinking that because mind is beyond form and color, one has recognized the mind's ultimately uncontrived nature. It is a mistake to think that merely understanding that mind is beyond sensory or material limitations is the same as knowing or realizing the nature of mind.

Refuting only two of the four extremes to establish the view. This last mistake is pervasive. Because the mind's nature is beyond form and color, it is not existent. Because the mind has clear awareness, it is not nonexistent. Although only two of the four extremes have been cut through, some lamas or scholars describe this as the luminous dharmakaya. Alternately, we might also misunderstand what it means to cut through the other two extremes of *both* and *neither.* We might understand the extreme of *both* to mean two statements regarding what the mind's nature *is:* it *is* of clear awareness and it *is not* of form, shape, and color. We could understand *neither* to mean two ways that the mind's nature does not exist—its clear awareness does not *exist,* and color, form, and shape do not *exist.* However, these two statements simply mean the same thing; *they cannot be the way to cut through the extremes of both and neither.* The mind cannot break through this circular logic.

Regarding the dharmakaya or nature of mind itself, keep in mind the words of the great master Sakya Trakpa Gyaltsen, "If grasping is present, it is not the view." In order for the view to be completely uncontrived and free of extremes, we must cut through all four extremes. If grasping at any aspect of existence or nonexistence is present, however subtle, it cannot be the view of Dzogchen. If we are not completely free of grasping, experiencing a thoroughly nondual state, we cannot directly see the face of the mind's nature. Thus, we are unable to meet the great dharmakaya.

Three Aspects of the Nature of Mind

Generally when we talk about the mind's ultimate nature, we say that the nature of mind is beyond the four extremes and endowed with three primordially present aspects or qualities. Although these three aspects are understood and experienced as an indivisible, singular state, we do distinguish between them at the conventional level. These are:

- The aspect of uncontrived emptiness.

- The aspect of clarity, which again is distinct from ordinary mind's clear awareness.
- Omnipresent compassion, sometimes referred to as all-pervasive capacity.

It is difficult to explain in words how the nature of mind is of these indivisible three qualities. The key is to understand Mipham Rinpoche's assertion that emptiness, just as it is, appears as ordinary mind's motion. Motion, as it is, is also uncontrived emptiness.

Dharmakaya as the Soul

Cutting through all four extremes is a problem that many practitioners will have as they explore this topic more deeply. Mipham Rinpoche says that the mind's basis of existence or nonexistence is kept within the mind. When we cannot go beyond cutting through the extremes of existence and nonexistence, we find ourselves subtly grasping at the nature of mind as though it is a soul, or the eternal Self that is presented in many non-Buddhist religions. In the root text, Mipham Rinpoche calls this the "inconceivable self." "Inconceivable" refers to the fact that in naming the soul, we attempt to label and relate to something that is actually beyond all concepts and extremes.

Mipham Rinpoche's Understanding of Perfect Purity

The nature of mind is distinct from the descriptions of ordinary mind and the inconceivable self. The mind itself and all phenomena that appear within samsara and nirvana have a primordially empty essence. They have no true existence, yet their appearances are expressions of all-encompassing, limitless, unobstructed, interdependent origination that naturally arises as indivisible clarity and emptiness, or the singular, natural state beyond all extremes of existence, nonexistence, both, and neither. It is beyond mental concepts and inexpressible in words. Seeing the pith of this nature, which is naked, indestructible, indivisible awareness and emptiness without any mode of grasping present whatsoever, is called *perfect purity*.

Grasping at Selflessness Is Not a Bad Thing Early on the Path

In the next section of the root text, Mipham Rinpoche asserts that grasping at the concept of selflessness is not necessarily bad for a beginning practitioner. Mipham Rinpoche often gives teachings for an ideal audience, such as yogis of profound experience. But in this section of the text, he points out that practitioners who are not realized yogis may actually need to grasp at a concept of selflessness in order to be able to move beyond it. This is similar to using the concept of the non-affirming negative as a conceptual basis for meditating on emptiness, as we talked about in topic one.

It is easy to understand why this is true. We can think about this section of the text as a prophecy for modern Dharma practice in the West. A lama buys a plane ticket and arrives in the West. He or she gives a teaching on Dzogchen and says something like, "If there is any grasping at all present, it is not meditation." This is the only instruction that the student is given. The student is not prepared through listening and contemplation before receiving the teaching. The student's experience is something like, "Wow, my mind is constantly grasping! Whether good or bad, I'm always having thoughts."

The lama's words and the student's mind seem completely contradictory. What is being taught and what the student experiences are like fire and water. This causes confusion. For this reason, Mipham Rinpoche advocates using the concept of selflessness as a way to connect the student's experience to the meaning of the teaching.

Grasping at selflessness has purpose when we are beginning practitioners because it reflects the reality of our experience. The scriptures state, "First, one grasps at the self and thinks 'I.' This gives rise to grasping at outer objects as 'mine.'"

Grasping at "I" and "mine" leads us to take birth in samsara. No matter how many times we examine this, we will probably end up knowing that our self-attachment is illogical. Yet simply knowing it is illogical does not make it easier to cut through. For a beginner, it is incredibly helpful to practice by using selflessness as a concept or support for practice.

Mipham Rinpoche asserts that merely thinking, "I don't actually exist," or "There is no me," will not really help us go beyond intellectual knowing. We have to effortfully engage in analysis. *Especially, we have to question where the self arises from, where it abides, and where it passes.* Then we bring our contemplation into our experience by working with meditation—by alternating between this analytical style of contemplation and then either resting in the mind's nature or trying to experience what is meant by "resting" if we are a less experienced practitioner.

Mipham Rinpoche uses the metaphor of someone seeing a poisonous snake to show what it means to go beyond intellectual knowing or mere intellectual certainty. If you see a poisonous snake and then, to alleviate your fear, you simply tell yourself, "There is no snake," you will still be frightened. As far as you know, the snake is still there. But if you see the same snake, and analyze the snake in an outer, inner, and secret way to see if it truly exists, and if you start to feel certain that there is no snake, then your fear will naturally dissolve. This metaphor describes the dissolution of an afflictive emotion; it not to say that conventionally, one need not beware of snakes. It is the same thing with selflessness. Merely thinking "There is no 'I'" will not really help you, whereas a thorough analysis combined with meditation will be of great benefit.

Work in Stages

The great master Longchenpa said that practitioners should work in stages. For example, it is not appropriate to tell a beginning practitioner that the nature of all phenomena is uncontrived or that all phenomena are empty. This teaching can give rise to a kind of false arrogance. Our shallow understanding of the nature of all phenomena can cause us to lose conviction in karma. We start to confuse conventional and ultimate reality. We think that things do not actually exist and that we do not have to really deal with them. Therefore, working with selflessness as a concept is a helpful stage in between grasping and cutting through grasping.

The great master Shantideva also said that if one can meditate on the concept of grasping at nothing at all, then this, too, will slowly be abandoned through proper guidance on the path. On one hand, we do not want to cultivate the idea that grasping is a good thing. On the other hand, we need to grasp at intellectual ideas like selflessness when we begin.

Mipham Rinpoche's vision of the path is one that develops in stages and requires us to work consistently with practice, rather than to try to realize something right away. For example, if I jumped into a lake when I did not know how to swim, I would probably die. However, if I went into shallow water as a child and slowly moved into deeper water as I became a more skillful swimmer, then one day I could jump into the lake without fear. Mipham Rinpoche is really advising us to become prepared and skillful so that we will be ready for deeper and more profound levels of practice as we develop further on the path.

Perform the Analysis Over and Over

Mipham Rinpoche also says that engaging in this analysis once and not finding a lasting or permanent self will not bring us to the level of experiential certainty. We will need to engage in this analysis hundreds or even thousands of times, because we are so habituated to our self-attachment. One great thing about this style of contemplation is that it does not need to be done as sitting practice. We can do it while we are taking a walk, at work, or in any other part of our daily routine.

We can also engage in formal daily practice to find out how many times we react with extreme self-attachment during one day. When we engage in this practice, we should not only keep a tally but also use it as a condition to sharpen our mindfulness. I sometimes have students keep a bag and black beans with them, and tell them to drop a black bean into the bag every time they notice a strong reaction. This will probably give us thousands of chances to practice each day!

The Benefits of Repeated Analysis

There are two benefits to continuously engaging in analysis or examination on the mind's origin, abiding, and passing. The first is that the mind gets tired of examination. When the mind gets tired, it becomes easier to enter the experience of the nature of mind once we are directly introduced to it.

The second has to do with how habituated we are to our ordinary way of thinking. When we examine the origin, abiding, and passing of mind, it is like holding the key to the primordial, unborn nature. It helps us relate to the nature of mind, which is something we are not habituated to doing.

Khenpo Kunpal's commentary says that both scholars and fools know that the mind is not permanent, but this does not make either one of them realized, because their knowledge is mere intellectual understanding. Mipham Rinpoche makes a similar point when he says that even if we examine someone's head a hundred times to look for the horns of a cow before concluding that there are none there, continuing to look for horns does not help us at all to realize the emptiness of the person's head.

Use Your Own Analysis and Meditation to Develop Experiential Certainty

At this point, I will give practice instructions based on this topic. *Each day, analyze the origin, abiding, and passing of an afflictive emotion or situation at least ten times.* This will allow you to train in mindfulness and recall these teachings. *Engage in analysis of the mind's origin, abiding, and passing.* When you do not find the origin, abiding, and passing, abide in that which you do not find. Alternate between this analytical style of meditation and resting. Become skillful and flexible at using each one, and moving back and forth between them.

The Main Practice Is Free of All Modes of Grasping

We need to transition from a conceptual style of meditation to one free of reference points by cutting through all grasping, and abide in the great primordially pure nature of mind. Thus, constant training gives rise to certainty as we gain experience and are able to abide in the mind's primordially liberated nature. The experience of abiding gives rise to the *wisdom of superior seeing*, or insight, which is described to be like the clear flame of a butter lamp.

I summarized Mipham Rinpoche's advice for practice above. But I want to point out that it relies upon the same style or method that we ordinarily rely upon in Secret Mantrayana practice. This style is the root of our entire tradition of meditation. For example, in *ngöndro*, or foundational practice, we generate a visualization—a conceptual practice. When we complete the practice, we completely dissolve it and abide in perfection stage. Generally speaking, we first focus on a concept and then later we cut through the concept and abide beyond that concept. This is exactly the type of practice that Mipham Rinpoche is talking about.

Applying this same idea to the teachings in the text, we begin with a concept of selflessness. We then cut completely through the concept of selflessness and abide free of all concepts. Mipham Rinpoche says that if our meditation is endowed with certainty and we alternate between conceptual meditation and meditation free from reference points, our practice and experience will increase like the waxing moon.

Meditation on Wrong View Versus Perfectly Pure Meditation

This is a very important topic. We all love the practice of meditation, but we need to know exactly what we are meditating on and how to meditate, or else meditation is a waste of time. For this reason, Mipham Rinpoche distinguishes between what he calls a foolish person's meditation and perfectly pure meditation.

Recognizing the difference between a foolish person's meditation and perfectly pure meditation is easy. Mipham Rinpoche says we know the quality of meditation being practiced based on the signs of body, speech, and mind, just like how when we see the sign of smoke, we know that there is fire, or when we see water birds, we know that there is water nearby. If we are practicing pure meditation, our good qualities will continually increase. This will happen, if not on a day-by-day basis, then on a month-by-month or year-by-year basis, depending on our capacity. Mipham Rinpoche also says that in order to cultivate this kind of perfectly pure meditation, we absolutely have to engage in a period of examination. Studying a text like *The Beacon of Certainty* naturally creates this situation for us.

Foolish meditation based on wrong view often happens in the modern age. This is especially prevalent among Nyingma and Kagyu practitioners.

A student will receive an empowerment and maybe a short teaching—pointing-out instructions or something to that effect. They hope that, just based on this one empowerment and this one teaching, they will realize the nature of mind and attain liberation.

I do not want to discourage anyone from receiving empowerments and pith instructions. But if we put all of our hopes in these, we will find that realization will not ripen because we have skipped the period of examination. All we have done is receive a short teaching. We have not engaged in examination in order to experience the meaning of the teaching, or had our own personal experience.

We could say that simply sitting in a meditative posture and closing our eyes is meditation. But if we have not preceded that with a period of examination, then it is a foolish person's meditation. In summary, without a period of examination during which we develop certainty that serves as a bridge between our ordinary experience and realization, realization cannot manifest.

The Way to Completely Destroy All Modes of Grasping

It is possible to destroy all modes of grasping by alternating between focused, conceptual meditation and meditation free of reference points. This is what Mipham Rinpoche refers to as *ultimate meditation.*

How do we destroy grasping? We listen to and contemplate teachings on the uncontrived nature and the mind's elaborations. We analyze and examine, develop certainty, and learn to authentically abide in the mind's nature. Based on these activities, we finally come to a state where we genuinely do not see a difference between appearance and emptiness, samsara and nirvana. We experience a state that is free of partiality and limitations. This is sometimes referred to as "not seeing the great sight" or the "paramita of sacred seeing."

We must rely on the guidance of an authentic lama to help us to clarify our experience of *sacred seeing* and recognize if we have fallen into a wrong view, the empty void, or attachment to our experience. Mipham Rinpoche gives the metaphor of an inexperienced person tasting molasses for the first time. Because they are inexperienced, they may think it is molasses, but they cannot articulate their experience.

Although our intuition about our experience could be correct, it may also be wrong.

In this same way, when we lack certainty and the guidance of an authentic lama, we might misunderstand our experience. We might think, "I am experiencing it exactly right!" We might totally trust ourselves. However, our intuition might not be quite right. This concern gives rise to the tradition of "offering the view" to a lama with whom we have developed an uncommonly deep relationship, so that the lama might point out our mistakes or misunderstandings. Again, this tradition points to the crucial nature of a close and personal relationship with a lama to support our progress on the Secret Mantryana path.

CHAPTER SEVEN

The Fourth Question

—*Which is best: analytical meditation or actual abiding?*

A s we explore this question, we will find that some schools believe that analytical meditation, which we could also refer to as examination or contemplation, is absolutely the most essential part of practice. Other schools believe that simply abiding in meditation is most important. Mipham Rinpoche's position is that taking up each of these practices individually has both faults and good qualities. When we combine them properly, however, we attain the skills that allow us to abide in the uncontrived view of Dzogchen.

The position of simply trying to abide is advocated by some practitioners of the Nyingma and Kagyu schools. Their rationale is understandable. They say, "When you practice analytical meditation, aren't you just creating conceptual thoughts? When you examine and study things, aren't you just making the mind busier?" For this reason, they advocate just trying to abide in a nonconceptual state the best that you are able. They believe "just sit there, clear the mind, and do nothing" is the pith of all upadesha instructions.

As discussed in the third topic, this is a common idea among Western Buddhists as well. Many Western Buddhists think, "Why bother to study Madhyamaka philosophy? Isn't it complicated, just bringing you more mental activity? Meditation is about clearing away your conceptual thoughts."

These types of yogis also existed in Tibet. When they met somebody who was studying philosophy, they would say, "There is no need to study all these texts! All you need to do is directly receive Dzogchen teachings and practice them!" However, if we recall the story of Atisha meeting such practitioners when he first arrived in Tibet, he told them that realization based on these means was impossible.

Mipham Rinpoche refutes this position by saying that "just trying to abide in meditation" is not sufficient. You cannot attain liberation from samsara by *simply trying* to abide in the nature of mind. This position is supported by the fact that some practitioners are able to abide for a long time in the state of formless meditative absorption, but yet they do not attain liberation from samsara. Thus, Mipham Rinpoche says that in order to attain liberation from samsara, we first need to understand and gain certainty in emptiness.

Without analysis, how can we understand or experience emptiness? Likewise, without analysis, what do we meditate on? When we merely hear the word "emptiness," we cannot know what it means without further analysis. Gaining intellectual certainty in emptiness is like gaining the eyes that see the perfect path of liberation. Without it, the wisdom of insight cannot dawn in the mind, and we will not even attain a state similar to liberation from samsara. For this reason, Mipham Rinpoche says that liberation from samsara is not possible unless we have first engaged in a period of examination on uncontrived emptiness. This was the primary theme of the first three questions and answers.

Next, Mipham Rinpoche says that as a result of abiding in samsara for countless lifetimes, the obscurations that cover the mind's ultimate nature have become heavy and thick. Because of the strength of our obscurations, we must engage in many types of analysis, trying hundreds of different doors and using logical methods to reverse our self-attachment. Without using myriad methods, the darkness of our obscurations is too thick for the sunlight of wisdom to shine through.

If we have very, very extraordinary karma, as did Longchenpa and Jigme Lingpa, then just receiving an introduction to the nature of mind would be enough for us to attain perfect realization of the Dzogchen teachings. However, Mipham Rinpoche says that this kind of practitioner is as rare as a star in the daytime sky.

On the other side of this debate, some practitioners—mainly those of the Later Schools—teach that practicing meditation free of analysis is like the experience of sleeping. They claim that analysis is absolutely necessary any time that we practice. I actually agree with this to a great extent. Analysis and examination are extremely important and it would be foolish not to use our intellect to understand the teachings. But Mipham Rinpoche says that such philosophers go a little bit too far, because they do not believe meditation should ever transcend analysis.

Introducing Indivisible Wisdom

Next, Mipham Rinpoche gives a brief presentation of his own view. He states that in order to cut through any doubts that we have regarding uncontrived emptiness, we need to perfect the view of the Prasangika Madhyamaka. We will discuss the view of Prasangika in more detail in the seventh topic, but we should know that holders of this view have completely cut through all extremes and mental contrivance. This perfect Prasangika view can only be gained through perfect examination and analysis.

Mipham Rinpoche goes on to point out that the view of primordial emptiness of the Prasangika school and the primordially pure view of Dzogchen are the same in one respect, but different in another. Their ways of describing the ultimate view are the same regarding the aspect of the empty essence. However, in order to reverse our attachment to the empty void, the Secret Mantrayana also teaches the *wisdom of great bliss*, which we also call the *spontaneously present wisdom of luminosity*, or *self-manifesting wisdom*. Thus, we should know that the view of the indivisible wisdom of great bliss and the empty expanse, which we call the dharmadhatu, is the indivisible state of equality in which the knower and object known are completely beyond all duality. This is the unsurpassable defining characteristic of the Indestructible Vehicle of the Secret Mantryana. There are many synonyms that describe this spontaneously present display of wisdom. It is often referred to as the nature of luminosity, self-arisen wisdom, rigpa, or unobstructed, spontaneously present appearance and emptiness, and so on.

In the opening verses of this topic, we have already learned one of the major differences between Madhyamaka philosophy and the tantras. From the point of view of the empty essence, the teachings on the mind's nature in the Madhyamaka and tantra are the same. However, from the point of view of the nature of clarity, the tantras have an uncommon, defining characteristic that is not found elsewhere.

We began to explore rigpa in the preceding chapter. Building on our prior study, we can now define rigpa as the union of the unobstructed, empty nature and spontaneously present clear light or radiance. Rigpa, the nature of mind, has three aspects that we also discussed in the last chapter. However, each of the three characteristics is also aligned with one of the three *kayas* (Skt.; enlightened embodiments). Thus, rigpa also has the potential to express the three kayas.

- The unobstructed, uncontrived empty aspect is the *dharmakaya*
- The aspect of clarity is the *sambhogakaya*
- The all-pervasive aspect or aspect of omnipresent compassion is the *nirmanakaya*.

Ground, Path, and Result

In the tradition of the Secret Mantrayana, we say that the number of vehicles or methods to attain enlightenment is as many as there are conceptual thoughts. However, they are most often described in the scriptures as either nine vehicles, three vehicles, or one vehicle.

Ultimately, we need to be able to unify all of the vehicles into one. For example, we have said that the water in all of the streams in one watershed will flow into one river, and could pass beneath the same bridge. In the same way, while there may be many vehicles within the Secret Mantrayana, eventually all of these vehicles will condense into one. This one vehicle is the pinnacle of the Secret Mantrayana path: the teachings of Atiyoga Dzogchen.

All paths, whether they are of the Madhyamaka, Vajrayana, or any other school, are always described in terms of the ground, path, and result. We generally see these three as being distinct. We see the ground as being separate from the path and the path as being separate from the result. Ultimately, the place where the ground, path, and result come together—what Mipham Rinpoche calls the "place of convergence"—is what is called the fourth empowerment, or the Precious Word Empowerment. This empowerment, given by a lama to a student, directly points out the nature of mind. In part, this is done energetically, at a time when the connection between the lama and student is sufficiently developed and the student's devotion and prior training is strong enough to allow him or her to recognize the experience. Most of the teachings in the sutra and tantra give a hidden, masked, or buried meaning. But in the Atiyoga Tantras, the highest class of tantras, the fourth empowerment directly reveals the pith, essential meaning of the Secret Mantra. It is not hidden or buried; it is completely clear.

Supreme Certainty Is a Necessary Condition for Indivisible Wisdom to Arise

Of the ground, path, and result, we are discussing the stages of the ground and path. At this time, we need to cultivate supreme certainty, because it is only in reliance upon supreme certainty that the actual wisdom expressed by the fourth empowerment appears to the mind. However, the cultivation of supreme certainty is not something we ever leave behind. Once we have cultivated supreme certainty, we have to continually renew it by resting in it again and again.

The phrase "supreme certainty" indicates that we have reached a new stage in our development of certainty. In the third topic we were concerned with the *experience* of certainty; in this topic we are concerned with *resting in* or *abiding in* certainty.

Some of us have gained a measure of intellectual and experiential certainty. However, only effort made at continuous practice carries us along the path toward the result. All of us will face obstacles in moving beyond our current level of experience on the path.

Those of us who are very intelligent face a significant obstacle. We understand things too easily, and for this reason, we are lazy. We lack diligence, so while we may have an experience of certainty one day, we may never think about improving it or increasing our capacity because we understood things so easily to begin with. Those of us who are of middling intelligence often make much more effort. Once we attain certainty, we work much harder to keep it. But, no matter what the tendencies of our own personalities, we should reflect on our good qualities and faults in relation to our practice.

Mipham Rinpoche says that certainty should be maintained like the constant flame of a butter lamp; growing clearer and clearer as the flame burns, continually increasing its clarity. This is only accomplished through constant abiding in the certainty that the ground, path, and result converge as the expression of spontaneously present intrinsic wisdom. Without certainty, we are unable to cut through the mind's elaborations and doubts.

This point is easily understood through a modern example. If we go before a lama and receive a profound upadesha instruction but do not have a solid foundation in examination and analysis, although we may have a gut response to the teaching, we will not be sure how to practice it. What if we were to then go to a retreat house, sit down alone on a cushion, and try to practice that teaching? We will know whether or not we actually understand the view when we actually face this situation. Again, without prior analysis or examination, we simply will not have the certainty we need to cut through the mind's elaborations. We will not know how to practice.

Regarding this lack of certainty, I often like to tell the story of a lama from Amdo who wanted to stay in a serious, solitary retreat. There is a lake called "Blue Lake" in Amdo, Tibet, that freezes over for only part of the winter. The lama decided to stay in retreat on an island in the middle of the lake, so that he would be forced to stay in retreat a full year until the ice returned in winter and he could cross back over to the mainland.

Once in retreat, the lama recognized his lack of certainty. He simply did not know how to practice the instructions he had been given. He had very little to do in his retreat hut. He had few belongings, but he did have a woven carpet with him. The story goes that he unraveled the carpet and then rewove it many times during that year to occupy his time after his lack of certainty shook his ability to practice.

The Faults of Meditation Without Analysis

Mipham Rinpoche next describes the virtue of analysis as it relates to meditation. His position is that we develop certainty gradually by working with analytical meditation, and over time, we are able to abide directly in that certainty. When taking this up as a practical instruction, we should return to analysis whenever the mind becomes distracted. This is similar in principle to many of the meditation instructions we may have received as beginning practitioners, which use the breath as a point of concentration. In this case, certainty is the focal point. When we feel a sense of trust or conviction in the uncontrived view or the ultimate nature of phenomena as a result of our reflection—what we call *ultimate analytical wisdom*—we rest in that. When the mind becomes distracted, we again use reflection or analysis to recultivate that feeling of certainty. While we are still progressing on the path, certainty and the actual experience of wisdom have not yet converged as one. However, "resting in" the experience of certainty will, over time, induce this convergence. It is extremely important that we rest over and over again in the experience of certainty, so that it might one day dawn in the mind as actual, intrinsic wisdom due to the support of the view.

Mipham Rinpoche lists the logical consequences that occur as a result of not training in analytical meditation. First, if we do not engage in a period of examination, then excellent certainty in the uncontrived state of equality, the nature of indivisible appearance and emptiness, cannot arise. If excellent certainty does not arise, then the concept of self and other and the mental elaborations will not "set" in the manner of the setting sun. If the mental elaborations do not set, then the winds of karma will not stop blowing. If the winds of karma do not stop blowing, then we will not transcend samsara. If we do not transcend samsara, then we will not abandon suffering. Thus, Mipham Rinpoche shows us that without analysis as the basis for meditation, liberation from suffering is not possible.

State of Equality

Mipham Rinpoche then asks, "What is excellent certainty?" He answers by saying that when we lack certainty, we see samsara and nirvana in contradiction even though they are primordially in a state of equality. Although we may abandon the suffering of samsara based on excellent certainty, still this does not establish nirvana. As we know, arhats reach a level of realization that releases them from the suffering of samsara, yet they do not reach the level of supreme enlightenment. From our conventional point of view, samsara and nirvana appear as a dualistic pair. However, their actual way of abiding is free of any dispelling and fixing, taking up or abandoning; in this way, we say they are in a spontaneously established state of equality. They are an expression of indivisible wisdom. Therefore, certainty is the key to recognizing, experiencing, and abiding in indivisible wisdom.

What does the phrase "state of equality" mean? From the ultimate point of view, all phenomena within samsara and nirvana are of a singular, indivisible, unborn nature. We are fixated on conventional appearance, however, where we perceive samsara and nirvana to be like fire and water. The cultivation of supreme certainty enables us to bring together conventional appearance and the unborn ultimate nature of all phenomena as one.

When we bring our supreme certainty together with the direct introduction to the nature of mind bestowed by the lama, and continually increase our supreme certainty, we begin to trust in the state of equality. This gives rise to *irreversible certainty*, certainty that cannot be stolen by anyone or lost in any situation.

When Chupur Lama, the Dzogchen yogi who raised me, was young, he constantly rested in the nature of mind. He was always practicing in *drubchens* (Tib.; great accomplishment gatherings), or doing retreat. But as he became older and even more experienced as a practitioner, he actually began to take up analytical meditation. He did this for the benefit of his students. He did not want to set the example of simply just leaving all that behind. He started to do more ritual practice, recited mantras, and engaged in analysis. Despite the fact that his realization was at a level that did not rely on the support provided by formal ritual practices—which give us repeated opportunities to catch a glimpse of the mind's intrinsic nature and to experience certainty—he made sure to leave an impression of the proper way to take up the path.

However, if we do reach a point where we truly achieve supreme certainty and are able to abide in that one-pointedly, but we continue examining, Mipham Rinpoche says this is a little bit foolish. It is like searching around your house and finding a snake and then continuing to look for it. Once realization of the uncontrived state of equality has naturally arisen in the mind, then what need is there to apply logical arguments, make inferential assumptions, or engage in reasoning? For example, if one can directly see a fire, trying to deduce that the fire exists based on the sign of smoke is frivolous.

The Shortfalls of Only Relying Upon Analytical Meditation

The next section of the text discusses the other position, that any meditation free of analysis is improper. Mipham Rinpoche believes this position is too extreme. He clarifies some of the faults of this position and then presents his own view.

Mipham Rinpoche begins by examining the assertion, "Meditation must be endowed with analysis to be meditation." He replies, "If this were true, then not only the ultimate nature cannot be established, but also the wisdom of the noble ones' equipoise, or the Buddha's omniscience, cannot be established."

Here is the reasoning behind his answer: The buddhas as well as the noble bodhisattvas abiding on the bhumis experience no conceptual thoughts or mental analysis. Thus, if this position of constant analysis were true, then the realization of the buddhas and bodhisattvas could not be authentic wisdom. When a being manifestly experiences the nature of suchness completely free of contrivance, there is no opportunity to think about this or that. There is no opportunity for conceptual grasping.

Mipham Rinpoche says that when the mind grasps at defining characteristics like *empty* or *not empty*, this is like a silkworm binding itself in its own silk. In other words, we bind ourselves to samsara with our own minds. The metaphor of the silkworm points out that once we attain supreme certainty, we must make more effort to abide in that certainty and decrease our reliance on analysis.

When the first Adzom Drukpa, a famous realized Dzogchen yogi of the modern era, initially gave Longchen Nyingthig teachings, he first gave teachings on analytical meditation for what seemed like years. All of his students listened to them month after month until they had attained certainty in their meaning. After this, Adzom Drukpa gave them the introduction to the nature of mind and then used a very special method to train them. Some people know that Tibetans love to do circumambulation and pray while counting on malas. He took all of those supports away. He would not let any of his students use a mala or any other ritual items. They had to just sit and abide in certainty. In other words, they had to decrease their reliance on outer conditions. I am not advocating that we all do this. I am just illustrating the meaning of Mipham Rinpoche's advice. Especially in the West, it is important for us to accumulate merit in order to dispel obscurations so that the wisdom of realization can dawn in the mind

Individually Self-Cognizant Wisdom Is Experiential

Abiding in the experience of certainty and receiving the fourth empowerment allows us to glimpse what is called "individually self-cognizant wisdom" (Tib. *so so rang rig pa'i ye shes*). Individually self-cognizant wisdom is the uncontaminated vision of the dharmadhatu: self-manifesting, primordial, clear light wisdom, or the wisdom of the noble ones' equipoise free of all duality. Individually self-cognizant wisdom is an experience beyond dualistic notions of empty and nonempty, existent and nonexistent.

When we experience individually self-cognizant wisdom, we experience the primordially unborn nature just as it is. From the point of view of conventional valid cognition—ordinary perception—individually self-cognizant wisdom is not possible. Normally, it is simply not possible for the mind to see or cognize its own ultimate, nondualistic nature. But it is possible in our tradition, based on the introduction to the nature of mind given in the fourth empowerment.

The word *individually* at the beginning of this term seems confusing to many students. Here is a way to think about it: self-cognizant wisdom is individual because it is an experience, and experiences relate to an individual person. *Individual* refers to a unique person and a unique experience. But confusion arises if a student thinks that because wisdom must be experienced individually, that wisdom is unique and distinct in each person.

To work through this confusion, we should reflect on the difference between conventional appearances and their actual nature. It may appear to us that there are differences in the experience of wisdom, because conventionally, people have individual experiences. We do not experience the same thing as everyone else due to our karma and habitual tendencies. However, it would be completely absurd to say that the nature of mind realized by Padmasambhava is different from the nature of mind realized by Vimalamitra.

Also, if each and every person who attains realization were realizing something distinct, then the number of classifications of wisdom would fill the entire sky! There would be no ultimate nature because it would not be unified. For this reason, we qualify that perfect wisdom is indivisible and singular in nature.

What is the difference between ordinary wisdom, which arises from a mind endowed with subject/object grasping, and individually self-cognizant wisdom? Ordinary, conventional *superior wisdom arisen from intellect* differentiates between subject and object, this and that, whereas these defining characteristics of ordinary mind are nowhere to be found in individually self-cognizant wisdom. There is no ordinary apprehension or conceptualization whatsoever. Thus, to recognize the level of wisdom that is being expressed by the mind, we must become skillful at noticing and cutting through any mode of grasping.

Stainless, superior wisdom arisen from intellect enables us to engage in the sublime path when it is accompanied by excellent certainty. Through taking up the vehicle of perfectly pure meditation, we reach the primordial ultimate nature itself, the wisdom of the noble ones' equipoise, which is the definitive meaning of meditation in the Mahayana. Because this vehicle is unequalled by others, it is called *great*.

Regarding all this, the great master Longchenpa said:

> When a thought arises, look right at it.
> When certainty is in the mind, [rest] on top of it.
> Although there is not any meditation, keep on meditating.
> Maintaining freedom from distraction is my heart advice.

This is one piece of advice taken from the *Thirty Pieces of Heart Advice* by the omniscient Longchenpa. As this advice points out, supreme certainty allows us to have an authentic experience of the mind's primordially pure nature.

The Meaning of Lineage

There are an inconceivable number of teachings and an inconceivable number of empowerments contained in the four lineages in Tibetan Buddhism as well as in the Jonang teachings. However, we can condense the entire meaning of the sutra and tantra into a very small number of words. Some practitioners might wonder, "Why are there so many different empowerments and teachings when the meaning can be condensed into something so small?" or "Why do we need to have so many different teachings in different lineages?"

There is a reason for having such a great variety of teachings; they account for differences in individual personalities, devotion, and karma. In order to benefit all different kinds of beings, we need an inconceivable number of teachings in the sutra and tantra.

All of these teachings are organized into something that we call a lineage. Lineages are naturally organized based on lamas giving empowerments, transmissions, and upadesha instructions on how to practice the meaning of certain texts or teachings to their heart students in a continuous, unbroken line. When students keep *samaya* (Tib. *dam tsig*, words of honor) and practice properly, that particular lineage will not be cut. Thus, when a teacher has an authentic connection to the lineage, then the blessings of that lineage will not degrade. This enables the same teachings to keep benefitting beings in future generations, even though a master may have first given them a long time ago. The teachings of the Longchen Nyingthig are such a lineage, and they contain the pinnacle of all vehicles, the teachings of Atiyoga Dzogchen.

The Good Qualities of Atiyoga Dzogchen

Induced by the experience of supreme certainty and the fourth empowerment, the Precious Word Empowerment mentioned above, it is possible to see the way that phenomena actually abide. Seeing the way that phenomena actually abide is called the *wisdom of the noble ones' equipoise*. One who is introduced to, trains in, and abides in the wisdom of the noble ones' equipoise while keeping samaya will attain realization either in this life, at the time of death, or in the bardo. Even if it takes a long time, the result will come within three lifetimes. For this reason, the vehicle of Atiyoga Dzogchen is also called "great."

Atiyoga Dzogchen is the supreme of all tantras, the pinnacle of all vehicles. It holds the essence of the teachings of all vehicles and the root of all Buddhist teachings within it. It is the pinnacle of Buddhist philosophy and the king of tantras. The teachings and the view of Atiyoga Dzogchen are the basis of all upadesha instructions given in the lineage teachings. Atiyoga Dzogchen is the supreme intention of all the buddhas and the essence of all paths. These are just some of the qualities of the unsurpassable innermost secret teachings of Atiyoga Dzogchen. We should all take a moment to reflect on how fortunate we are to meet with these teachings. We have all accumulated merit and prayed for countless lifetimes to receive this chance.

Next, Mipham Rinpoche asks, "How is it that we understand Atiyoga Dzogchen to be the pinnacle of the tantras?" Generally we describe the tantras in a series of four. These are the Kriya Tantra, the Upa Tantra, the Yoga Tantra, and the Anuttarayoga Tantra.

Of these, the Anuttarayoga Tantra is said to be the unsurpassable tantra. This particular series of tantras contains a series of four empowerments. The Precious Word Empowerment is not taught as being its own vehicle. It is contained within the Anuttarayoga Tantra, but it is the pinnacle of the Atiyoga Tantra Dzogchen teachings. The good qualities of this particular empowerment are that it is unobstructed, it is not hidden, and it is direct. For these reasons, it is considered the pinnacle of the Atiyoga Dzogchen teachings. This is why Mipham Rinpoche emphasizes the Precious Word Empowerment in the text when he teaches about the vehicle of Atiyoga Dzogchen.

While receiving empowerments is definitely beneficial, we should understand the tradition of giving empowerments. From a very traditional point of view, each lineage has its own series of empowerments. Each empowerment has its own blessing and good quality. When a lama gives an empowerment, there is traditionally an uncommon introduction or pointing out that is given in conjunction with each empowerment in that series. Especially in our tradition of the four empowerments, the second, third, and fourth empowerments are given along with an uncommon pointing-out instruction.

Empowerments normally are given to maybe three or four students—never to a room full of hundreds of people or to people that the lama does not know. This tradition of giving empowerments to a restricted number of students still does exist in Tibet; it has not disappeared, but it is never advertised. Most empowerments given in the West in modern times are a mere shadow of this tradition. Receiving empowerments enables us to make a karmic connection or receive a blessing from a certain master, but we should be sure to cultivate an uncommonly deep relationship with an authentic master so that when we are ready, we might properly receive the Precious Word Empowerment, which is also called the empowerment that is the expression of the energy of rigpa.

In summary, because the uncommon introduction to the nature of mind is given through the Precious Word Empowerment and this is a part of the teachings on Atiyoga Dzogchen, Mipham Rinpoche names it "the pinnacle of all vehicles." We should be aware that this is done for a logical reason and not because of any prejudice or partiality on Mipham Rinpoche's part.

Atiyoga Is the Supreme Tantra

Mipham Rinpoche goes on to explain why the teachings of Atiyoga itself are the unsurpassable, the most supreme of all the tantric series. Just as the Kalachakra Tantra takes the seat as the king of all the tantras for the Later Translations schools, so the teachings on Atiyoga Dzogchen are the king of all teachings in the Nyingma tradition.

In the same way that gold that is smelted sixteen times becomes extremely refined and pure, such is the purity of the teachings of Atiyoga Dzogchen. We can understand the gradual purification of the teachings as they move toward the pinnacle of Atiyoga in this way. Starting with the Causal Vehicle, and then moving through the outer and inner tantras, the clarity and depth of the teachings increase at each stage. The Anuttarayoga Tantra, also called the unsurpassable inner tantras, include the three stages of the Maha, Anu, and Atiyoga tantras. In turn, the Atiyoga tantras include the three series of Dzogchen called the *semde*, *longde*, and *mengnagde*. Within these three series, the Precious Word Empowerment, or the empowerment that is the expression of the energy of rigpa, reigns supreme. It is the path of wisdom itself, which enables you to directly see indivisible rigpa and emptiness. For this reason, the teachings of Atiyoga Dzogchen are supreme, meaning that they are the most direct, most clear, and unobscured.

But just saying that the teachings of Atiyoga Dzogchen are important is not enough. We need to receive these teachings. Receiving them is not enough. We need to develop certainty in them. And even that is not enough; we need to abide in that certainty.

Many Americans or Westerners are receiving Atiyoga teachings on *trekchöd* (Tib.; cutting through) and *todgyal* (Tib.; directly crossing over) almost effortlessly. When we do not have to make effort to receive teachings, we tend not to make those teachings very important. We do not see their value; we become lazy and faithless. This is a great obstacle to the accomplishment of the Secret Mantryana path. Do not let that happen to you!

Stainless Certainty

Mipham Rinpoche says that if we have *stainless certainty*, as expressed by the teachings and realization of the great Nyingma scholar and Dzogchen master Rongzom Pandita, and we abide in that, then we become completely free of doubt. We obtain certainty that can never be stolen by anyone—*irreversible certainty*. What a jewel!

When reading the teachings expressed through Kuntuzangpo, Vajradhara, and the great realized masters like Longchenpa and Rongzom Pandita, we notice that each lama has his own special quality. The way lamas each express their realization has its own special quality. Mipham Rinpoche has great confidence in the realization of great masters like Rongzom Pandita and Longchenpa, and that confidence shows in his composition of this text. When I read this text myself, I have the feeling that there is no need to doubt anything. His words bring to my mind a perfect feeling of certainty.

Conventional and Ultimate Aspects of the Path

We can engage in an examination of the path from two different points of view. The first is from a point of view that is temporary or conventional. From this temporary point of view, we examine the path and phenomena using valid cognition, through the study of Madhyamaka and through the paramitas.

From the ultimate point of view, the ultimate aspect of the path, if we do not put aside logic and reasoning, mental elaboration and concepts will obscure the nature of suchness. We will never be able to go beyond characteristics like form and color, or the mind's labeling, saying, "This is something, that is something."

The ultimate nature of Atiyoga Dzogchen is indivisible self-manifesting wisdom, free of all fixing and dispelling. This is the definitive essential meaning of all the sutras and tantras. But it is too extreme to apply only analysis, to engage only in analytical meditation. We will definitely fall into partiality regarding the uncontrived view. Some of the kinds of partiality that we can fall into include belief in true existence or non-existence and generally the dualism of ordinary mind.

The ultimate nature of the clear light wisdom of Dzogchen must be beyond arising from the superior intellect of ordinary mind. If the mind's nature is bound by concepts, that nature will be obscured and flawed. However, this part of Mipham Rinpoche's teaching runs contrary to our tendency in the West; most practitioners just want to try to rest without going into any analysis or examination at all. In Tibet, it is more likely that khenpos, scholars, and geshes will engage in so much analysis that they never get to a point where they put these tools aside. They will try to make meditation on the nature of mind fall within the sphere of the activity of dualistic mind and analysis, which is also not possible.

Mipham Rinpoche says that if all grasping does not melt away, then based on the ordinary mind's perception of logic and concepts, our experience will contradict the actual nature of suchness. If by words we try to establish that which is beyond words, this will also contradict the nature of suchness. It is not the intention of the bodhisattvas to try to use words to establish that which is beyond words.

In summary, when we arrive at the place where all analysis has naturally exhausted itself, we should set analysis aside and focus on meditation. We have talked about a three-stage process, where in the beginning we work mostly with analysis and examination. In the middle we work with both analysis and meditation. Finally, when we have gotten to a place where analysis is no longer appropriate, we simply meditate.

The Importance of Understanding the View of Trekchöd and Practice of Todgyal

Inseparable rigpa and emptiness is realized through resting in the view of trekchöd in union with todgyal. In order to abide in the essence of primordial great emptiness, we need to know the view of trekchöd. In order to completely realize the aspect of clarity, one needs to abide in todgyal. This clarity is expressed as the vast, spontaneously present wisdom and kayas. In order to practice todgyal properly, it is extremely important that we first master the view of trekchöd completely, which can only be done through building a strong foundation based on the preliminary practices, guru yoga, and relying on the yidam deity.

Semde, Longde, and Mengnagde

The ultimate meaning or the essence of all the teachings in the sutras and the tantra are indivisible with the meaning of Atiyoga Dzogchen. From a logical point of view, the ultimate meaning or essence of the teachings must be indivisible with the Dzogchen teachings or else Buddhist philosophy would be full of contradictions.

In general, the teachings of Dzogchen are divided into three series: the outer, inner, and secret. The outer series is called *semde*, or the *mind series*. The essential meaning of some of the upadesha instructions contained within the semde is essentially the same as the teachings of Mahamudra, the teachings of indivisible samsara and nirvana, and the teachings of the Great Middle Way. Of course, these are the pinnacle practices of the Kagyu, Sakya, and Gelugpa lineages. We can say that they are distinct in category, but the essence of all of them is self-manifesting clear light wisdom, which is indivisible from the ultimate meaning of the pinnacle of the semde series of Atiyoga Dzogchen. From this point of view, all scholars and siddhas speak with one voice and have a singular intention.

Mipham Rinpoche points out that some members of our own Nyingma tradition would assert that the teachings of Dzogchen are very different and more profound than the teachings of other schools. Mipham Rinpoche questions whether this is really true. If a tradition leads one to the realization of wisdom beyond ordinary mind, however it is, then this is the realization of the nature of the dharmadhatu. It is the direct vision of the state of equality, or indivisible wisdom. If we do not see this, then we have not seen the ultimate nature. All four schools have a singular intention. When that singular intention is realized, that realization is of a singular expanse.

But even though Mipham Rinpoche says that there is no reason for arrogance, he still differentiates between the teachings of Atiyoga Dzogchen and teachings in other traditions. For example, in the teachings of Mahamudra, the Great Middle Way, or indivisible samsara and nirvana, the origin of wisdom or indivisible emptiness and rigpa are the same, but the explanations are quite different. From the point of view of the teachings in Atiyoga Dzogchen, they are the clearest, most elaborate, and not hidden. This is true in all three of the cycles of Atiyoga Dzogchen, but they are especially the most clear in the inner teachings, or middle cycle of longde, or the expanse series.

The secret cycle is called *mengnagde,* or the upadesha cycle. Additionally, mengnagde has an outer cycle, an inner cycle, and a secret cycle, and then an innermost, more secret cycle—the unsurpassable innermost secret cycle. There are explanations in the teachings of mengnagde, especially, that are not mentioned in any other text. Additionally, the teachings of mengnagde are passed through a whispered lineage, or a lineage of teachings that come from the mouth of the lama and are heard by a student. Many uncommon oral lineages exist within this cycle. However, Mipham Rinpoche says that even though there are distinctions between the lineage teachings, falling into arrogance is not appropriate.

Atiyoga Dzogchen Brings About the Quickest Result

Finally, Mipham Rinpoche points out why the teachings of Atiyoga Dzogchen bring about the quickest result for a Vajrayana practitioner. Even when we are bound by the shackles of the afflictive emotions, it is still possible, through the teachings of Dzogchen, to train in wisdom in accordance with realized masters of our tradition. There is a series of three types of wisdom that enables us to do this. The first is exemplary wisdom, the second is actual wisdom, and the third is inseparable wisdom.

Exemplary wisdom is similar to the experience of the wisdom of the noble ones' equipoise, which is why it is called exemplary. As tantric practitioners, many of us have the wish to actually, authentically, and nakedly experience wisdom right from the beginning. We do not realize that because we are shackled by afflictive emotions, the only thing that we can experience at this point is exemplary wisdom. If we have too much attachment to the experience that we want to have, we will not even experience exemplary wisdom. We will keep ourselves from experiencing it.

Mipham Rinpoche gives an analogy to understand the relationship between exemplary wisdom, actual wisdom, and indivisible wisdom. He says that the first, exemplary wisdom, is like seeing a drawing of the moon. The second, actual wisdom, is like seeing the reflection of the moon in water—this is much clearer and more vivid than the drawing, but it is still not seeing the moon itself. Seeing the actual moon in the sky is of course even clearer, and this is the Buddha's experience of indivisible wisdom.

When an ordinary being experiences exemplary wisdom, it is like seeing the drawing of the moon. A bodhisattva who achieves realization of the first bhumi is said to see actual wisdom, which is like seeing the moon in water. When a buddha experiences complete realization, the Buddha sees indivisible, primordial wisdom, or the moon directly in the sky.

In summary, Dzogchen can be practiced even when we are completely ordinary beings. Additionally, Dzogchen becomes the heart of one's practice. It pervades every other practice—even those classified as foundational or preliminary—if one knows how to practice it correctly.

Other Buddhist traditions describe stages for how one follows or practices the path. For example, a person begins training and eventually attains the state of an arhat, then they have to enter the Mahayana path, where they practice the path of the six paramitas. The practice of Atiyoga Dzogchen can be practiced right from the beginning, but it is more profound and much quicker than the paths that are described in other traditions. But how do we practice it authentically?

Mipham Rinpoche tells us that it must be on the basis of ever-deepening certainty.

CHAPTER EIGHT

The Fifth Question

—Of the two truths, which is most important?

ALL PHENOMENA condense into the two truths of conventional and ultimate reality. Logically speaking, they *must* condense into the two truths, because we cannot even intellectually conceive of anything beyond the conventional and the ultimate. Even though this is true, there are still those who assert that either the truth of ultimate reality or the truth of conventional reality is more important than the other. It is rare to find a philosopher who asserts that ultimate and the conventional are equally important.

The equality of the two truths is an idea that we must master through examination until it becomes experiential. This topic may seem simple; it may seem that it is only important for beginning practitioners who are having their first lessons on Madhyamaka. But mastery is perhaps even more important for serious Vajrayana practitioners, because it helps to build a foundation for working with the practices of generation stage and perfection stage.

This chapter is divided into three sections. The first section covers the tradition of the other philosophies, starting with those that focus on ultimate reality as the most important and then moving to those philosophies that emphasize the conventional. Next, we'll see how Mipham Rinpoche teaches on his own tradition. Finally, we'll explore his teachings on abandoning wrong view.

Some Assert that Ultimate Reality Is the Most Important

Mipham Rinpoche first introduces the position held by some philosophers and scholars, that ultimate reality is the more important of the two truths. We may think that we already believe in the equality of the two truths. Most people find the position of these scholars logical—even experienced Dharma practitioners.

Why is it tempting to believe that ultimate reality is the most important? Our dualistic minds see samsara as a delusion; it is conceptual, it is an expression of the mind's grasping. We could even say that samsara itself is merely confused appearances. Ordinarily, we think that confused conventional appearances should be abandoned, and so we grasp at the idea of abandoning them. As a result, we then conclude that ultimate reality is undeluded perfect purity.

However, to realize either of the two truths in isolation is in contradiction to the nature of indivisible wisdom, the realization that results from taking up the path of the Secret Mantrayana. Mipham Rinpoche asserts, "Even if you practice for a hundred years based on one of the two truths in isolation, you will never realize the true essence of Dharma."

Isolated Ultimate Reality Is Illogical

Why is it illogical to have an isolated ultimate reality that is separate from the conventional? To answer this question, we could start by saying that to all of us ordinary beings, the appearance of conventional reality *seems* to be undeluded. For each type of sentient being, there is an unconfused conventional appearance that beings of that realm agree upon. Animals perceive in a certain way. Humans perceive in different way. Gods perceive in yet another way. If we say that these seemingly undeluded appearances are true or real from their own side, then ultimate emptiness is impossible. It cannot be posited.

In other words, there is no logical way to posit an ultimate reality that is isolated or separate from appearances. If all phenomena are empty of themselves, then undeluded conventional appearances must be primordially empty. And yet all phenomena that are empty, by definition, do appear. If we posit them in isolation or as being separate, we have put space between appearance and emptiness as we talked about in topic one. We are forced to distinguish them; they cannot be like two sides of the same coin. Based on our study of this text so far, we should have a gut feeling that isolated appearance and emptiness does not accord with the view of Madhyamaka. If this position is not consistent with the view of Madhyamaka, it is even farther away from the view of the Secret Mantrayana.

The scriptures say, "There is no ultimate reality that results from abandoning conventional appearances." Or, as we learned in the third topic, "Emptiness appears without losing any of the quality of emptiness. Appearances are empty without losing any of the quality of appearance."

The Union from the Outer, Inner, and Secret Point of View

The teachings of the Nyingma lineage are filled with references to the union of appearance and emptiness. It is important for us to gain certainty in what this means. When we reflect on the teachings and their multifaceted levels, the meaning of this union seems to change. These different presentations will be difficult for us to follow if we do not properly understand the meaning of inseparability, which is the root of everything.

When studying the many layers of teachings, we may wonder, "What *is* the union of appearance and emptiness?" The outer, inner, secret, and the unsurpassable, more secret points of view approach the union of appearance and emptiness in slightly different ways. The teaching that Mipham Rinpoche gives here is the root or the essence of them all. If we cannot understand the root of indivisible appearance and emptiness, then it will be difficult for us to understand how the outer, inner, and secret teachings each relate to the union of appearance and emptiness. If we do not understand these teachings intellectually, it is very difficult to experience them.

In this text, Mipham Rinpoche only indirectly gives teachings on the outer meaning of appearance and emptiness at this point, but we should know that we have already worked with the outer meaning in the first topic. Mipham Rinpoche's answer emphasized that the method for understanding the union of the conventional and the ultimate begins by intellectually knowing that ultimate reality can be posited as nothing other than the expression of appearance. We have been trying to gain a deep intellectual understanding of what this means through our study and practice thus far.

Mipham Rinpoche's teachings on this topic are not just focused on the outer meaning, but also the inner and a bit on the secret meaning as well. He is guiding us so we can deepen our understanding and make it more profound. This helps us move toward the actual experience of abiding in certainty and to raise our experiential certainty to irreversible certainty—a certainty so deep that we are utterly and completely convinced, with no chance of wavering.

The inner meaning of the union of appearance and emptiness is often expressed symbolically during ritual practice. For example, there are sadhanas in which we use the bell and vajra. The bell is symbolic of female energy or wisdom and the vajra is symbolic of masculine energy or method. Using method and wisdom together creates the dependent arising or positive conditions for taking up the path of indivisible wisdom. This is one way of expressing the inner union.

Secret practice is generally done after one has developed deep certainty in the practices of method. The practices of liberation and union is taught in the Secret Essence Tantra. But if we take up such practices without a deep conviction, then it all becomes just samsaric action. We may start to wonder, "What is the point?" This kind of thinking will always be an obstacle to life-long practice. It is the expression of a lack of certainty.

From the point of view of the unsurpassable, more secret teachings—the teachings of Atiyoga Dzogchen—one relies on indivisible method and wisdom, resting in the vast expanse free of any partiality or limitations. In no way is appearance an obstruction to emptiness or is emptiness an obstruction to appearance. Mere appearance self-liberates. Mipham Rinpoche states that we need deep conviction and certainty in the indivisibility of appearance and emptiness, or else we will always find that in our personal experience, appearance is obstructed by emptiness or emptiness is obstructed by appearance. When we attempt to rest, we will not have the experience of resting in a vast expanse free of all partiality and limitations because these obstructions are present.

Dependent Arising and the Equality of Appearance and Emptiness

No ultimate expression can be free of or separate from conventional appearances; these two are primordially, spontaneously, and indivisibly present. Our first step to this understanding is intellectual; then we begin to work with meditation. We gain personal experience through meditation practice and becoming accustomed to naturally seeing appearance and emptiness in union. If we develop confidence in the nature of dependent arising, this will greatly support our personal experience of actual meditation. We could say that it is through our understanding of dependent arising that appearance and emptiness become equal.

Once we know the equality of appearance and emptiness, it is not difficult for us to understand the essence of Dharma. Some people may wonder, "Conventional method, ultimate wisdom—what does it mean to say they are in a state of equality? And why is dependent arising the method or the framework from which we would say they are equal?"

All phenomena arise in reliance upon many causes and conditions. Ultimately, whatever appears is primordially empty. Somewhat ironically speaking, our minds can only name something that appears but that at the same time has a primordially empty nature. To me, this is like watching a comedy; it makes me laugh when I think that whatever arises in reliance upon another could simply be called *primordial wisdom*.

Maybe you are not laughing as much as I am at this statement. But this is because most practitioners lack profound conviction in the nature of dependent arising. Whatever is empty must be dependently arisen, and therefore it appears. Whatever is dependently arisen and appears must be empty. If we do not understand and experience this, I guess it is not very funny after all.

What If We Made Ultimate Truth the Most Important?

Coming back to our original question: What would happen if we made the ultimate nature the more important of the two truths? What if we were to grasp at the ultimate nature and isolate and separate the two truths? As Mipham Rinpoche tells us, this not only deprecates the union of appearance and emptiness but also the entire Madhyamaka path. Additionally, the entire canon of teachings of Nagarjuna would be contradicted or contaminated.

Next, Mipham Rinpoche describes the fault of habituating to the intellectual notion or experience of isolated emptiness, the practice taken up by one who makes ultimate reality the most important. It is possible to habituate to isolated emptiness and confuse it with realization. In any case, our realization of that type of emptiness would be the realization of an empty void, or empty nothingness. In other words, if realization of the ultimate nature were possible by meditating on isolated emptiness, then the wisdom of the noble ones' equipoise would be the cause of destroying conventional appearances! Realization of isolated ultimate emptiness would actually cause appearances to cease—there could be no conventional reality. Recall that we mentioned this very flaw in the first topic.

If we understand that phenomena are empty of themselves, then this flaw will probably not arise in our practice. This flaw is a logical consequence from thinking of phenomena as being empty of other. For example, consider again the assertion of the philosophical school that says a pillar is not empty of itself; it is empty of the pillar's true existence. In this case, realization of isolated emptiness would be the cause for destroying the appearance; it would be just like a hammer that crushes a fragile cup.

Therefore, Mipham Rinpoche names this isolated emptiness the "empty void that dispels other." In other words, the empty void, or isolated emptiness, results in nihilism. It is not possible for duality to set based on this kind of realization.

If we rely upon the method of conventional appearances, however, we will not fall into the empty void. When conventional appearances are present, the extreme of the empty void ceases. We also will not fall into the side of mere conventional appearances. When the empty nature is present, the extreme of mere appearance ceases.

Mipham Rinpoche tells us that we should not understand what appears and what is empty in the way that we understand light and darkness. The proper way for us to understand them is as fire and warmth. In this way, we become skillful at understanding emptiness and dependent arising, dependent arising and emptiness. There is no more profound understanding of the view of Dzogchen than this.

The Play of Appearances

As we have touched on in earlier chapters, the words *expression* and *play* are very important in the context of the Secret Mantrayana. *Expression* describes the nature of all phenomena, which are of the nature of unborn emptiness. We could loosely say that *expression* means *potential for expression*. The word *play* is defined as all unborn, unobstructed appearances, whether they be recognized conventionally or as the expression of wisdom.

The expression of emptiness is the play of appearance. Play is not separate from emptiness; it naturally dissolves back into the vast, empty expanse. If play is the expression of emptiness, how could it be possible to place one before the other—temporally, spatially, or in any other way? From that point of view, emptiness and appearance are in a state of equality, like pouring water into water.

This is why outer appearances, sounds, and concepts are not distracting for a yogi. They are all expressions of the unborn nature. Although I just said that *expression* can be generally described as a sort of potential, this is not a concept to be grasped. If we take this too far, we will come to a point where we wonder, "Does this mean that phenomena are compounded? Are we positing expression as a cause of appearance?" No, we are not; this is an analogy, a way to convey a sense of the meaning; it is not a definition. Instead, use the analogy of a mirror. When a mirror is present, any form that is in front of the mirror, whether pleasing or unpleasing, is suitable to appear in the mirror's face. That is expression: it is the quality of being suitable to appear. The appearance itself, the actual appearance, is play.

Talking in this imprecise way, it could seem like expression and play are distinct or separate. Although they are two distinct words, do not think of them like that, either. In the same way that emptiness and appearance are not separate, expression and play are not separate.

Returning to dependent arising: if emptiness is not an *expression* of dependent arising, then appearance and emptiness, the conventional and the ultimate, must have a causal relationship. Most of us tend to understand reality, and even Dharma, in this way, however. We think, one must be the cause for the other because we do not understand how it is that they express coemergently. This discussion should begin to help us understand the words *expression* and *play* more clearly. Emptiness cannot be a cause or a result because it is uncreated, unborn, and uncompounded.

Focus on the pith of these teachings. If you know the root, everything else becomes easy; everything else falls into place. The quote from the Heart Sutra, "Form is emptiness, emptiness is form," captures the meaning of the words *expression* and *play*. The unobstructed expression of form is never separate from the unborn natural state.

What If We Emphasize Conventional Reality?

Up to this point, we have talked about the perspective of those who would make the ultimate nature or emptiness the most important. There are a few philosophies or practitioners who make conventional reality the most important and set aside ultimate reality altogether. Again, faults arise as a result of focusing solely on the conventional nature. If, based on mere conventional appearances, we try to assert or differentiate the teachings of the sutra and tantra, and especially to understand the view of inseparable wisdom, flawless understanding is impossible. When we separate conventional phenomena from the ultimate nature, we are simply focusing on appearances that are arisen from confusion. This is not the view of indivisible appearance and emptiness.

As a logical consequence, there is no opportunity for self-improvement in this kind of situation at all. Without considering the nature of ultimate reality, how could self-improvement and realization be possible for an ordinary being?

Application to Generation Stage

Next, Mipham Rinpoche discusses one consequence of grasping at conventional appearances without relying on the inseparable expression of the ultimate nature. When such a practitioner takes up the Vajrayana practice of generation stage, then all the appearances generated as part of that practice also become mere conventional appearances—the unborn, ultimate nature is excluded from the practice altogether. This limits the practice to mere conventionality by definition.

Mipham Rinpoche calls such a practice "mere imagination." Imagination is a mental activity that falls outside the bounds of generation stage practice. When we imagine, we are pretending that an appearance is something that it is not. Just so, when we focus only on conventional appearances, it is not possible to truly see or experience phenomena as the mandala, or the pure expression, of the deity since its ultimate aspect has been excluded.

Generation stage is an incredibly important practice as we progress through the levels of the Indestructible Vehicle and the Secret Mantrayana. However, to be an effective form of training, it has to reach the level of authentic generation stage practice. For this to happen, we have to rely upon both method and wisdom, appearance and emptiness, and properly understand the relationship between them. When we understand generation stage as having the indivisible quality of fire and warmth, it surpasses mere imagination; it becomes an experience that we can truly abide in. If we authentically abide in indivisible method and wisdom, appearance and emptiness, then the techniques of dissolving generation stage into the expanse of perfection stage and also seeing the unobstructed expression of the appearances of generation stage arise from perfection stage are not difficult to master.

Additionally, whenever we engage in generation stage practice, we should work to develop three qualities:

- *Clear appearance:* see the details of the deity visualization clearly;
- *Pure vision:* see the deity as the unobstructed expression or appearance of the primordial nature;
- *Confidence:* remain within the confidence, or energy, of the deity.

Generation Stage Is Not Imagination

It's important to understand that generation-stage practice is not a practice of "imagination." I want to focus on this incredibly important point. I have had countless conversations with Westerners who believe that visualizing deities is part of Tibet's specific cultural heritage, and that it is unsuitable for Western practitioners. Those who profess such views have seriously misunderstood the essence of generation and perfection stage as the key to experiencing the indivisible two truths. To be clear, all of the techniques taught as part of generation stage are aspects of shamatha, or calm abiding practice, which enable us to focus one-pointedly and enter into a state beyond the mere conventional.

In the Nyingma school, we often talk about seeing conventional reality as the nature of the deity. I sometimes become concerned when I hear students talk about this. Most of the time it seems that this phrase is just lip service in the same way that we talk glibly about emptiness, Dzogchen, or Mahamudra. Mipham Rinpoche says that we often claim to subscribe to the inseparable view, but we do not actually have the view of indivisible method and wisdom. In this case again, the result is that we take up the view of the empty void, mere nothingness. This is something to avoid.

Mipham Rinpoche says the following about practitioners who merely give lip service to inseparable appearance and emptiness but fall into attachment toward one side or the other while practicing: "Even though one's examination might be like an excellent mother, the child who attempts to abide in meditation on the inseparable view cannot catch up." Even though there may be an excellent examination and intellectual engagement beforehand, when our actual meditation does not match it, it is like a child who gets lost and cannot reach its mother. This, again, results in habituating to mere isolated emptiness.

Certainty in the unborn nature and its unobstructed way of appearing will lead us to an authentic experience of primordial purity. We will begin to recognize with certainty that every expression, every appearance, is primordial purity. When we practice generation stage based on this certainty, then generation stage is not a way of thinking, a way of conceptualizing, or a way of imagining. It is a method to train in the authentic expression of primordial purity. Especially, working with generation stage as an instantaneous visualization becomes very easy after that point—whereas beforehand we were always working hard trying to "see" all these different things. We come at it from a completely different perspective.

The Explanation of the Nyingma Tradition

Mipham Rinpoche's own tradition presents the proper way to meditate as abiding in the indivisible two truths. The quality of inseparability or indivisibility is the uncommon, special feature of the Secret Mantrayana.

Meditation on the indivisible two truths does not fall into any limitations or extremes; for this reason, we describe it as being impartial or "beyond partiality." Generally, if we understand impartiality, we also understand freedom from limitations. Mipham Rinpoche asserts that the ground, path, and result of his own tradition are completely free of partiality and limitations. He describes the ground as the bodily aggregates, the spheres and sense perceptions, the path as the six paramitas, and the result as the experience of the view free of partiality and limitations. Thus, all phenomena without exception are ultimately free from partiality and limitations. Of course, the union of appearance and emptiness has this same quality. If appearance or emptiness is isolated so that our meditation is incomplete or lacking, then realization will not be possible.

One scripture says, "In the pure land free of partiality and limitations, the Buddha Samantabhadra primordially abides." On one hand, our Buddhist literature tells us that Samantabhadra is the primordial Buddha, but actually, at the very moment we abide free of partiality and limitations, that is Samantabhadra; that is the primordial Buddha. In the Nyingma tradition, we have no greater introduction to the nature of mind than this.

Also, the omniscient Longchenpa said, "Whatever appears is emptiness; whatever is emptiness can never be free of appearance." Thinking about the unborn primordial state is quite different than our ordinary understanding of emptiness. Even though the word "emptiness" is used in this quotation, we should think that this actually refers to the unborn primordial nature. That is why, whenever we see the face of indivisible appearance and emptiness, it is free of any partiality or limitation.

Sometimes the words and the teachings of the Indestructible Vehicle are extremely hard to explain. When we read them they make no sense.

But through increasing our devotion and through prayer, especially the practice of Guru Yoga, and all forms of accumulating merit, we catch glimpses of understanding. When we suddenly have a moment where we understand the pith of the vehicle, we never forget it because it is authentic understanding. It is not like ordinary information that we learn and immediately forget. We are all intelligent and we are all endowed with some faith, so we should pray and develop devotion to increase our understanding of these teachings. Then we will find that understanding the meaning of these teachings becomes easier.

In summary, if we rest in the expanse of suchness, conceptual mind will dissolve into the expanse of the dharmadhatu. This is the condensed meaning of the 6,400,000 tantras. This is the condensed meaning of the 84,000 methods that were taught by the Buddha Shakyamuni. But in order to understand this condensed meaning, each and every student's mind must become the ring of great devotion that the lama's hook can latch on to. It is the student's heightened devotion that makes these teachings meaningful.

Transformation into Gold

I would like to tell the story of the great master named Drukpa Kunleg, considered one of the most realized yogis in Tibet. Drukpa Kunleg had a married sister who is central to this story. Drukpa Kunleg was completely crazy, and displayed the worst, most offensive, and dirtiest kind of conduct that you could imagine. I think that is delightful for a realized yogi!

In any case, a group including Drukpa Kunleg's brother-in-law, who had incredible faith and devotion, brought thangkas and asked for them to be blessed. Drukpa Kunleg agreed, and then proceeded to spread his feces all over the thangkas. When they returned for their thangkas, they each took their thangka back home. The brother-in-law, who had incredible devotion, opened up his thangka, and found the entire thangka was ornamented in gold. When the other people took their thangkas home and opened them up, they perceived that the thangkas were covered in feces! Even an incredibly realized master like Drukpa Kunleg cannot change feces to gold for other people. But his sister's husband, with his incredible faith and devotion, could transform his own perception. That is why the relationship between student and teacher, and especially the devotion and connection between them, is incredibly important in terms of the manifestation of realization.

Appearances Are Imputed by the Mind

All appearances are said to be thoroughly imputed by the mind. Even emptiness is imputed by the mind. It is only our individually self-cognizant wisdom that has any experience of emptiness. Otherwise, emptiness cannot be pinpointed, it cannot be described, and it cannot be said to possess any of the characteristic qualities that we tend to express through language. Thus, like the introduction to the nature of mind itself, the union of appearance and emptiness is something that is experienced only by individually self-cognizant wisdom.

Because this is the sphere of activity of individually self-cognizant wisdom, the intellectual mind has no job. Intellectual mind has no need to label the experience as pure or impure; labeling itself has no purpose. Whether we are in the stage of examination, abiding, or experiencing the result, we should experience appearance and emptiness as equal, remembering that indivisibility is like pouring water into water, not like twisting white and black thread together.

The Words of Nagarjuna

There are several other quotations that may help us understand indivisible appearance and emptiness. The first is by the great master Nagarjuna, who said, "For whatever object emptiness is suitable, for that object everything is suitable. For whatever object emptiness is not suitable, for that object nothing is suitable."

This quotation brilliantly expresses the meaning and implications of the nature of indivisible appearance and emptiness. Based on the coming together of causes and conditions, no matter how something must appear, it is possible. Or another way to say this is that whatever causes and conditions have accrued can express in any suitable way. Thus, causes and conditions express as ripened karma in any way that is suitable. So, based on the coming together of causes and conditions, not only is appearance possible, but karma can ripen in any necessary way.

Here is another way to express the same idea: *For any entity that can be posited as empty, any appearance can manifest interdependently.*

Nagarjuna also said, "There is not even one phenomenon that is not arisen through interdependent origination." It is our samsaric vision that causes us to perceive emptiness and dependent arising as being distinct. We would never describe them as being synonyms from a strict scholarly point of view, although this may become our experience at some point.

Phenomena are dualistic from the point of view of samsaric vision. We see appearance and emptiness as separate, even though the nature of phenomena is primordially inseparable nature. Therefore, the great master Patrul Rinpoche said, "Confused mind follows after an object; this is conventional reality. That which is beyond confused mind and beyond words and thought is ultimate reality."

Realization

In the sutras, the words "ultimate realization" describe one whose experience of method and wisdom has become completely integrated, so as to express the meaning of inseparability. From the conventional point of view, the definition of ultimate realization is to completely and thoroughly mix method and wisdom.

Another way to understand realization is based on the words of Sakya Trakpa Gyaltsen, who said, "When grasping is present, it is not the view." Here, "grasping" refers to conceptual activity of any kind, no matter how subtle. If there is any establishing or refuting, or any position taken, then this is not the view of inseparable appearance and emptiness.

Again, the great master Nagarjuna said of the unborn, primordial nature: "It is beyond the object of speech, it is beyond the sphere of the mind's activity. Unborn and unceasing self-arising appearances are the nature of suchness beyond the experience of suffering." This quotation tells us that when we practice meditation, if the sphere of the ordinary mind's activity is present, this is not the view of Dzogchen. Of course, we should be realistic and remember that we have to work with conceptual techniques in order to get to this point. We have to start to understand what it really means for the sphere of the mind's activity to be present or not and be aware of that when we practice.

It is true that Nyingma and Kagyu lamas who teach Dzogchen and Mahamudra give instructions about "just relaxing and resting." Of course that is good advice, but if we do not have certainty—if we do not know how to rest and relax, if we do not know what we are resting in, if we do not know how the mind is to do that—then what will we rest in?

Therefore, the goal of Mipham Rinpoche's text and Khenpo Kunpal's commentary is that we learn the skill or "nonmethod" of how to relax and rest the mind. When the sphere of the mind's activity is present, we are incapable of seeing the cloudless, sky-like expanse of the mind's primordial nature. Slowly, however, based on inner certainty and diligent practice, a cloudless sky will appear in front of us.

We develop confidence and certainty in stages; we develop experience in stages. These depend on our habitual tendencies and our capacity. If we are diligent and faithful, we will experience the view. Again, although the view itself is not different, our experience or the way that it unfolds personally for us is different, because we are all different people.

If we can habituate ourselves to the indivisible path, then one day, in the very moment phenomena manifest as appearance, we will also see the nature of emptiness. We will gain a deep sense of confidence and trust that the nature of unborn suchness is clearly expressed as the nature of wisdom.

Characteristics of Realization

We could use this metaphor to describe realization: "When an old man is taking care of a small child, however much that small child plays, the old man never gets tired." It is just like watching a movie or drama, everything is like play; there is nothing to get tired of. This is like the experience of a person endowed with realization. We could also define realization by referencing a person who is not overpowered or controlled by any appearance, sound, or concept.

Mingyur Namkhai Dorje was a great, realized master. When he was very old, he would go outside to practice todgyal, one of the two main phases of Dzogchen, as the sun set in the evening. He was so realized that he did not even recognize the difference between night and day. Sometimes his attendants were awful and they forgot him; they would leave him outside all night. It is incredibly cold where he lived in Tibet; a place called Dzogchen. This area of Tibet is so named because it has been the seat of so many great Dzogchen yogis and also of Dzogchen Monastery. In the early mornings, the attendants would sometimes go outside and find him with frost on his clothing and hair. He would be sitting there stoically like a boulder and when the sun came up he would practice again.

Even if we cannot be like that, we still should work on not being overpowered by excellent or poor outer conditions.

Gaining Certainty in Indivisible Appearance and Emptiness

Gaining certainty in indivisible appearance and emptiness, and continually resting in that, is the root of the sutras and tantras, and the root meaning of the profound path. Through listening and contemplation, we should cut through our doubts about the meaning of the teachings. When we have deep certainty in the view, we should abide in that certainty. Based on doing this, we will experience an increase in our capacity to rest in the view in stages, and also an increase in our capacity to recognize it. If we continually keep this in mind, and dedicate ourselves by making effort, the result will surely manifest. It is just like when you have a field with good soil, good seed, and the conditions of water and sunshine. It is simply not possible for the seed not to sprout.

Mipham Rinpoche says that by attaining certainty in the pith of the inseparable view, there will be a day-by-day increase in the certainty and abiding for the supreme practitioner. For a practitioner of middle capacity, there will be a month-by-month increase.

When you have this type of certainty, grasping at conventional reality as good or bad will naturally be abandoned as a consequence of your certainty. It is a little bit like the metaphor of being in a very cold place— when you first build a fire it is impossible to experience any of the fire's warmth. After the fire has been burning for some time, the feeling of cold starts to fade away, and as the fire burns even longer, the feeling of being cold will eventually disappear. If we "strike the pith" of indivisible appearance and emptiness each day, our grasping will decrease. Although we may not notice a decrease in our grasping as much in the beginning, over a long period of time there will be a noticeable change.

The way that our experience or ability will increase is similar to how the stages of the tantric path move from less profound to more profound in terms of the view. For example, we move from the outer tantras to the inner tantras to the most secret Atiyoga tantras.

Mipham Rinpoche says that it is first necessary for us to see the pith of the inseparable view. Secondly, we must not just see it, but we are to experience it and habituate to it through our meditation. Based on this, we see the nondual empty expanse and wisdom. This pith of nondual appearance and emptiness arises in the mind as primordial wisdom and wisdom embodiments.

Conventional Appearances as the Deity

Mipham Rinpoche says that as a result of experiencing the ultimate nature over a long period of time, we develop uncommon certainty in conventional appearances as any of the yidam deities we may be practicing. From this uncommon certainty, forms, sounds, and concepts arise as unobstructed expression of the unborn nature of phenomena. One genuinely sees appearances as the nature of the deity and genuinely hears sounds as the nature of mantras. This enables one to awaken to concepts as the expression of enlightened mind. In this situation, the actual nature and the way things appear have come into complete agreement.

Thus, the appearance of wisdom embodiments is an expression of completely pure perception, an expression of realization. Otherwise, if the appearances of samsara are just seen as pure and impure in the ordinary way, this same awakening to perfect purity will not occur. Just thinking that shit is gold will not make it so. No matter how much we focus on turning black charcoal into white, it will never happen through mere mental wishing.

In general, we define samsara as impurity and nirvana as purity. However, the perception of samsara is nothing more than the result of subject/object grasping. When grasping is not present, this is liberation. There is actually nowhere to go; liberation does not transport us to some other place. When we see samsara as bad and the ultimate nature as good, however, we grasp at them as being contradictory. However, we should recognize that without samsara, nirvana is not possible. For a practitioner who has supreme, irreversible certainty, the great master Longchenpa said, "Samsara is Samantabhadra, nirvana is also Samantabhadra. In the expanse of Samantabhadra, neither samsara nor nirvana is primordially present. Birth and death are Samantabhadra. Pleasure and suffering are Samantabhadra. In the expanse of Samantabhadra, pleasure and suffering are not primordially present."

I feel that students will immediately think they are on this level being pointed out by Longchenpa. I caution you to constantly examine yourself with honesty and humility. Do not let your ego take over!

In different levels and styles of teachings, we are instructed to abandon samsara. We are also instructed that the ultimate nature is not to be abandoned. But for a skillful Vajrayana practitioner, the aspect of luminosity that is conventional reality will dissolve into the vast expanse. When it does, this is what we call being "beyond samsara." The literal definition of nirvana in Tibetan is "beyond suffering," or more specifically, "beyond samsara."

Classifying the Tantras

The tantras are classified based on a practitioner's ability to apprehend the appearance of primordial wisdom and wisdom embodiments. Subtle differences and levels in our meditation experience are described based on the ever-increasing experience of indivisible appearance and emptiness. Additionally, without taking up indivisible appearance and emptiness as the view, the tantras cannot be designated as higher or lower, more or less profound. For example, one cannot classify the tantras correctly simply based on conventional appearances that are devoid of the aspect of emptiness, or vice versa. However, as our actual experience of inseparable wisdom grows more and more refined, so too does the ability to classify the higher and lower tantric series.

Just as our view becomes more refined, so our meditation and conduct follows after it. If we practice properly and unmistakenly, we will see the actual nature just as it is, and beings and the world will manifest as the appearance of primordial purity.

Clarifying Wrong View

We have moved to the third section of this chapter, which clarifies different aspects of wrong view. First, Mipham Rinpoche clarifies the wrong view that asserts samsara as having an impure nature.

This teaching is unique to the Secret Mantrayana. The Causal Vehicle teaches that we must cultivate the renunciation of samsara very strongly; samsara must be abandoned. Additionally, samsara is taught as having an impure nature. Although we must also cultivate renunciation in order to motivate ourselves to take up the path, from the point of view of the Secret Mantrayana, it is a great mistake to think of abandoning samsara. Remember that "Samsara is Samantabhadra; nirvana is also Samantabhadra." From this point of view, it is wrong view to assert that samsara is impure.

This teaching is incredibly beneficial for our bodhisattva activity and in support of the generation of bodhichitta. When we understand that we are not moving beyond samsara to get to nirvana, but rather know that samsara also has a basis of purity, we are inspired to remain on the bodhisattva path. When we realize that all phenomena are in a great state of equality, and that samsara is just a state of mind, our fear lessens. We fear the activity of benefiting beings less, which can require great personal sacrifice and courageous selflessness, we fear remaining in samsara less, because we begin to realize that our own state of mind in relation to samsara will also change.

By now we are familiar with the way that Tibetan texts repeat themselves like waves in an ocean, going deeper into an idea over time. In this section, Mipham Rinpoche again asserts that without developing certainty in the primordial, pure, great state of equality of samsara and nirvana, then attempting to recognize the three mandalas, train in pure perception, and even the practice of generation stage become meaningless. It is like drawing a picture of fire—even though you have an image of fire, it lacks the characteristics that fire is supposed to have. In the same way, these practices would be like a drawing that would lack the true characteristics of the practice until they were properly developed.

To those who have ordinary, samsaric vision, the actual nature and the way phenomena appear are in contradiction, and the great primordial purity of all appearances is not seen. While these practitioners may try to use mental contrivance to make a putrid scent smell like perfume or to transform black charcoal into white, they will never achieve the purification necessary for beings and the world to express as wisdom embodiments. The vision of the realized masters is such that, based on perfectly pure, valid cognition where deities and mandalas naturally appear, their way of appearing and the actual nature are in harmony. This pure vision of reality itself is asserted as the Indestructible Vehicle.

Next, Mipham Rinpoche clarifies the wrong view embodied by the assertion, "There is no superior or inferior view." This assertion was made by Sakya Pandita and other Sakya scholars who said, "The view of the six paramitas that relies on the Causal Vehicle is the supreme view. If anyone were to assert that there is any more profound view than this, they would be incorrect." Mipham Rinpoche disagrees with this assertion for a few reasons. The first one is that even from a worldly point of view, it does not really make sense to us that there cannot be a more or less subtle presentation of the view. However, the statement also implies that there is no difference in the faculties or intelligence of beings. The idea that some have sharper faculties and some have a lesser faculty would not make sense, because the teachings would all be the same and we would all have to be the same to receive them. Additionally, it would imply that we all would attain realization at the same time. For example, it would not be possible for someone to receive a certain teaching that was more profound and then realize it more quickly.

Finally, Mipham Rinpoche also says that the differences between sutra and tantra would not be clear if this statement were true. One of the defining characteristics of the Secret Mantrayana is that its explanations are superior. It is clear, easy to understand, vast, and presents more methods than other vehicles. Saying that there is no difference in the view would imply, then, that if the view could only be taught in the same way without any difference in terms of subtlety or coarseness, the sutra and the tantra teachings would have to be the same.

In sum, Sakya Pandita's statement turns the idea of the outer, inner, and secret tantras on its head. The general idea is that the outer tantras present the view in a more coarse and general way, while the inner tantras present it in a more refined way, and then the Atiyoga Dzogchen teachings are even more refined. For all of these reasons, Mipham Rinpoche says that it is incorrect to say that the view cannot be expounded differently by different texts.

Mipham Rinpoche presents two specific faults that could result from this misunderstanding. The first is that once a supreme yogi has realizated the equality of samsara and nirvana beyong all differentiation of purity and impurity, good and bad, it would be illogical for that yogi to engage in the practices of the outer tantras such as visualizing the *samayasattva* (Skt.; commitment being, the self-visualization) as the impure deity and the *prajnasattva* (Skt.; wisdom being, the "in-front" visualization). While resting in the actual, primordial nature of the ground, there is nothing to be taken up or abandoned. However, in order to take up the outer tantras, a yogi would have to engage in this purposeless activity of differentiaing between oneself being ordinary and the in-front visualization as being superior.

The second example is of a practitioner who has trained in the outer tantras, and because he or she has not attained complete liberation, still grasps at the purity and impurity of phenomena. When that practitioner takes up the unsurpassable Secret Mantrayana conduct, which is based on the realization of the equality of samsara and nirvana, such as the practices called liberation and union, the conduct would be called "reckless conduct" because the yogi is not endowed with realization. Khenpo Kunpal calls such conduct "boasting about realization" since the yogi is not at the level of a true master.

Also, if a practitioner realizes the state of purity and equality of all phenomena based on the teachings of the paramitas, is it not illogical that he or she then must take up the outer and inner tantras?

The Purpose of the Nine Vehicles

It is precisely because the view can be presented differently to different beings that we have the outer, inner, and secret tantras and that the series of nine vehicles were posited. This is the final section of the topic explaining the purpose of the nine vehicles based on the teachings of the view.

Generally, we present nine vehicles in the Nyingma tradition. These nine are differentiated based on the faculties, personalities, and abilities of individual practitioners. We should not think that the existence of nine vehicles is definitive, however. We could even say that because the vehicles are classified in various ways, they are innumerable in a sense. A great scholar named Ngari Panchen said, "For however long the mind is afflicted, for just that long the vehicles will not exhaust themselves. But when the mind's afflictions are exhausted, then there are also no vehicles." In any case, we should not think that nine is an absolute number.

In Summary

The chapter ends with a summary. Those who see the great purity and equality of all phenomena, based upon habituation to the indivisible nature of the two truths, will see the strength of their inner wisdom increase. The increase in the strength of inner wisdom will lead to an increase in pure vision and in turn, the way that things appear and the way that they abide will begin to agree. This agreement will manifest more fully in direct relationship to the strength of inner wisdom. When we have some inner wisdom, it is possible to see the manifestation of wisdom embodiments. As the mandala of the deity manifests more fully, we will also see the setting of duality and will see appearances, sounds, and concepts as the three-fold mandala. Based on deep certainty in the indivisible path, we will develop inner wisdom and experience the manifestation of indivisible wisdom.

Finally, from the point of view of the ground, path, and result:

- All phenomena are primordially indivisible appearance and emptiness. This is the ground.

- Meditation on the path allows us to have an experience and gain at least a glimpse of indivisible wisdom.
- The result is nondual, indivisible, ultimate wisdom, which is the continuous experience of the limitless dharmakaya.

CHAPTER NINE:

The Sixth Question

—Is the perception of sentient beings based upon common objects?

WHEN MIPHAM RINPOCHE talks about different ways of perceiving a common object, he is referring to the six different types of beings, and how each type perceives the outside world differently. Some of us may think, "This particular teaching does not seem as useful as some of the other things we have talked about." You may think that way, but this topic actually adds a very useful perspective to our discussion of the Secret Mantrayana, especially in regards to the display of pure appearances.

To understand the basis of this question, we will first focus on our understanding of perception, which we can frame in terms of a discussion of "valid cognition." Buddhist philosophy teaches that it is possible to perceive outer objects in a way that is conventionally valid; this is called "valid cognition." Valid cognition is an undeceived or unmistaken perception, or perception that is in agreement with how other like beings perceive. As the scriptures say, "The perception of the object by the perceiver is undeceived by any *immediate cause of confusion.*" An "immediate cause of confusion" is anything that might cause us to perceive an object differently from other like beings, such as an eye cataract. The presence of an immediate cause of confusion results in *mistaken cognition.*

That said, the question arises, "Do all sentient beings perceive the same thing in the same way?" According to Mipham Rinpoche's own lineage, our ability to perceive things in an undeceived way is based on our habitual tendencies and intelligence. The purity of perception, or the degree to which a being can cut through deceptive appearances, depends on his or her own spiritual practice and purity of mind.

This topic teaches us that even though our own point of view may be unmistaken valid cognition in a certain moment, it is not necessarily true for every other being nor is that way of perceiving pervasive for every being at every level of realization. We should interpret much of this chapter as helping us to cut through grasping at our own thoughts and our own point of view as being supreme. Also, as previously stated, this chapter gives us a way to understand the development and display of pure appearances.

The ability to distinguish between unmistaken valid cognition and mistaken cognition is very important in Madhyamaka philosophy. In fact, the scriptures say, "Unmistaken valid cognition is like the stairway to the roof, without which we cannot reach the top of the perfectly pure palace." This palace is the pinnacle of realizing ultimate reality.

We should not feel discouraged if this topic seems complex. This is one of the most difficult philosophical ideas in the entirety of Madhyamaka. Be patient and try to take from it what is most meaningful for your own practice.

The Presentation of the Later Scholars

Mipham Rinpoche will first present the position of other traditions, starting with the Later Scholars. The object of the Later Scholars' examination is called "an instance of water." First, we should know that one instance of water is perceived differently by the six types of beings (gods, asuras, humans, animals, hungry ghosts, and beings in the hell realms). It is logically impossible that different types of beings would perceive the water in the same way, because then their realms and experiences would also be identical.

Mipham Rinpoche describes how beings in the hell realm see water as molten iron, hungry ghosts are said to see water as pus, and gods perceive water as nectar. Their perceptions are different because beings' minds and habitual tendencies are different.

Despite the fact that beings perceive differently, the philosophy presented by Tsongkhapa says that water is a common object to all six types of beings. There is the wish to say that while water appears differently to different types of beings, at the same time water is a common object for them all. We have to take at face value that this is the argument presented whether or not we personally agree with it. However, Mipham Rinpoche and some other great scholars find this position problematic.

Gorampa's Explanation

For water to be a common object for the six types of beings, the water must have a quality of true establishment. In other words, there must be something lasting or unchanging in the water in order for it to be common to these different types of beings. Otherwise, it is not possible to establish Tsongkhapa's position.

The way in which the great Sakya master Gorampa taught Tsongkhapa's position makes it a little easier for us to understand. Gorampa explains that water contains the aspects of all possible appearances within it. Again, in order for the different types of appearances to abide within the water, there is a sense of true establishment or permanence in the water. Gorampa critiques Tsongkhapa's position by saying, "If there is some sense of permanence to water; if it inherently contains these other potential appearances, then conventional valid cognition is illogical."

Take the example of a cup of tea. As Tsongkhapa asserts it, while I am drinking a cup of tea, I am also drinking nectar, pus, and molten iron, and other things at the same time because there is an inherent aspect of each within my tea. This is illogical; it does not make sense conventionally. Conventionally, we all know that this is water. As long as we do not have cataracts or a mental illness that causes our perception to be completely different from other human beings, we all agree that this is water. Conventionally, it does not make sense that while we are drinking water, we are also drinking the aspects that appear to another being.

Again, the premise is that all six ways that water could appear to six types of beings are actually present in this cup of water. Because each is considered to be an aspect of the water, philosophers who argue against this position describe it as an aspect of true establishment or permanence, or something that implies that the water is not completely empty. If the water were completely empty, how could it have the aspects of other things within it?

No one should think that Tsongkhapa's position is strange; he has a reason for making this assertion. Again, he is a great, realized master—an emanation of Manjushri. When we studied the first topic, we learned that the Later Scholars place a strong emphasis on not contradicting conventional reality. So, from the point of view of a being who perceives pus, pus conventionally exists for that being. In just the same way, the Later Scholars say that water is not empty of the essence of water; it is empty of true existence. This style of teaching helps those beings that cannot directly accept that "All phenomena are empty." This current argument builds on the same philosophical idea. Once we consider the emphasis toward concern for beings in this philosophy, the argument makes more sense.

The Later Scholars' Position Makes Valid Cognition Impossible

The way that Mipham Rinpoche explains the Later Scholars' position is that according to this philosophy, water has a *slightly truly established nature*. Furthermore, Mipham Rinpoche asserts that when water has a slightly truly established nature, we cannot differentiate between valid and mistaken cognition.

Let's understand why this is so. The Later Scholars assert that the six types of beings see a common object, i.e., they all see water. That water contains the six different aspects of appearance within it. Thus, six appearances will be seen and all six perceptions will be valid cognition for that being. Each different type of being sees the aspect of the water that makes sense based on that being's habitual tendency and way of thinking.

One complication is that valid cognition is based on the fact that it *is* possible to perceive phenomena in different ways. Valid cognition can only be posited when there is also mistaken cognition, or a different way to perceive. So the first thing that Mipham Rinpoche asserts is that if water is a common object for the six beings, valid cognition becomes impossible because each being must perceive it in the same way. If we have the common object of water, doesn't it make sense that a being in a hell realm and a hungry ghost would both see water? This is why

Mipham Rinpoche asserts that this position leads to concluding the water is "slightly" truly established.

As a result, the six aspects of the water cannot be established through valid cognition, even though they are supposed to somehow be within the water. What actually would happen is that every being must see the water in the same way. Any difference in perception becomes impossible based on the idea of a common object. If everybody has to start out seeing the same thing, then any variation becomes impossible. This is why valid cognition becomes irrelevant; if everybody sees phenomena in the same way, there is no contrast; there can no mistaken cognition.

The Second Flaw of the Later Scholars' Position

Regarding the statement that water contains all six aspects that could appear to the six types of beings, Mipham Rinpoche goes on to say that if each type of being sees an uncommon appearance suited to that being's own habitual tendencies, then why do we need to assert a common object?

Thus, the next argument is not about the water itself as a common object, but a characteristic of the water. The Later Scholars respond by saying, "Okay, so water doesn't work as a common object, but what about just the characteristic of dampness? Could that be the common object?" But the same logical problem arises as a result of this statement.

When we start with a common basis of appearance, how is it that a different appearance can arise from it? If water has a common basis of appearance, as we said, then water would have to be seen as water by everyone. Here, we meet the same problem; even though we are trying to describe dampness as a mere characteristic, again it has a sense of permanence or inherent existence because we want to make this one characteristic the basis for different perceptions.

Dampness could only work in this way if we think about dampness as being something that is distinct from water. But Mipham Rinpoche says that we only understand something to be water because it is damp. If dampness were not present, we would not be able to perceive water. So, this argument only works if we can come up with a mental way to divorce dampness and water.

Basically, we should understand that the ability to distinguish between dampness and water is artificial. For this reason, dampness is not a logical common object. It does not get us away from the problem of water, because dampness and water are singular and indivisible.

In summary, the idea of perceiving a common object of perception has logical flaws, whether or not we try to name that object as water, or if we try to name that common object as a characteristic of water such as dampness.

Appearance Depends on Dependent Arising

In summary, we could say that the only way that it is possible for us to designate names like "water" in the case of humans, or "pus" in the case of hungry ghosts, is based on dependently arisen phenomena. We only know that something is perceived as water by a human being based on our habitual tendencies, obscurations, and karma. When we consider the habitual tendencies, obscurations, and karma of a hungry ghost, we can designate the appearance of water as something else.

We should begin to have the sense that valid cognition is an expression of dependent arising; in other words, the way we perceive is dependent on causes and conditions. There are no phenomena that can withstand ultimate analytical reasoning. We will always find phenomena's emptiness once we engage in examination. Thus, we can only designate the name or characteristics of a phenomenon from the point of view of the appearance being an *unexamined, mere designation* of that phenomenon.

Avoiding the Limitations of the Mind-Only School

The next assertion that logically arises is that if there were no such thing as the agreeable appearance of a common object, then, as the *Cittamatra* (Skt.; Mind Only) school asserts, external objects would appear based only on one's own habitual tendencies.

This is a problem. Because mind is truly established in the Mind-Only school, it does not reach the level of true Madhyamaka. The Later Scholars would reply, "If everything is dependent on the mind's habitual tendencies, then don't we become just like the Mind-Only school?" If external objects are reflections of our mind's tendencies, our philosophy cannot rise to the level of the Prasangika or even Svatantrika Madhyamaka because mind has the quality of true existence.

However, Mipham Rinpoche says we can avoid falling into the position of the Mind-Only School. He asserts that external objects are projections of the mind, and also that the perceiving mind is not truly established. He does not mind sharing some philosophical ideas with the Mind-Only school. In fact, the teachings on Mahamudra say that all objects are established by the mind. This is a very common idea that we accept as part of Secret Mantrayana philosophy.

The Mind-Only school refutes the idea of a common object. Generally, the Nyingma teachings say that all phenomena are established by the mind, and then we examine where phenomena originate, where they abide, and where they pass. If our examination is proper, we find that they do not arise, abide, or pass anywhere.

The Mere Appearance of a Common Object

Mipham Rinpoche asserts that while there is no actual common object, there is the *mere appearance* of a common object. The mere appearance of a common object has to do with conventional agreement. For example, humans agree that water is water. Hungry ghosts all experience water as pus. However, this is only possible when we understand the ultimate nature to be free of partiality and limitations. It is only possible when we understand that the nature of reality itself is indivisible appearance and emptiness, since this is the only circumstance from which any possible appearance can display. This again illustrates an idea from the fifth topic, which said, "For whatever object indivisible appearance and emptiness is suitable, for that object, everything is suitable."

It also relates to the idea of expression and play. Play appears to us as either an ordinary, agreeable appearance or the recognition of wisdom based on our own habitual tendencies. So, the mere appearance of a common object is simply the play of appearance.

When we see an unexamined, unanalyzed mere appearance—for

example, if a human perceives a dancer—Mipham Rinpoche says that a dissimilar appearance will be perceived by a god. But the expression of that dancer's movement must still be able to be seen, even though the specific appearance is seen differently. Mipham Rinpoche says that the ability to see varying expressions of movement is different than asserting a common object.

Here is a very succinct way to understand Mipham Rinpoche's position: *We cannot posit a common object if we also say that the common object has been thoroughly examined. But we can posit an interdependent mere appearance of a common object, as long we are not asserting that examination of the true nature of that appearance has taken place.*

In summary, Mipham Rinpoche asserts that it is the fundamental nature of the appearance and emptiness of phenomena that enables the variety of possibilities or expressions to be seen. As soon as we isolate either appearance or emptiness, conventional reality and valid cognition fall apart. It simply does not work at all.

This is how Mipham Rinpoche avoids contradicting conventional reality. Asserting the mere appearance of a common object is Mipham Rinpoche's way of saying, "Whatever people understand, whatever people think about the conventional world is true from an unexamined, unanalyzed point of view." Mipham Rinpoche is not bothered that the essence of this unexamined, unanalyzed object is empty of itself.

An Overview of Mipham Rinpoche's Approach

We find in this chapter that, again, indivisible appearance and emptiness is where all things converge, just as all rivers ultimately converge in the ocean. Such is the relationship of indivisible appearance and emptiness to any other teachings, which ultimately converge within it.

Once we properly understand the teachings on indivisible appearance and emptiness, it then becomes possible to designate cause and effect, and to also make any conventional designation, free of contradictions. It is because of the indivisible nature of appearance and emptiness that any appearance is possible; that phenomena can manifest in accordance with the habitual tendencies and disposition of beings.

For each type of being, an appearance will manifest based on that being's sense faculties meeting with the object. We could say that in a sense, it is based on the strength of their point of view that a certain appearance will manifest. That is why water can appear as a home to a fish, or can appear as molten iron to a being in a hell realm. In our own tradition, we focus on inseparable appearance and emptiness. We also call this the state of equality. Its essence is beyond all contrivance, sides, stages, partiality, and limitations.

From this point of view, it is now possible to posit the mere appearance of a common object. The mere appearance of a common object is the unborn, unobstructed expression of the nature of suchness. If we attribute other characteristics to emptiness and appearance than impartiality and a freedom from limitations, such as giving it a size, a particular shape, dimensions, then conventional and ultimate reality will both be destroyed.

There is a great pith found within this topic. When we reflect on indivisible appearance and emptiness, and especially when we reflect on the phrase "free of partiality and limitations," we should wonder to ourselves, "What is that like?" We should actually try to understand it. We should understand that conventional designations can be made *only* because the nature of appearance and emptiness is free of partiality and limitations. This actually acts as a sort of indirect proof. When we gain certainty in this idea, we approach what is called the "great pure equality" of the ultimate nature.

When the ultimate nature is free of size, direction, and other dualistic concepts, then the expression of any phenonema, shape, or form can appear. It can have three sides, it can have four sides, it can be as big or as small as it needs to be. Alternatively, if the expanse of space had a size and shape, then anything that expressed or formed within that expanse of space would have to conform to that shape. There would be limitations. Not everything would be possible.

For this reason, it is said that because all phenomena are indivisible appearance and emptiness, conventional designations are possible. If the expanse of space had size and shape, it would not be possible for everything to manifest; there would be obstruction. This is why it is said that designations such as appearing or not appearing, valid cognition or mistaken, invalid cognition, nirvana and samsara—all of these designations are possible because of the indivisible nature of appearance and emptiness.

Tasting indivisible appearance and emptiness is like tasting honey. When you have a small taste of honey, you are not satisfied and you want more and more. When you taste indivisible appearance and emptiness, you hunger to increase your experience of it.

That is a basic overview of Mipham Rinpoche's approach. We will now go into the details.

Valid Cognition and Mistaken Cognition

What is the difference between valid cognition and mistaken cognition? To review, we said that whatever conventionally appears as itself, as it is, without an immediate cause of confusion that obstructs either the object or our own samsaric mind, is valid cognition. When there is some immediate cause of confusion that interferes with perception, this is mistaken cognition.

At this point in the text, Mipham Rinpoche wants us to understand valid cognition is the interdependent result of an object, a being's mind, and the interaction between these two. Not only that, but for cognition to be valid, there must also be a lack of an immediate cause of confusion. Perception should have the quality of interdependence rather than independence, a quality of impermanence rather than permanence. So, the text is pointing out that valid cognition is based on dependent arising, and that neither phenomena or the mind are truly established.

We confuse mistaken cognition for valid cognition when we are overpowered by self-attachment. Historically, when scientists began to question the earth-centric layout of the universe, the Catholic Church persecuted or imprisoned them. Actually, neither the scientific presentation of the universe nor the way that the Church described it has to be designated as valid cognition, because conventional truth is always relative and colored by our own habits and prejudices, but conflict arises because we are attached to one viewpoint or the other.

In the same way, the Buddhist understanding of the universe differs from science. But is it really necessary to have to take the step of picking which one is right and which is wrong? When our self-attachment drives us to do that, we have conflict with others as a result of trying to establish our own position. So we have come back to the Madhyamaka idea of remaining free of positions.

As yogis, of course, the wish to do things our own way will cause huge problems for us. This is why there is a very specific way that we take up the path as Vajrayana practitioners. We start out with listening and contemplation because we need to gain some understanding of the Dharma in general. Once we do this, we gain a little bit of experience, and then we rely on a lama in order to gain direct experience. When we develop a very close relationship with a lama, we go before him or her, we ask questions, we offer our experience, we clarify our ideas, and we receive feedback. Many Americans have an idea to practice the path independently and just do it on their own, which causes them to make mistakes. As yogis, we need to rely on all these different aspects of practice to make sure that we are not acting out of self-attachment.

The Importance of Conventional Valid Cognition

It may seem purposeless to talk about valid cognition from the ultimate point of view, because valid cognition seems to be a purely conventional experience. But as we have learned in this topic, this is not actually so. We need to understand valid cognition and have the proper understanding of our world, because when we do not have a correct understanding of the ordinary conventional world that we live in, then there is no way for us to properly relate to the ultimate. For this reason, conventional valid cognition is important. When we understand valid cognition properly in a conventional sense, we also will have a good condition or support for properly understanding the ultimate state.

Temporary Valid Cognition

With this in mind, Mipham Rinpoche begins to classify types of valid cognition. This is actually quite helpful. He starts out with what he calls "temporary valid cognition" and then moves to "unmistaken ultimate valid cognition." The level of one's valid cognition depends on the mind of the particular being. The idea of "temporary valid cognition" is especially useful to us, because it points out that the valid condition that we perceive, since it is not ultimate, is always changing. In other words, the way we perceive phenomena will change as the mind becomes purified.

Thus, we could say that without properly understanding temporary valid cognition, ultimate valid cognition will not be properly understood. For this reason, valid cognition is seen as something like a continuum that becomes more and more purified over time.

Temporary valid cognition has two levels. The first is conventional valid cognition that is impure samsaric vision. Next is conventional valid cognition that is pure vision. Finally, there is ultimate valid cognition.

Samsaric Vision and Valid Cognition

The next section discusses the definition of the *valid cognition of impure samsaric vision*. Remember that samsaric vision is dependently imputed, as we name and designate phenomena based on causes and conditions. In samsaric vision, there can be both valid cognition and mistaken cognition.

Valid cognition from the samsaric point of view is simply to be able to see what other people see conventionally. When there is a cup of water before us, we see water as water because the eye faculty is intact. When the eye faculty itself is flawed, as in the case of a cataract or jaundice, perception, too, can be flawed or colored. The object is not seen in the way others see it, and for that reason, even in the realm of samsaric vision, there are mistakes in perception, or mistaken cognition.

This is a useful metaphor in terms of understanding how habitual tendencies color the way that we see in general. For example, Mipham Rinpoche says that even a hungry ghost does not perceive water in the way that humans do. When a hungry ghost sees water, it appears as pus because of habitual tendencies and karmic obscurations. But still the perception of pus is valid cognition from the being's own point of view.

Mipham Rinpoche goes on to say that one day, based on the purification of obscurations, it is possible that the hungry ghost will see what a human sees as water. And in the same way, we can understand that even though a human sees water as water, this also is not ultimate valid cognition; it is temporary samsaric valid cognition. Once the karmic obscurations are purified, we may perceive what we see now as water as nectar, such as is perceived in the god realm.

Thus, samsaric vision is impermanent. It gradually changes through purification. Faith, devotion, and pure perception are all inferential forms of valid cognition. In other words, all of these aid in the gradual purification of valid cognition until perception is completely pure.

Conventional Valid Cognition Based on Pure Vision

Conventional valid cognition that is based on pure vision is defined as the perspective of a being who is able to see a situation ultimately. However a situation is, that being sees it directly. From the point of view of *conventional valid cognition based on pure vision*, even a human's perception of water as water is delusion. When we see the essential nature of phenomena itself, there can be no characteristic designations. This is described as pure vision. As an example, it is often said in the tantras that a buddha or bodhisattva will see conventional phenomena like water as the dakini Mamaki. This is an example of seeing the essence of something just as it is.

When worldly people like ourselves reflect on this idea of the ultimate nature of phenomena, we come to realize that anything other than abiding in the ultimate nature of suchness is all mistaken cognition. But from our own point of view as worldly beings, such perception is valid.

Conventional Valid Cognition as a Temporary Method

None of us are able to abide in indivisible emptiness and appearance until we are free from the delusion of duality. Valid cognition is gradually purified based on practice, in the same way a cloud gradually disappears so that the sun nakedly appears in the sky. When the sun appears directly, we experience the pure vision of the noble ones.

In sum, Mipham Rinpoche described both types of valid cognition as being temporary—conventional valid cognition that is impure samsaric vision and conventional valid cognition that is pure vision. This word *temporary* has to do with the fact that it is a method to realize the ultimate. For example, if we want to reach the far side of an ocean, we need an excellent boat. Without the proper boat, we cannot cross the ocean. But once we get to the other side of the ocean, there is no more need for the boat. In the same way, these two types of conventional valid cognition represent the boat we must use to cross the ocean; they are temporary in that sense. Without relying on the method of these two, we cannot reach the experience of ultimate valid cognition.

Ultimate Valid Cognition

When Mipham Rinpoche describes ultimate valid cognition, he says that it ultimately establishes "singularity." Why does he say this? It has to do with the fact that while abiding in the nature of suchness itself, we cannot designate anything like samsaric vision or pure vision. It is a singular, indivisible experience. At that moment, great indivisible wisdom cannot be described as having any dual or conventional characteristics, such as having a size, shape, or color. For that reason, the name that is associated with it is *indivisibility* or *singularity*.

In this section of the text, then, Mipham Rinpoche points out that ultimately, seeing suchness just as it is, is ultimate valid cognition. Because it is nondual, it is singular in nature; there is nothing else that can be seen. At this point there is only one indivisible truth; there are not two truths. If the essence of all phenomena were not uncontrived indivisible appearance and emptiness, then how could ultimate valid cognition be established as being completely singular and indivisible in nature? This is why the establishment of valid cognition depends completely upon the fact that a phenomenon's own essence is completely empty.

Establishing the Conventional Realm as Great Purity

Based on the teachings of temporary and ultimate valid cognition one gains certainty in, and eventually experiences, one of the defining characteristics of the Nyingma school, called "establishing the conventional realm as uncommon, great purity." All Vajrayana Buddhist traditions teach the equality of samsara and nirvana, which is shown by the fact that an ordinary being can transcend the nature of the ordinary world and experience the state beyond suffering, or nirvana. However, it is a special feature of the Nyingma school to teach that the conventional world itself is of the nature of great purity. For conventional phenomena to be of the nature of great purity, they must be intrinsically empty, and of the nature of indivisible appearance and emptiness. It is important that we use intellectual logic to understand this. But if we only rely upon intellectual logic and do not go beyond it with actual practice and developing certainty, then while we can *say* that the conventional world is uncommon great purity, this does not mean that we will necessarily realize it experientially.

The realization of the conventional world as uncommon great purity begins with training in intellectual understanding, and then gaining experience and understanding through practice. When we combine the intellectual with the experiential, then what we see and experience directly is the play of suchness. In that case, even if we saw in a conventional way, we would still see through perfectly pure eyes. We would be able to see that the conventional world does not obstruct primordial purity.

This particular teaching on uncommon great purity was described as the Great Lion's Roar of a great Nyingma scholar named Rongzom Pandita. His texts give the method for establishing conventionality as primordial purity. This was elaborated on by other scholars in the Nyingma tradition, such as Longchenpa and Jigme Lingpa. For this reason, it has become an uncommon attribute of the Nyingma path.

The basic thing to remember is that even though you may think to yourself that the conventional world is primordial great purity, this does not enable you to experience it.

There are other texts or teachings that describe conventionality as great purity. One of them was a tantra that was held by and spread by Nagarjuna called the *Hevajra Tantra*. It was said that Nagarjuna went to the palace of the dakinis in Orgyen Khamdroling. The palace was full of tantras, and he took a text! It was said that because he was equal to a buddha in realization and the abandonment of faults, the dakinis were unable to retrieve the text, and thus, they named him the holder of this tantra.

This topic is is also described at length in the Uttaratantra. But the way that one actually achieves this realization is by relying on the method that Mipham Rinpoche presents; developing certainty through intellect and practice.

Mipham Rinpoche gives a subtler explanation of great indivisible purity in the next section of the text. He begins by asserting that to establish uncommon great purity, it is not possible for appearance and emptiness to be isolated or partial in any way. If they were, then the great view of pure perception cannot dawn. Instead, phenomena will be the expression of a mere empty void. In review, the empty void occurs when phenomena are not empty of their own essence, but instead are empty of something else so that there is a gap between appearance and emptiness rather than them being like two sides of the same coin.

What we learned in the first topic has now become quite useful. When we have a phenomenon that appears that is not empty of itself but is empty of something else, i.e., its inherent existence, then the connection between the emptiness and appearance is lost. There is no relation between the apparent object itself and its emptiness. In other words, the empty void makes the indivisibility of appearance and emptiness impossible. Mipham Rinpoche says that in this kind of situation, space could have a function like that of a vase and even functional entities like vases could be a void, like space. It mixes up the order of everything.

If a particular apparent entity is not empty of itself, and we are asserting emptiness, then the entity must be empty of something else. But when the emptiness we are asserting is an empty void, which we also call isolated or partial emptiness, then appearance cannot manifest from that emptiness. Again, there is no connection between the apparent entity and the empty void. Mipham Rinpoche says they are like mountains in the south and the west, devoid of connection.

An empty void is like a nonentity. When something is a nonentity, then how could it appear as an entity? This is contradictory; it is impossible. Mipham Rinpoche says to Je Tsongkhapa and his followers, "You still have to establish that appearance and emptiness are connected, because your philosophy asserts that they are. How are you going to do that?"

The Flaws of Mere Appearance Being Separate from Emptiness

Mipham Rinpoche goes on to say that mere appearance, or appearance separate from emptiness, causes the same types of problems. When appearance is isolated, it could never be an expression of great primordial purity. Logically speaking, how could appearance be separate from emptiness?

While we are purifying temporary valid cognition, we must gain experience and certainty in the indivisibility and impartiality of appearance and emptiness, emptiness and appearance. It does not make sense to reflect on this from the point of view of the samsaric vision of ordinary worldly beings. As practitioners who are training in the view, however, our development is focused by reflecting on ordinary examples, for example, contemplating that the pillar is emptiness and emptiness is the pillar.

When we begin to have more certainty in appearance and emptiness, and also expression and the appearances that arise from expression, this will greatly benefit us, especially in our training in the generation and perfection stages. Take the example of meditating on a deity. From the point of view of ordinary beings, meditating on or visualizing a deity can be a very strange thing to do. We could have the sense that an impure being is just trying to conjure up a pure deity. However, if we have confidence based on our training that the actual nature of all conventional phenomena is uncommon great purity, then we start to realize that the visualization or the focus on the deity is actually just the situation as it is, because primordial purity has never been obscured. This meditation training eventually will enable us to recognize the uncommon great purity of all conventional phenomena.

The Unified, Pure, and Equal Indivisible Two Truths

Mipham Rinpoche introduces the ultimate nature in this section of the text and how one achieves realization of the ultimate nature. This method includes everything that we have discussed in the chapter up until now—all the conventional designations that we have been talking about and the gradual purification of valid cognition.

Mipham Rinpoche defines the ground or the basis as the actual nature or the actual situation of all phenomena. It is the indivisible nature of suchness. He also defines realization as the agreement of the way things appear and the way they actually are. We can then define the actual situation as the uncommon state of purity, the primordial nature itself as seen by the wisdom of the noble ones' equipoise.

A realized practitioner directly sees the way that things actually are. That is the aspect of emptiness. What does it mean for a yogi taking up the path to see appearances? It has to do with seeing suchness directly. The realization, the manifest knowing, of the indivisible nature of wisdom is defined as appearance. This is ultimate valid cognition of indivisible appearance and emptiness. The actual situation, or the ground, and the manifest experience seen by the yogi are in complete agreement.

It is important that we mix the conventional and the ultimate in this section of the text. When we talk about the ultimate state or ultimate valid cognition, we are talking about the indivisible, uncompounded experience of primordial wisdom. Yet we also know that this begins with mere intellectual knowledge. We start with intellectual knowledge, we gain personal experience, we are introduced directly to a more profound experience, and then we abide in this.

Ultimate Reality Is Great Equality, Conventional Reality Is Great Purity

The section that follows establishes ultimate reality as great equality, and then it again establishes conventional reality as great purity. This explanation is subtler than that given in the overview.

Ultimate reality is described as great equality, and conventional reality is described as great purity. If ultimate reality were not established as great equality, then it would also be impossible to establish conventional reality as great purity.

Conventional reality must be established as great purity because ordinary appearances as seen by sentient beings are impure. That impurity has to be established as primordial purity through gradual purification and practice. From a practitioner's point of view, this requires great effort. Thus, from the point of view of purifying impure appearances so that we naturally perceive their primordial purity, we call conventional reality "great purity."

Ultimate reality is in a state of equality. It has primordially always been that way. Because it is in a state of equality, there can be no variation, no purity and impurity. We just understand it to mean that however it is primordially, in whatever situation it is, it is just that. So to say that it is in a state of equality is simply descriptive of that state that has always been. We do not need any effort in order to make it that way.

We can understand what this means though the example of yogis who are actually practicing. Yogis take up the teachings on great equality just as taught, and they have an unmistaken experience of that result in their own mind streams. Based on this experience, they are able to establish conventional reality as great purity. On the other hand, if they do not take up the great purity of conventional reality, they cannot realize the meaning of the great equality of ultimate reality.

Another way to understand this is through the method of realizing ultimate great equality using any of the so-called "practices" of self-liberation such as *Rangdrol*, *Shardrol*, etc. (Tib.; self-liberation, liberation on appearance). When conventional appearances are self-liberated, this is the expression of the great purity of conventional reality.

Ultimate Great Equality

We can understand ultimate great equality in this way: the five aggregates are the play of appearance, but at the very instant they appear, they are illusory, like a magical display. Their appearances are indivisible from the vast, empty expanse. Recognizing this is seeing play as the pure realms. Whatever play expresses conventionally, it is none other than the nature of primordial wisdom. This is how we can understand conventional reality as great purity.

The perfectly pure vision of a buddha is beyond any establishing, asserting, or positioning. Pure vision simply sees the naked expression of suchness. From this point of view, there can be no ordinary designation of valid cognition. This is ultimate valid cognition. Again, this state is characterized by the agreement of the appearance of phenomena and the way that they actually abide.

Gendun Choepel, a Tibetan meditation master and brilliant philosopher who lived during the twentieth century, made the assertion that conventional reality has no real essence. When he said this, others criticized him. Many people said that he was deprecating conventional reality. But what Gendun Choepel meant is that conventional designations are temporary. They cannot be trusted with certainty because they are not lasting and unchanging. This is true of any kind of valid cognition until it reaches the level of ultimate valid cognition. It is only when we see ultimate valid cognition that there is anything than can be trusted or unmistaken.

Notice that Mipham Rinpoche gives this teaching from both points of view. He explains how, if we start with great equality or ultimate reality, that will bring us to understanding or realizing the great purity of the conventional state. At the same time, when we recognize and experience the great purity of conventional reality, we also are able to experience ultimate reality as great equality. There is no hierarchy between them. One brings us to the other. No matter where we start, one brings us to the other.

When we do not recognize that the nature of suchness is also the great purity of the conventional world, we experience samsaric suffering. We simply do not realize the primordially pure nature of appearances as they arise. The only possible way to be liberated from this is to recognize suffering the moment it arises. As a result of taking up the perfectly pure path, we will one day recognize the great equality of the nature of suchness. All suffering and fear will be self-liberated at that moment.

It is good for us to reflect on the difference between great purity and great equality, the great purity of the conventional state and the great equality of the ultimate state. Know the difference between these and how both of them are of benefit to a practitioner on the path.

Our Experience Depends on Purifying Obscurations

Most importantly, our own experience depends not only on how much we practice but on how much we purify our obscurations. Sometimes we get into negative thinking, "I am not the kind of practitioner who can experience this. A lama or a yogi experiences that, but I experience only suffering." This is not a good pattern of thinking. Just focus on what is pragmatic; focus on what is in front of you. You have to eat what is on your plate or drink what is in your cup. You cannot put more in your stomach than it will hold, so there is no reason to be frustrated with yourself about it. All you need to do is slowly work to increase your aptitude. It is important that we practice each day. Not only do we study the teachings on *The Beacon of Certainty*, but we also must try to integrate the meaning of these teachings into our practice.

The Good Qualities of Establishing Great Purity and Equality

From the point of view of the nature of great purity and equality, we gain certainty that any phenomena can appear and be designated. Appearance and emptiness, existence and nonexistence, samsara and nirvana, all of these are able to appear and be designated because of the ultimate nature of great purity and equality.

When we gain certainty in the ultimate nature free from partiality and limitations, we see the arising of all phenomena just like a movie. Samsara and nirvana manifest as undeceiving, unobstructed, dependent arising. At this point, we begin to gain certainty in the state of equality that cannot be stolen by anyone. When we develop this certainty, our samsaric suffering begins to lessen because there is nothing stronger, no greater good quality than our own confidence and certainty in the state of great purity and equality.

The Importance of Purification and Pure Perception

Mipham Rinpoche gives us a reminder at the very end of this chapter. He gives a short teaching about the patience that it takes to develop our understanding and the ability to experience and abide in the view.

We should remember that ordinary people do not understand the indivisible view of Atiyoga Dzogchen. It is only understood by a few who have the prior karma and supportive conditions in order to practice and realize and abide in the view. When our prior habituation comes together with supportive conditions in the present, Atiyoga Dzogchen is understood almost effortlessly. But we should also remember that without prior supportive karma and if we have strong obscurations, the view will be difficult to understand. For this reason we have to work to purify our obscurations.

Mipham Rinpoche also says that even if we worked for one hundred years to simply understand the teachings on valid cognition, this would not enable us to realize the view of Atiyoga Dzogchen. We have to work to purify our obscurations and also train in pure perception. Simple blind effort will not enable us to realize the view.

CHAPTER TEN:

The Seventh Question

—In our own tradition of Madhyamaka,
is any position taken?

THE FINAL QUESTION asks, "Does the uncontrived Madhyamaka take any position?" Another way of translating "take any position" is "make any assertion." We can look at it that way if it makes more sense.

As we discuss Mipham Rinpoche's response to this question, you will find that most of the information here is not new! This seventh chapter synthesizes and brings together the meaning of all the previous topics. You will recognize many of the concepts from earlier topics; this is intentional. Now that we have gone through and understood each of the earlier topics in detail, Mipham Rinpoche will present a unified and comprehensive understanding of the uncommon defining qualities of the ground, path, and result of Madhyamaka, which is distinct and uncommon from other philosophies. We should already know that Mipham Rinpoche's teachings follow after those of the omniscient Dharma king Longchenpa.

When we read the teachings of the ground, path, and result of Madhyamaka philosophy from the point of view of other philosophies such as the Gelug and the Nyingma schools, they seem very similar. There is a reason for this; their target is the same. All schools claim that not only do they hold the view of uncontrived Madhyamaka but that their presentation is also consistent with the Middle Way philosophy called Prasangika, which is considered the pinnacle of all Madhyamaka philosophy. The difference between the schools, therefore, has to be contained within the logic and methods used to reach this goal.

Although this may seem confusing because the philosophical presentations seem so similar, the small distinctions do really matter. We need to pay close attention to them.

Does Madhyamaka Take a Position?

We have two questions to contemplate as we study this topic. First, what does it mean to say that Madhyamaka takes a position? Secondly, does Madhyamaka take any positions?

The first question is for the benefit of students who are not familiar with the language used in Madhyamaka reasoning. What is a position or assertion as used in this context?

A *position* or *assertion* is a statement of relative or ultimate truth that says, "This is so." In the language that we have used throughout our study of the uncontrived Madhyamaka, we would say that any of the four extremes is a position. For example, to exist, to not exist, to both exist and not exist, and to neither exist nor not exist are all positions, and we call these positions the four extremes. As for the second question, Mipham Rinpoche answers by exploring the views of the "ancient scholars."

The View of the Ancient Scholars

When we hear about the "ancient scholars," we often think of the Nyingma lineage because it is known as the "Ancient Translation School." However, it is important for us to know that the ancient scholars in this text are scholars from distinct lineages who came to Tibet from India. While some Nyingma scholars are included in the catchall phrase "ancient scholars," the text is not referring to the Nyingma lineage in general.

When the ancient scholars examined the uncontrived Madhyamaka, Mipham Rinpoche says that they spoke with one voice; they were in complete agreement that Madhyamaka asserts no position. This is a very simple idea—if it is truly Madhyamaka, truly the Middle Way, how could any position be taken? If you were to ask the ancient scholars why no position could be taken, their answer would be that the uncontrived Madhyamaka is necessarily beyond the four extremes. Therefore, no position could possibly be taken.

Madhyamaka Must Be in Accord with the Assertions of Nagarjuna and Chandrakirti

At first glance, the positionlessness of Madhyamaka seems like a flawless assertion, but Mipham Rinpoche brings up a point that helps us to see its potential contradictions. Any presentation of the view, meditation, and conduct of Madhyamaka must be in accord with the great Prasangika Madhyamaka scholars Nagarjuna and the glorious Chandrakirti. Mipham Rinpoche references Chandrakirti's text, *Entering the Middle Way* (Skt. *Madhyamakavatara*), in which Chandrakirti discusses the aggregates, elements, sense bases, interdependent origination, the path of the ten bhumis, and the resulting ten powers. These are all very clearly presented in Chandrakirti's great text.

Since Chandrakirti discussed these topics, it must be incorrect to absolutely assert that the Madhyamaka takes no position. How could we say that the path of Madhyamaka is positionless if we can discuss these aspects of the path, even relatively? If Madhyamaka were truly positionless, we would not be able to acknowledge or even discuss the aggregates, the elements, the sense bases, or the paths and bhumis. So Mipham Rinpoche concludes that the singular voice of the ancient scholars contradicts the Madhyamaka treatises of the glorious Chandrakirti.

Was Chandrakirti Truly Taking a Position?

The question might arise: How did Mipham Rinpoche know that Chandrakirti, when he described relative phenomena such as aggregates, elements, and sense bases, was not describing it from the point of view of abiding in inseparable appearance and emptiness?

That could make sense, but only from the point of view of a yogi who is constantly self-liberating appearances. But Chandrakirti's text is not talking from the point of view of a yogi abiding in his or her experience of realization. This text is taught from the point of view of an ordinary practitioner who is learning the way to follow the path. For that reason, Mipham Rinpoche understands it to be establishing relative phenomena because it is the way that ordinary people are relating to the path and the teachings.

The Eight Great Lions Who Asserted that Madhyamaka Does or Does Not Take a Position

Centuries ago, scholars gathered at a shedra near Lhasa named *Tsangphu Netang*, which was built in the place where a hawk dropped a *kata* (Tib.; offering scarf) held in its beak from the sky. Later, eight of the scholars were given the name the Eight Great Lions, and these Eight Great Lions are who we know now as the ancient scholars. Among the Eight Great Lions, some asserted that the Madhyamaka takes no positions, while others asserted that a position must be taken.

Mipham Rinpoche says that both sides have good qualities as well as flaws. For example, to say that there are absolutely no positions taken in Madhyamaka establishes uncontrivance. But it contradicts the scriptures of Chandrakirti, who does take conventional positions in the text of *Entering the Middle Way*.

On the other hand, for those who assert that a position is taken, this position must be examined very carefully. Although this statement is in accordance with Chandrakirti's text, we also must be able to establish uncontrivance. Uncontrivance is a defining quality of the ultimate view of Madhyamaka. For that reason, we can understand Mipham Rinpoche's own way of relating to Madhyamaka as not taking either of these sides but as looking at both of these sides as extremes.

As we know, the Later Scholars are usually defined as Tsongkhapa and his followers. The school that Tsongkhapa established, as we can recall from topic one, places high importance on following after worldly opinion. That is, they do not analyze conventional reality but leave it alone, as it is, so that it can be perceived and understood in the way of ordinary people.

The Teaching of Longchenpa: Meditation and Post-Equipoise

Mipham Rinpoche does not find the approach of either the ancient scholars or the Later Scholars to be satisfactory. Rather, he follows the philosophy that was established by the omniscient king, Longchenpa. This philosophy is stated in great detail in the *Wish-Fulfilling Treasury*, and it is very easy to understand.

Actually, from the point of view of the great teachings that have been given in the history of our lineage, we practitioners of the Nyingma lineage have little merit. Longchenpa composed more than two hundred texts, but only around twenty-six remain. There were great, elaborate teachings on the Causal Vehicle among these two hundred, as well as detailed teachings on Atiyoga Dzogchen. Unfortunately, we only have these few texts left to study.

Again, Mipham Rinpoche presents Longchenpa's teaching as the teaching of his own tradition. In order to understand Mipham Rinpoche's presentation, we need to differentiate between the period of actual meditation and the post-equipoise period. He describes what these mean in great detail.

Actual meditation is described as being *transcendent* or *beyond the ordinary*. More specifically, actual meditation is resting in the uncontrived view, which we have discussed throughout our study of this text. We are able to rest in the mind's uncontrived nature for only instants at a time. According to Mipham Rinpoche's presentation, at the exact instant in which we abide, no position can be asserted. This statement is also in accordance with the teachings of the Buddha Shakyamuni who also taught that in order to be flawless, the ultimate state must be free of all positions.

We can only experience freedom from all positions while we actually abide. Once we enter the post-equipoise period, positions must be asserted. This makes sense if we think back to Chandrakirti's text, which asserted the aggregates, elements, sense bases, and so on. According to Chandrakirti, positions are asserted as part of our conventional experience, as well as our experience of the path. In summary, when we abide in meditation, no positions can be asserted. In any moment that is in the post-equipoise period, positions must be asserted.

Uncontrivance Is Not Shamatha Practice

Many teachings describe the states of calm abiding, meditative stabilization, or actual meditation. But here Mipham Rinpoche uses the phrase "actual meditation" to specifically refer to *one-pointedness endowed with inseparable wisdom*. While many of us engage in ordinary shamatha practice, actual meditation and the post-equipoise period do not describe shamatha practices and techniques.

When we practice mindfully, our one-pointedness generally lasts for a very short period of time when, suddenly, the mind is moved by either an afflictive emotion or the karmic wind, which we could loosely describe as discursive energy. Once the afflictive emotion or karmic wind appears as the mind's motion, our experience is no longer actual meditation.

Whether the karmic wind expresses as a discursive thought or an afflictive emotion, it is easily understood if we think about the word *movement* as opposed to *one-pointedness*. Any movement of the mind causes a break from one-pointedness. When the karmic wind arises, we are unable to rest one-pointedly. In other words, when we are unable to rest one-pointedly, it is because the karmic wind has moved and we have moved into the post-equipoise period. For that reason, it is impossible to make a statement like, "I have been resting in the nature of mind for six months," because that implies that the practitioner has not subtly examined the karmic wind and all of the times that the mind moved between the experiences of actual meditation and post-equipoise.

Additionally, to be called actual meditation, inseparable wisdom must be present. Thus, we must learn to distinguish between ordinary mind and the presence of inseparable wisdom, or rigpa. If the mind is one-pointed and rigpa is present, we are truly resting in meditative equipoise, actual meditation. As we talked about in earlier chapters, in order to properly recognize and rest in rigpa, we need to be introduced to the nature of mind through the fourth empowerment. However, even though we may have received the introduction to the nature of mind and are able to abide in the mind's nature for an instant, the karmic wind will rise up again and we immediately move into the post-equipoise period.

This should help us understand that Mipham Rinpoche describes something much subtler than the general way we understand meditation and the post-equipoise experience. We usually understand meditation to mean sitting down on the cushion, but here there is much more subtle awareness being placed upon what is happening in the mind. Actually, we could have ten, twenty, or even hundreds of actual meditation experiences while sitting on our cushions, and between each such experience, we would also experience the post-equipoise period. In the same way, in ordinary life, any moment that we are resting in rigpa would be an experience of actual meditation, even though we are not sitting on the cushion. *Mipham Rinpoche calls on us to change our way of thinking and look at our lives as a series of moments that are either actual meditation or post-equipoise.*

Positionlessness and Superior Intellect Arisen from Ordinary Mind

We have described actual meditation, or the experience of meditative equipoise, as opposed to the post-equipoise period. We also noted that while we are abiding in the wisdom of meditative equipoise, no position can be asserted. However, nearly any Madhyamaka scholar will say that when we examine inner and outer phenomena using ultimate analytical wisdom, we establish the uncontrived view of appearance and emptiness. This is a style of positionlessness that is based solely on *superior intellect arisen from ordinary mind*. It has nothing to do with our personal experience or habituating to the experience of actual meditation.

Based on superior intellect arisen from ordinary mind, many skeptical philosophers come to trust the *idea* of positionlessness simply because it is logical. It is also very easy to establish through debate. When we debate, we can easily cut through any position that anyone else tries to assert.

However, there is a different kind of positionlessness that we should relate to as practitioners. This style of positionlessness is directly understood, or is the sphere of activity, of *individually self-cognizant wisdom*. If we recall, individually self-cognizant wisdom is beyond the sphere of activity of ordinary mind, but can be glimpsed when one is introduced to it properly by an authentic lama.

Therefore, when we assert either that Madhyamaka must be free of positions or that Madhyamaka must take positions, both of these statements are made from the point of view of not only the post-equipoise period, but also from the superior intellect arisen from ordinary mind rather than the experience of indivisible wisdom.

As meditation practitioners, our experience is paramount. When we think about positionlessness, again, we should understand this to be the object of the wisdom of meditative equipoise. Positionlessness is first, of course, the object of our superior intellect and intellectual certainty, but we must move beyond this so that it becomes an actual direct experience. Even as we read and study philosophical teachings, we should always understand that meditation is the most important part of our tradition.

For most Western practitioners, our understanding mostly comes from our intellectual processing, our tendency to think and analyze. It is rare to find a practitioner who has had genuine experience of the meaning of the teachings. So when we discuss the view, meditation, and conduct of Madhyamaka with ordinary practitioners, we are usually talking from the point of view of superior intellect arisen from ordinary mind.

However, it is important for practitioners of Madhyamaka, whether we be Svatantrika Madhyamaka or Prasangika Madhyamaka, to assert that Madhyamaka is positionless. The key is to differentiate whether we are in the actual experience of meditative equipoise or in the post-equipoise period. Using this guideline, we are able to properly understand and contextualize our listening, contemplation, and meditation. We especially should understand that listening and contemplation then become very important bases for actual meditative experience.

Positionlessness Is an Extreme

Both Longchenpa and Mipham Rinpoche teach that asserting that Madhyamaka is positionless is an extreme. Asserting that Madhyamaka takes positions is also an extreme. If we have understood the discussion so far, it also follows that, from the point of view of resting or abiding in the natural state itself, there can be no position. Conventionally, however, we must assert all kinds of positions. This understanding of Madhyamaka is right in the middle. It is not too big or too small. This pith is easy to explain and not easily forgotten. It is an uncommon defining quality of Mipham Rinpoche's philosophical explanation, and it is the essential meaning of the final topic.

Differentiating the Meaning of the Teachings

From the point of view of the post-equipoise period, there are five paths (the paths of accumulation, preparation, seeing, meditation, and no-further-learning), the practice of meditation, and the result of omniscient wisdom. All of these must be asserted from our point of view as practitioners on the path who start from ordinary mind. However, while we actually abide, what is the path? What is the result? What is wisdom? From the point of view of actual abiding, none of these can be expressed. Just as it was said in the omniscient Longchenpa's *Treasury of the Dharmadhatu*, while abiding in on the path, there is no passing from bhumis or paths. However, for a bodhisattva who is abiding on the bhumis and who is in the post-equipoise period, there is the experience of progressing on the path, no matter how subtle that progression may be. There is such thing as deepening realization. There is such a thing as accomplishing a result. Even though this is different from the experience of abiding described above in the *Treasury of the Dharmadhatu*, whenever we read a text, it is very important for us to differentiate whether it speaks from the point of view of wisdom itself or if it speaks from the point of view of beings who are attempting to achieve wisdom. When we make a mistake about which point of view a text is speaking from, we may lose faith, or lack motivation to practice bodhichitta. We become arrogant, and we become selfish. It is incredibly important to know the context that a text is written from.

This is important for all of us. If we are practicing meditation and have been introduced to the nature of mind, then when we abide in the wisdom of meditative equipoise, we should recognize whether or not a position is being taken, or perhaps more accurately, whether a position seems to be expressed in that meditative experience. If we notice a position is taken, then we should recognize that this is not the actual view; this is not what is being pointed out by the upadeshas. It is a sign that we are unsure of what has been introduced by the lama, and that our minds remain obscured. We should not only work to purify our obscurations, but we should also return to our lama and request further instruction.

When we are in the post-equipoise experience, we should continue to work diligently to develop bodhichitta and meditative stabilization, and study philosophy. These will all increase our ability to experience actual meditation. Every aspect of the path will become clear and easy as a result of these efforts.

For the purposes of this text, I teach Mipham Rinpoche's view as my own and as the perfect, unmistaken view. However, we should remain aware that Sakya, Kagyu, and Gelugpa philosophers each have their own presentations that bring their practitioners to the experience of certainty.

A Shortcut to Dzogchen?

A person I have known for a couple of years came to me and said, "There is another way to realize Dzogchen. Do you know what it is? Eat plants."

This is not a joke. Apparently, there is a drug that is extracted from plants that gives some sort of experience to the person who eats it. According to this student, "When you eat it, you do not have to work from the bottom to reach the peak, you just automatically jump up to the top. You will see what you need to see."

I said, "Thank you very much, but I do not need to eat plants to be able to realize the view of Dzogchen. Dzogchen realization does not come from outside of you. While eating plants may cause you to have visions or see something out of the ordinary, that experience is impermanent. However, when realization arises from inside of you, it will never change." Remember that wisdom will never arise based on the cause of an outer condition. Outer conditions will benefit you if your inner realization is strong enough, but realization comes from within and is based on your practice.

Refuting the Later Scholars

Next, Mipham Rinpoche refutes some of the other philosophical traditions. If we recall topic one, we know that the Later Scholars take the position that conventional reality exists. They say, "We must follow after worldly opinion in just the way that others assert it. If we do not, we will deprecate conventional reality."

Mipham Rinpoche says that this cannot be correct. The reason is that the Later Scholars do not differentiate between the experience of actual meditation and the post-equipoise period. In other words, they make a broad statement that Madhyamaka must be completely uncontrived, and they also make a blanket statement that conventional reality exists.

The word *exists* is the problem here. If we take conventional reality as it is at face value, if we fail to analyze it to determine that its true mode of existence lies beyond the four extremes, this directly contradicts saying that Madhyamaka is positionless. The contradiction surfaces because both statements—phenomena exist as they appear and Madhyamaka is uncontrived—must be true at the same time. However, if we assert absolute positionlessness, then the post-equipoise period, or conventional reality itself, must also be positionless. However, we know that, based on the text of Chandrakirti, the post-equipoise period has stages and paths and conventional differentiations that everyone accepts.

Prasangika and Svatantrika Madhyamaka

At this point, I need to say a few things about the two different styles of Madhyamaka philosophy, which are the Prasangika and the Svatantrika. Prasangika Madhyamaka is generally known as the uncommon style that all Tibetan Buddhist scholars assert to be the most profound. Prasangika Madhyamaka was established by great scholars like Nagarjuna and Chandrakirti, which is why Mipham Rinpoche uses the texts of these scholars as a benchmark to measure whether or not we are reaching the level of true, uncontrived Madhyamaka.

The Svatantrika is asserted by other great scholars such as Yeshe Nyingpo, Lhakden Jed, and Khenpo Bodhisattva. Svatantrika is also a very profound style of Madhyamaka, but the Prasangika philosophers attribute three kinds of faults to the Svatantrika, which were introduced in topic one.

All three flaws attributed to the Svatantrika have to do with the application of ultimate analytical wisdom. If ultimate analytical wisdom is not in agreement with Madhyamaka philosophy, then a particular philosophy cannot reach the level of authentic Madhyamaka. Why would I say that? If all phenomena are of an uncontrived nature, then we must be able to establish them as being unborn and beyond extremes. On the other hand, if phenomena can withstand ultimate analytical reasoning, this results in the inability to establish phenomena as being ultimately unborn. This is one of the three flaws that are in contradiction to Chandrakirti's logic. The three flaws are summarized as follows:

- *The first flaw is that conventional truth can withstand analysis.* If one asserts conventional existence, then phenomena will withstand analysis. In other words, phenomena cannot be harmed or broken down by logical analysis.

- *The second flaw is if we take the position of conventional existence, birth cannot be refuted ultimately.* In other words, if something exists, we cannot logically establish it as being of an unborn nature. Birth is a position, abiding is also a position; these are both forms of existence. If something exists, it cannot be unborn. So, the second flaw is a logical consequence of the first flaw.

- *The third flaw is if conventional phenomena exist, then the wisdom of the noble ones' equipoise destroys conventional phenomena.* If phenomena exist, and the wisdom of the noble ones' equipoise is realized, then conventional phenomena must be completely excluded or destroyed in order for that experience to be possible. Otherwise, we must assert existence and nonexistence simultaneously. The third flaw is also a logical consequence of the first.

What is most important to understand is that if a phenomenon can withstand ultimate analytical wisdom, it cannot be established as unborn. The idea that phenomena are not of an unborn nature contradicts the essence of Madhyamaka reasoning. All the other flaws arise from the inability to establish phenomena as being of an unborn nature.

Based on this discussion, it logically follows that all those who follow

Madhyamaka philosophy want to establish themselves as being of the Prasangika Madhyamaka school, since it is asserted to be flawless. No matter which lineage or school a scholar belongs to, he or she will say, "I am a Prasangika Madhyamaka philosopher. You others are merely Svatantrika."

If we assert the position of existence at all, these three flaws will arise no matter what we state our philosophical beliefs to be. We should keep in mind that throughout this text, Mipham Rinpoche does not assert conventional existence. He asserts only the *mere appearance of conventional reality*. Mipham Rinpoche does not say that phenomena exist as a consequence of following after worldly opinion; he just says conventional phenomena merely appear to exist. This is a subtle but very distinct assertion.

Additional Flaws

Mipham Rinpoche says that additional flaws arise from the view of the Later Scholars. First, phenomena are not truly established in the Prasangika presented by the Later Scholars. But at the same time, from the point of view of unexamined worldly opinion, phenomena exist. The Prasangika presentation of the Later Scholars is stated in such a way that both statements must be accepted at the same time.

This is logically problematic. The Later Scholars say that phenomena are not truly established from the point of view of the ultimate nature. But at the same time, they are established from the point of view of worldly opinion. If both statements are true at the same time, we assert existence and nonexistence simultaneously, which is illogical. If only one of them is true, then the philosophy is inconsistent with its own words. Actually, the only way to make these two statements logically consistent is to differentiate between actual abiding and the post-equipoise period.

The text goes on to present further flaws that result from this argument. However, what we should understand is that it is impossible for us to both assert existence and nonexistence at the same time unless we shift the point of view from which we are speaking, because it is simply not possible to assert existence and nonexistence simultaneously.

In topic one, we mentioned the need to qualify from what point of view we were speaking. As a result, we say things like, "Ultimate reality is qualified as taking no positions and conventional reality is qualified as taking positions." But ultimate and conventional reality can actually be described as being of a singular, indivisible, equal nature if we simply talk about them from the point of view of either abiding in meditation or the post-equipoise period. This allows us to resolve the problem of having to qualify that they are different. In topic six, we established the conventional and the ultimate as being in an equal state. From that point of view, it would be very problematic to qualify the conventional as being in one way and the ultimate as being another way. They lose their equality when we do this.

The Nyingma and Gelug philosophies differ in another important way that accounts for the differences in the way they describe the view. A realized Nyingma practitioner will probably have begun by making intellectual examination the most important part of their training. But after they have gained some certainty in the view, their focus will shift and meditation will become preeminent. Examination merely becomes a support to meditation at that point. However, in the philosophy of the Later Scholars, examination is and remains the most important part of the practice. The majority of one's life is devoted to examination, logic, and debate.

You may have noticed that much of the language that Mipham Rinpoche uses relates to actual meditation instruction and explaining how to bring examination into our meditation practice. Because the focus in the Nyingma tradition is very much on meditation and the experience of meditation, the words used are very different from other styles of Vajrayana philosophy.

The Elaborate Explanation of Longchenpa's Philosophy

This section begins with a question: *How can we understand the two truths in accordance with the teachings of Longchenpa, free of any confusion, stainless in understanding?*

Mipham Rinpoche begins by summarizing Longchenpa's position. If we assert the Prasangika in accordance with the defining characteristics of the Madhyamaka school—and also in a way that it cannot be harmed by the doubts of skeptical philosophers—then while resting, all phenomena must be of an unborn, primordially pure, empty nature, and in the post-equipoise period, positions must be taken. This is an uncommon defining characteristic of Nyingma philosophy because this explanation enables us to assert Madhyamaka properly and without the danger of being harmed by any logical arguments.

When we properly understand the wisdom of the noble ones' equipoise as being nondual wisdom, then all of the subtle extremes, without exception, will be fully pacified. We know from this statement that if dualism is present, it is not the wisdom of the noble ones' equipoise. Just so, if duality is present when we are attempting to abide, then we are not resting properly in the nature of mind. For this reason, we can understand that nonduality is one defining characteristic of the wisdom of the noble ones' equipoise. When we are introduced to the nature of mind, we experience nonduality for an instant. We know this as *exemplary wisdom*, an experience similar to the wisdom of the noble ones' equipoise.

In this section of the text, even though the Madhyamaka teachings are being given in accordance with the Causal Vehicle, the text uses language that is very similar to that of the Secret Mantrayana. This language exemplifies the way in which this text acts as a bridge between sutra and tantra. This occurs because a beginning practitioner starts by using ultimate analytical wisdom to establish the unborn nature. We call this type of wisdom "ultimate analytical wisdom" because it is completely intellectual; we go through all the stages of examining phenomena. However, this does not establish the unborn essence of the ultimate nature. Rather, this style of examination remains within the sphere of superior intellect arisen from ordinary mind. The wisdom of the noble ones' equipoise is completely different; it is free of all duality. It is based on one's personal engagement in ultimate analytical wisdom that the setting of duality begins to dawn in the mindstream.

Next, the text revisits topic one as it relates to having a partial or incomplete understanding of the view. Topic one examined whether the nonaffirming negative could be posited as the ultimate view. We found that if the nonaffirming negative correctly expresses the ultimate view, then positionlessness is impossible. As we know, the nonaffirming negative asserts the extreme of nonexistence, what we called the empty void. For this reason, the view as posed by the nonaffirming negative is incomplete or merely partial.

The two different extremes presented so far in this topic—taking a position or not taking a position—are analogous to the extremes of existence and nonexistence that were discussed in the preceding topics. For example, the extremes of nonexistence and positionlessness can each be likened to the empty void. In the same way, the nonaffirming negative cannot be indivisible appearance and emptiness; it is simply the empty void, the extreme of nonexistence. Of course, asserting a position is asserting permanence or existence.

The only way to have true philosophical consistency is if phenomena are an expression of indivisible appearance and emptiness. As we have just seen, nonduality is impossible based on the style of Madhyamaka asserted by the Later Scholars. Additionally, the experience of inseparable appearance and emptiness is also impossible.

Ultimate Madhyamaka Is Completely Uncontrived

Mipham Rinpoche says that if we are going to assert Madhyamaka, we need to assert ultimate Madhyamaka. What is the definition of *ultimate Madhyamaka*? It must be completely uncontrived. The teachings so far tell us that if we claim that Madhyamaka either asserts a position or it asserts no position, then uncontrivance is impossible. It will always be incomplete or partial Madhyamaka, rather than uncontrived Madhyamaka.

The first thing to know about the word "contrivance" is that ordinary mind is not without contrivance for even an instant. The philosophical meaning of contrivance has to do with the words that we attach to things, for example, whether an object is empty or not empty, it exists or does not exist, or when we talk about the four extremes of existence, nonexistence, both, and neither. These are the contrivances that we are talking about.

There is also ordinary contrivance. These are qualifiers, or the mind's coloring of things. The mind never represents something to us without engaging in activities like overlaying or superimposing. This is the essence of the word "contrivance." It is the ordinary mind's creating or doing. We should know that our perception is always colored by ordinary mind.

The essential definition of Madhyamaka, then, must be uncontrivance. Other ways to understand uncontrivance are to be beyond establishment and refutation, or to be free of fixing or abandoning. If none of these are present, then this is ultimate Prasangika Madhyamaka. The contrived mind is the mind that thinks in terms of existence, nonexistence, accepting, and refuting. Uncontrivance must be beyond these. When we are unable to rest in uncontrivance, the mind is not pacified. In other words, as the mind gets busier, we accumulate more and more negative karma as we react to emotions and concepts, so that the time of realization will never come. Thus, Mipham Rinpoche asserts that if any contrivance is present, it is not Madhyamaka. And, if we cannot rest in uncontrivance, nondual wisdom cannot arise.

Anticipating the Challenges of Other Philosophers

Mipham Rinpoche composes the next section of the text to refute any possible faults that other philosophers may attribute to his own philosophical presentation. He starts from the premise that many disagreements have arisen as different scholars assert Madhyamaka philosophy, and he has discovered inner contradictions during his own examination of other philosophical presentations. Then he asks himself, "*Won't all of these inner contradictions come as a result of my explanation as well?*"

To illustrate why this is not true, Mipham Rinpoche uses the context of consciousness and wisdom, although all of the different examples given in the text are analogous to these. For example, when he uses the "way of appearance" as opposed to "the actual state," these phrases are analogous to consciousness and wisdom. He says that when we view phenomena from the point of view of consciousness, we must accept that mere positions can be asserted. If you remember, Mipham Rinpoche has also used the word *mere* to describe *mere appearance*, which is distinct from unqualified appearance. Unqualified appearance is true from its own side, whereas mere appearance is inseparable from emptiness.

Wisdom is the expression of all phenomena in the primordial state of equality. It is beyond the dichotomy of position and positionless. All phenomena are included within the two truths, and when we examine their primordial nature, not even one of them can withstand analysis. This is the expression of wisdom that is reliant on mere appearance inseparable from emptiness.

Mountains in the East and Mountains in the North

Mipham Rinpoche says that if the two truths become separated like mountains in the east and mountains in the north, they lose their relationship to each other. Consciousness and wisdom are not like mountains in the east and mountains in the north. They are expressions of one and other based on a practitioner's experience in meditation.

From Mipham Rinpoche's point of view, the assertions of conventional and ultimate reality of the Later Scholars are like mountains in the east and mountains in the north. First, we have an assertion that conventional reality exists. That is like mountains in the east. And then we have the mountains in the north: reality's ultimate nature. When we cut through the true existence of the ultimate nature, then the two truths become separated.

From Mipham Rinpoche's point of view, the relationship between the two truths is like fire and warmth, or consciousness and wisdom. We can describe the border between these two as recognition: whether we recognize wisdom in a certain moment or whether the experience in that moment is ordinary consciousness. No contradiction arises since we are not talking in absolutes. We are talking based on the actual experience of the practitioner.

Further Classifying Madhyamaka

In Mipham Rinpoche's tradition of philosophy, not only do we differentiate between actual meditation and the post-equipoise period, but we also differentiate between consciousness and wisdom. Because of this differentiation, no inner contradictions arise.

For example, when we talk about the valid cognition of conventional and ultimate truth, this is the sphere of ordinary mind. It is contrived. It is the sphere of the superior intellect arisen from mind and therefore positions are asserted. When we talk about nondual uncontrivance, we are speaking from the point of view of wisdom, which is not ordinary mind. By differentiating in this way, faults will not come to Mipham Rinpoche's own tradition.

Mipham Rinpoche details further classifications of Madhyamaka that will help us to understand Secret Mantryana texts more precisely, including the *path of Madhyamaka that differentiates between relative phenomena*, and the actual *Madhyamaka of equipoise*, which is completely nondual. The path of Madhyamaka that differentiates is just like it sounds—during the post-equipoise period, we differentiate between conventional and ultimate reality and understand things in the sphere of ordinary mind.

Mipham Rinpoche also classifies these as coarse and subtle Madhyamaka. Coarse Madhyamaka again refers to the path of Madhyamaka that differentiates, which is the sphere of ordinary mind or superior intelligence. Subtle Madhyamaka is the actual Madhyamaka of equipoise. By naming these classifications, Mipham Rinpoche seems to suggest to the Later Scholars, "There is nothing wrong with your philosophy, but if you were to adopt these ways of classifying or differentiating what you are talking about, it would clarify your philosophy so that it becomes free of inner contradiction."

Mipham Rinpoche also presents the classifications of *symbolic Madhyamaka* and the *Madhyamaka of suchness*. Symbolic Madhyamaka consists of the teachings and the practice of the path, as anything symbolic is contrived. The Madhyamaka of suchness is the ability to abide in suchness after being introduced to these symbols based on an uncommonly deep relationship with a spiritual friend.

He also names the even *more subtle Madhyamaka of suchness*, which is the experience of individually self-cognizant wisdom itself. In this experience of the ultimate nature, there are no assertions of positions or of being beyond positions.

These are only some of the classifications named in the text. I include them here because when you study Mipham Rinpoche's other texts in the future, and he uses the word "Madhyamaka" in a way that you are not used to hearing, you will need to figure out for yourself what the reference means. You will need to decide, "Is he talking about the post-equipoise period or the actual experience of meditation?" We will need to take responsibility for our own learning.

Great Madhyamaka

Most importantly, for our purposes, Mipham Rinpoche uses the term "Great Madhyamaka" in the root text. When he says "Great Madhyamaka," he is talking about resultant Madhyamaka or indivisible Madhyamaka. The wisdom of meditative equipoise itself is Great Madhyamaka. It is abiding in actual meditation.

Sometimes, by making one assertion, another assertion is made indirectly, as in the affirming negative. For example, to say, "I do not sleep at night," implies that it is possible that I sleep during the day. In just the same way that this statement has an indirect implication, if we say that Great Madhyamaka takes no position at all, that implies that there is a lesser, or small Madhyamaka that does take positions. We should be very clear that Mipham Rinpoche is not interested in saying that Madhyamaka does not take positions in general. He only says that Great Madhyamaka does not take positions. Great Madhyamaka refers to the ultimate state. Small Madhyamaka talks about the way of appearance, or the causal Madhyamaka. From the point of view of small Madhyamaka, the two truths merely appear and can be intellectually understood.

When we study the way that things appear—for example, when we think of the ultimate state, we have a mental understanding of nonexistence, and so we refute existence. When we think about the conventional state, we establish it in our own mind as being existent. This is the mere appearance of the two truths.

Specifically, the phrases "the way of appearing" and "the actual state" are two of the most important phrases in the Secret Mantrayana. We may think that the *way of appearing* and the *actual state* are synonymous with conventional and ultimate reality, but they are not used in quite the same way. The *actual state* is synonymous with Great Madhyamaka, and the *way of appearing* refers to small Madhyamaka, coarse Madhyamaka, or causal Madhyamaka.

From Mipham Rinpoche's point of view, the positionlessness presented by the Later Scholars is a position in itself. From the point of view of conventional reality, asserting existence is obviously a position. However, Great Madhyamaka, the actual nature, is an expression of the two truths in dependence upon each other. Great Madhyamaka enables us not to need to assert the ultimate state as positionless and conventional reality as taking positions. For example, Mipham Rinpoche might say, "I accept that to understand emptiness, I must rely on the appearance of phenomena. And I understand that I must rely upon the appearance of phenomena to understand emptiness."

Conventionally, appearance and emptiness must be posited as interdependent. When the two truths are posited in dependence upon each other and their mere appearance is placed in the larger context of the natural state, we are not forced to say that one exists and one does not exist. We can simply understand them through their interrelationship.

This is different than the presentation of the Later Scholars. For example, let's say we were to use a prayer wheel to represent ultimate reality and a pair of sunglasses to represent the conventional appearance of the two truths. The Later Scholars' goal is to put them together on the same side. And because they are being put together, we have to say that they both exist and do not exist at the same time.

Mipham Rinpoche does not need to assert existence and nonexistence together in this way. He accepts that there can be the mere appearance of the two truths and that they can be reliant upon each other, and that they express the nature of inseparability. The logical fault of trying to overlay existence upon nonexistence goes away.

Whenever we talk about analytical valid cognition, we have to put that on the side of conventional reality. There is no reason to have to establish existence and nonexistence together. We can simply deal with it in the conventional sphere itself.

Distinguishing the Nyingma Position from the Later Scholars

Next, Mipham Rinpoche anticipates another criticism of his position. Somebody might say, "What you assert philosophically is really no different from the Later Scholars."

This comes back to distinguishing between the way that phenomena appear and the natural state. When we use Madhyamaka logic to understand the conventional nature of all phenomena, we conclude they are not truly established. But from the point of view of our conventional valid cognition, as addressed in topic six, things do appear to be established. So when we talk about phenomena from the point of view of appearance, we are always either refuting or establishing. We are always caught up in these two extremes.

Mipham Rinpoche thinks that it is fine to accept the mere appearance of these extremes and to describe them as the two truths, but we should know that this is only from the point of view of superior intellect arisen from ordinary mind. We also know that the actual state is beyond these extremes; it is beyond all refuting and establishing. When we know that the actual state is beyond refuting and establishing, there is no need to even talk about whether or not there are positions taken or if it is positionlessness.

In summary, the topic for this section was: *Is a position taken or not?*

Mipham Rinpoche's answer is: Great Madhyamaka is even beyond asking that question!

Cutting Through the Three Flaws

Next Mipham Rinpoche anticipates the criticism, "The three flaws attributed to Svantantrika Madhyamaka also arise based on your philosophical explanation."

The reason this is not true is that Mipham Rinpoche consistently asserts the mere appearance of the two truths, or the mere appearance of conventional reality. Because of this, existence is not truly established existence. It the mere appearance of existence.

Based on this, we can start to understand why the three flaws of the Svatantrika do not apply to his philosophical explanation. The first flaw is that phenomena can withstand ultimate analysis. That is not a problem for entities that merely appear, because we know that entities that appear are dependently imputed. Their appearances arise through interdependent origination.

As part of not falling into this first flaw, Mipham Rinpoche also has to refute that the ultimate state, which we impute as the extreme of non-existence, can withstand analysis. He does this by explaining that like the conventional state, the ultimate state is also dependently imputed. We only understand the ultimate from our ordinary point of view, or conventional reality. Therefore, there is no problem. We do not have to say whether ultimate reality exists or not. We are beyond that because everything is a function of dependent arising. So the flaw of withstanding analysis does not arise either for entities that seem to exist or the kind of nonexistence that we impute to the ultimate state.

When we talk about dependent imputation, we have to go back to topic one and to the Later Scholars' argument that the pillar is not empty of itself; it is empty of its true existence. If we recall this argument, its consequence is that the Later Scholars put space between the conventional appearance and the ultimate nature of the pillar. It cannot work in the same way that Mipham Rinpoche describes it, which is that *we understand the ultimate nature based on mere appearance.*

Why is it that Mipham Rinpoche relies on dependent arising consistently when he explains his own philosophy? This comes back to his main assertion in topic three: *A cup can appear without losing any of its quality of emptiness, and a cup can be empty without losing any of its quality of appearance.* All the layers of meaning that are coming together right now are incredibly profound. If we keep this idea in mind, everything else makes sense. Even from a conventional point of view, we can understand everything as arising interdependently. There is no need to put space between apparent phenomena and their ultimate nature.

As the second two flaws attributed to the Svatantrika Madhyamaka arise as a consequence of the first, there is no need to refute them.

Is the Essence of the Two Truths the Same or Distinct?

As covered in topic one, the "nominal ultimate" refers to the empty nature of the unobstructed way that conventional reality appears. However, when we talk about the interdependence of the two truths, we need to ask, "Is the essence of the two truths the same—is it one—or do they have distinct essences?" If we answer the question by saying that the essence of the two truths is distinct, four flaws will arise. If we answer that question by saying that the essence of the two truths is the same, four flaws also arise.

First, if the two truths are not of the same essence, then there is no connection between them, like mountains that are in the north and the west. However, if they are of the same essence, then how would we even distinguish between conventional and the ultimate? These would be exactly the same.

Each of the four schools of Tibetan Buddhism has its own way of positing the two truths, and there is a lot of debate among them. We will not give great details on the debate, but we should know that the Gelugpas, Nyingmapas, Sakyapas, and Kagyupas each have their own way of positing the two truths. Some scholars—including a few Nyingma scholars—describe the relationship between the two truths as being of *one essence and two aspects*. We touched on this in topic one, and at that point, we accepted the construct of one essence and two aspects as being logical. A metaphor for understanding what it means to be two aspects of the same essence is a shell and its white color. However, logical problems do arise if we assert the nature of the two truths in this way. The Later Scholars also assert the relationship between the two truths as a singular essence with two aspects.

We should be able to identify the reason that this explanation is problematic by recalling what we learned in topic one. The Later Scholars say that a pillar is not empty of the pillar's essence; it is empty of the pillar's true existence. Thus, the object of refutation is not the thing itself but the object's true existence that is "stuck on the side," and indivisibility can never really be posited. If appearance and emptiness are disconnected in this way, it does not work to say that phenomena are of a singular essence.

Appearance Refutes Emptiness, Emptiness Refutes Appearance

Some Sakya scholars also assert *one essence and two aspects*. The great scholar Gorampa said that based on this, all eight flaws will arise. From the point of view of having the same essence, the four flaws of singularity will arise, and from the point of view of having distinct aspects, the four flaws of distinctness will arise. Even though *one essence and two aspects* sounds reasonable from a logical perspective, there is no sound way to posit the two truths within that framework.

Gorampa describes the two truths using the phrase "distinctions that equally refute." The meaning of this is that from our own point of view as ordinary beings in the conventional world, appearances refute emptiness. Equally so, if we have deep certainty and conviction in emptiness, emptiness refutes appearance. This is the way that we perceive, and for that reason both sides, appearance and emptiness, seem to refute each other, and they refute each other equally.

The Flaws that Arise if the Essence of the Two Truths Is Distinct

The four flaws of distinctness are given from the point of view of one who has realized ultimate reality.

- The first flaw is that if the two truths were distinct, even if one realizes ultimate reality, because they will not have realized conventional reality, they cannot attain omniscience as a result of their realization. Since there is no connection between the ultimate and the conventional, they have not realized the nature of all phenomena. Even though they have realized the nature of suchness, they have not attained nirvana.

- The second flaw is that if the conventional and the ultimate are distinct, then conventional reality is not of the nature of suchness. If conventional reality is not of the nature of suchness, then even if one attains realization, it is not realization of conventional reality. The nature of suchness becomes lost, in a sense.

- The third flaw is if the two truths are distinct, then even though one may realize the unestablished nature of the self, they only realize that it is merely unestablished, they do not realize that it is ultimately unestablished. In the same way as the second flaw pointed out, phenomena and their suchness are disconnected. So even though one realizes that the self is unestablished, this is not the same as realizing the ultimate nature. Because they are distinct, realization of the conventional nature is not the same as realization of the ultimate nature.

- The final flaw is that even after one has realized ultimate reality, because they have not realized the ultimate nature of conventional reality, they are not free from samsara. Karma and afflictive emotions still arise. Realization cannot actually be posited if the essence of the two truths is distinct.

The Flaws that Arise if the Essence of the Two Truths Is the Same

There are an attendant four flaws of singularity if the two truths are considered to be as one, or the same.

- The first flaw is that whatever is seen by beings as conventional reality must also be ultimate reality, since they are of one essence. So to see the conventional must be also to see the ultimate.
- The second flaw is that in conventional reality, karma and afflictive emotions increase based on contaminated afflictive emotions. Thus, ultimate reality must also be a condition for causing contaminated afflictive emotions to increase in this same way.
- The third flaw is that in the same way that ultimate reality cannot be classified or described, conventional reality also cannot be classified or described.
- The fourth flaw is that since we can all see and hear conventional reality, we would also have to be able to see and hear ultimate reality.

Mipham Rinpoche on the Relationship of the Two Truths

You may be wondering, "What's the point of hearing all of these flaws of asserting the two truths in this way?" There is a very important reason! It is said in the sutras that no matter whether you think the defining characteristics of karmic formation and ultimate reality are one or distinct, either way you will engage in wrong view. Mipham Rinpoche says it is our own human tendency to always grasp at things as either being one or distinct. It is only by surpassing our tendency to grasp at singularity or distinctness that these eight flaws will not arise.

When the two truths are free of both singularity and distinctions, we actually realize why it is important for Mipham Rinpoche to assert the two truths in this way. No matter if the two truths were singular or distinct, sentient beings and buddhas would have the relationship of cause and result, rather than being in a continuum. The way that Mipham Rinpoche posits it, rather, is that there is a way things appear, and in dependence on that, there is also the expression of the actual ultimate nature. If we posit sentient beings and buddhas as cause and result, then the Secret Mantrayana teachings are exactly the same as those of the Causal Vehicle. Instead, it is posited that we are ordinary sentient beings, but we are also primordially buddhas. This is a very different kind of assertion. It asserts the view of the Resultant Vehicle. If buddhahood were a result, then it would have to be created by causes and conditions; it would be impermanent or subject to destruction. It would be compounded rather than uncompounded.

Mipham Rinpoche says that the relationship between sentient beings and the buddhas is such that the buddha nature is obscured based on adventitious obscurations. From the point of view of being unable to see the buddha nature or the expression of wisdom, one is a sentient being. But from the point of view of those obscurations being cleared away, or the essence of the being itself, one expresses the ultimate nature or buddhahood.

There is disagreement about whether buddha nature itself is compounded or uncompounded. I am confident that Nyingma scholars would answer that buddha nature is of the nature that we call the *great uncompounded*. Because buddha nature is uncompounded, there are no contradictions from the point of view of the nature of wisdom. If buddha nature is compounded, then logical difficulties can arise.

Mipham Rinpoche's understanding of *compounded* is a bit different than we might assume. He describes *compounded* as being created by something and being impermanent. Something that is uncompounded, because it is uncreated, has a quality of permanence. But Mipham Rinpoche calls this "sacred permanence" rather than ordinary

permanence. This points to the fact that although something which is ,
uncompounded is uncreated, it is not obstructed from expressing the
qualities of wisdom, such as expressing the three kayas.

The Nyingma school is often criticized for viewing the buddha nature
as being permanent, since we assert it is uncompounded. Some of the
Later Scholars assert the buddha nature as impermanent because they
view the buddha nature as being compounded. The general fault that
is attributed to the view of buddha nature as impermanent is that anything impermanent is of the nature of suffering; it is samsaric. So even
though one completely realizes or manifests buddha nature, one would
still suffer in samsara.

The Relationship between the Two Truths Is Like Fire and Warmth

In the next section of the text, Mipham Rinpoche asserts that the two
truths have a relationship that is like fire and warmth without falling
into any side whatsoever. The relationship between them is interdependence. For example, knowing that something is fire depends on it having the quality of warmth, and the quality of warmth is present based
on fire. This is also the relationship between appearance and emptiness.
We understand emptiness based on appearance, and all that is empty
appears. We may think that this sounds the same as *one essence and two
aspects.* Why is it different? The reason is because we are actually using
the language of interdependent origination in the statement. It is in
dependence on fire that we know warmth, and warmth depends on the
presence of fire.

In other words, the two truths are not of one essence nor are they
distinct, because there is no refuting or establishing. For example, we
do not have to abandon conventional reality in order to grasp the ultimate, and we do not have to abandon ultimate reality in order to grasp
at conventional reality. When things are interdependent there is no
need to refute one and establish the other. That is the defining quality
of interdependence.

We should know that this is an uncommon quality that Mipham
Rinpoche asserts in the path of the Secret Mantrayana. In all four lin-

eages of Tibetan Buddhism, Mipham Rinpoche is the only scholar to describe the relationship between the two truths in this way. The reason his teachings are flawless and unmistaken is because this text is written using the voice of realization. It is written from the point of view of his actual experience of meditation. It is only when we describe the relationship between the two truths as being devoid of singularity and distinctness that the view can rise to the level of profound, ultimate Madhyamaka.

Additionally, we can understand the relationship between the two truths, free of contradiction, from both the point of view of our superior intellect arisen from ordinary mind and also from the nature of suchness. For example, from the point of view of superior intellect arisen from mind, even when we understand the two truths to be the nature of fire and warmth, we can logically understand them to be beyond having a singular nature or distinct natures. When we examine them from the point of view of suchness, there is no need to even discuss this. This is uncommon because we usually only understand things to be without contradiction from the ultimate point of view rather than the conventional—not to mention both!

However much you study this text, you will become more and more convinced that Mipham Rinpoche is an actual emanation of Manjushri. Many texts have inconsistencies—what you read in the beginning changes in the middle or the end. There also may be flaws that the author has not anticipated, and so the text is easily taken apart through logic. However, this particular text is completely consistent in the beginning, middle, and end. It is in complete agreement. The meaning becomes more and more profound as we move from the first section of the text and then finally to this last section of the text that synthesizes the entire meaning.

Mipham Rinpoche says that if we posit the way of appearing and the actual state as having the relationship of fire and warmth, then many of the refutations and establishments that happen with conventional and ultimate reality become obsolete. For example, oftentimes, the ground, path, and result are either said to exist or not to exist, depending on the point of view. In actuality, we can posit their mere appearance and their ultimate way of abiding perfectly and without contradiction.

In summary, if we properly understand the relationship between the way things appear and the actual state, then no matter what we examine, whether it be the ground, path, or result, all can be understood interdependently and there is no contradiction in the way that the teachings are presented.

The Big-Mouthed Meditator

Conventionally, we can say that there are *mere* positions based on the way of appearing and that positionlessness is accurate according to the way that things actually are. Each time we examine the teachings, this aspect of differentiation encourages us to ask: From what point of view is this assertion being made? It brings the experience of the particular practitioner into the examination.

This is a very important pith of the Secret Mantrayana teachings. If we can understand this pith clearly, it enables us to understand the nature of the two truths, free of all doubt. This particular point is raised for the benefit of practitioners who the great master Sakya Pandita described as "meditators who have mouths as big as frogs and empty stomachs." This phrase describes practitioners who not only have no experience but who do not even realize that they are missing anything.

Whenever we engage in listening and contemplating, we should be precise. For example, some practitioners do not differentiate which position they are speaking from. This causes these practitioners to mix the ideas of conventional reality with the way things actually are. We might even hear Dharma practitioners say things like, "All phenomena are of an equal state; we don't really need to differentiate between good and bad, that is just labeling." From the point of view of our conventional lives, we do need to differentiate; we do need to be precise. We need to have standards for conduct and we need to pay attention to karma. For this reason, the great master Padmasambhava said, "Even though my view is as high as the sky, my attention to cause and effect is finer than flour." These words are for the benefit of the big-mouthed meditator!

Refuting the Argument That Many Teachings Establish and Refute the Two Truths

Next, Mipham Rinpoche anticipates another fault that a philosopher could raise. Many sutra, Madhyamaka, and *Prajnaparamita* teachings contain discussions that either establish or refute one of the two truths. For example, from the point of view of consciousness and ordinary perception of the ground, path, and result, we establish that the ground, path, and result exist. But from the point of view of the primordial nature, we often establish that the ground, path, and result do not exist.

Mipham Rinpoche responds that a given section of a particular text is simply trying to describe what it has set out to teach. For example, if a text talks about the conventional ground, path, and result, it is being presented from that point of view. None of these texts has the goal of establishing that the two truths are in contradiction. Again, it is important when we study any text to try to understand the point of view from which it is being taught. The author always has a point of view or a goal in mind when he or she teaches something in particular.

In this text, the two truths are discussed in a level of detail that you rarely read in other Dharma texts. If we become skillful at the two truths, we become very skillful not only as Dharma practitioners, but at helping others understand Dharma. Most people are not skillful at understanding the two truths. When we read most texts or talk to most people, they lump the two truths together because that is as far as ordinary practitioners can go. Of course, from the point of view of someone who experiences all phenomena as being in a state of equality, there is no need to take up or abandon anything. Judging by the fact that there are very few of these beings around us, it does benefit all beings and especially our Dharma communities to be skillful at understanding the two truths, because that is what helps people develop their understanding and their practice of Dharma.

Can Conventional Phenomena Be Existent?

Mipham Rinpoche presents another criticism that a philosopher might raise. This one relates to topic six and the qualities of water and wetness. *Can we understand conventional reality to not be of an empty nature, or to have an established quality? Can we say, from the point of view of consciousness, that we relate to conventional phenomena as being existent?*

The answer to this question is, of course, no. All phenomena—both their appearance and the way that they actually are—are primordially unborn. They are beyond concepts and characteristics. Regardless of the way we conventionally perceive phenomena to exist, they are of a primordially pure nature. Again, this is the reason we talk about "mere appearance," and posit the "mere existence" of phenomena. We can never posit or describe the two truths in isolation. The two truths must always be presented as being inseparable. "Indivisible wisdom" is a name that describes this inseparable nature.

Why Can't There Be One Truth?

Then, Mipham Rinpoche raises another question: *If we describe the two truths as being like the nature of water and wetness or fire and warmth, then why do we have to describe them as being two? Why can't there just be one truth?*

What is the purpose of teaching the two truths as being distinct? In this text, especially in topic six as well as other topics, we talked a lot about the analytical valid cognition of the two truths, and how valid cognition is like a continuum that becomes more and more subtle until we see with perfect purity, which is ultimate valid cognition.

Mipham Rinpoche says that without the analytical valid cognition of the two truths, our minds have no method for the realization of ultimate indivisible wisdom. In order to give us a method for realization, the two truths must be presented as differentiated ideas, rather than being presented in a singular manner.

So, in order to give beings the method for realizing ultimate indivisible wisdom, we absolutely must present and teach on the two types of valid cognition, and more specifically, analytical valid cognition. The teachings on analytical valid cognition make up what is called the path of Madhyamaka, or small Madhyamaka. We have talked about Great Madhyamaka, the Result Madhyamaka, or realization, but Mipham

Rinpoche describes small Madhyamaka as working with analytical valid cognition.

The result of Great Madhyamaka has three defining characteristics. It is profound, pacified, and uncontrived. When we realize Great Madhyamaka, we realize the profound, pacified, uncontrived, nondual nature of wisdom. If we want to realize the mind's nature, then training in the two types of analytical valid cognition must precede our realization.

Introduction to the Nature of Mind Using Symbolic Words and Methods

Another reason that the indivisible two truths are taught as such is because of the methods relied upon in the Secret Mantryana. There is a threefold method for introducing the nature of mind in the Secret Mantrayana: symbol, method, and upadesha. In other words, there are three different ways in which we could be introduced to individually self-cognizant wisdom. However, without the indivisible two truths as support, these methods cannot be relied on to further realization.

This section directly refers to the discussion of the absolute word empowerment that we engaged in topic four. It was said in the *Tantra of the Indestructible Essence* that indivisible wisdom must be shown through symbolic words and methods. This is because the essence of the mind, or wisdom, cannot be nakedly perceived by a dualistic mind.

The two terms *symbol* and *method* can also be described as "symbolic words and symbolic methods," which I think is a little easier to understand. They point out why it is so important to never discard the ritualistic aspects of Secret Mantrayana practice, saying they are just "cultural" styles of practice. For example, offering the mandala or working with the bell and vajra are not mere ritualistic gestures; these are included in the threefold methods of symbolic words, methods, and upadesha that are used to introduce students to the nature of mind. If we discard these aspects of practice, our dualistic minds cannot be introduced to the nature of mind properly. So, rather than discarding these aspects of practice, it is more important for us to develop the ring of faith within our own heart, and then when the hook of that introduction is presented by a lama to whom we are closely connected, we will recognize it ourselves.

Even though symbolic words, methods, and upadesha are conventional aspects of practice, they are the methods used to introduce us to the unborn primordially pure nature. *Returning to the main question: Why do the two truths have to be explained in differentiation? Why can't we present them in singularity?* Again, even though the two truths are like fire and warmth, we differentiate between them because if we did not, then these symbolic words and methods would not be useful to us. We would not be able to rely upon them to understand or recognize the ultimate nature. It is nearly impossible to find a method to introduce an ordinary, dualistic-minded sentient being to the nature of mind without relying upon this tradition that has been established and has the power of blessings and succession of lineage practitioners behind it.

Practicing with the Two Truths

Our discussion of Mipham Rinpoche's text provides valuable insight as to how we can bring the two truths together. As ordinary beings who experience the world dualistically, we begin practicing the two truths by alternating between them. But the strength of this practice can lead us to experience the result of indivisibility. Of course, if we are a being who experiences no distinction between actual abiding and the post-equipoise period, then presenting two truths is not necessary. However, for a practitioner who experiences a distinction between a moment of actual abiding and his or her post-equipoise experience, then presenting the two truths distinctly as they have been in this text is not only reasonable, but it is purposeful and supportive.

If the two truths are not presented and differentiated, we will become confused about which truth we are talking about. If the two truths are presented in singularity, then we ordinary beings have no way to talk about anything. Longchenpa differentiates between them so that we can then precisely understand the meaning of the scriptures without contradiction. If we take this differentiation away, then Longchenpa's instructions that should clarify our understanding of the two truths—a defining characteristic of Mipham Rinpoche's own lineage teachings—

goes away. As a result, we are unable to understand the meaning of philosophical texts without contradiction. Also, we might apply the ultimate view to the conventional or the conventional logic to the ultimate, as there would be no clear way to distinguish them.

As we examine the two truths, many texts, such as the *Prajnaparamita*, present realization as being blocked by obscurations and obstructions that must be cut through. This is the dualistic manner through which we experience progress on the path. Again, this is presented from the point of view of beings who perceive in a dualistic manner. When we read teachings like these, we should understand that they are presented from the point of view and for the benefit of beings who perceive conventionally.

The ultimate nature is described as suchness, a state of equality. Many synonyms that describe that state are presented in the Secret Mantrayana teachings, such as the "view of Dzogchen," the "wisdom of great bliss," or "inseparable rigpa and emptiness." But this is just like a person who has more than one name. There are no classifications within the nature of suchness. However, there are different ways of expressing or trying to describe this experience, one of which may be more appropriate in a certain context.

We should understand that the purpose of differentiating between the two truths has to do with the perception or the point of view of the specific being reading the text, whether or not his or her mind abides in duality or beyond it. If we study further in the canon of texts, such as the *Prajnaparamita* texts, we will notice that they all focus on the nature of the two truths because this is the pith for understanding the Secret Mantrayana. It is said that "all the teachings of the victorious buddhas rely upon the nature of the two truths." When we reflect upon the implication of this quotation, it makes sense that the two truths could be the topic of an entire major treatise like this one.

In summary, we can say that if we were to describe the difference between a Dharma practitioner who is truly skillful and one who is not skillful, the line between them would be drawn based on how well that practitioner understands the meaning of the two truths and understands the relationship between them. *For example, how do the two truths work? How does one take up and practice the two truths? How do the two truths relate to each other?* If we understand the two truths properly, we naturally become skillful because it becomes easy to properly relate to the world around us. We properly understand karma, the nature of cause and result, and other important aspects of the path.

Realizing the Mere Empty Void Obstructs the Two Types of Omniscience

What are the consequences of realizing the empty void? If only the empty void is realized, then appearance and emptiness have become isolated or separated as we talked about in topics one and three. The result of separating appearance and emptiness is that the two types of omniscience—omniscience of the conventional and the ultimate— cannot blossom. Of course, each of the two types of omniscience is aligned with one of the two truths.

Even though we can say that a practitioner has realized the ultimate nature based on the realization of the empty void, this experience is incomplete; it is not the same as the authentic realization of the Secret Mantrayana. For example, the aspect of clarity does not appear in the realization of the empty void, so the knowledge of all conventional phenomena is not present if we understand clarity as appearance. Realization in this case is the mere result that is attained on the shravaka and pratyekabuddha paths.

Emptiness and dependent arising are taught to be inseparable for this same reason. Conventional appearances express based on unobstructed interdependent origination and are indivisible from the point of view of their unborn, empty nature. As a result, the two types of omniscience can be expressed. We could say that the pith of this explanation in our own lineage is that the way that things appear and the way that they actually abide both need to be placed within the context of Madhyamaka.

Understanding this point makes everything clearer. The Later Scholars' explanation of the ultimate nature can be said to be part of Madhyamaka because it is positionless; it technically fits the definition of Madhyamaka. But their presentation of conventional reality just follows after worldly opinion. This is something separate. In our own lineage of Madhyamaka, the way that things appear and the way that they actually are can both be placed within the context of the Madhyamaka and there is no separation between them.

When we really think about the inability to attain the two types of omniscience, the clearest example we can use is the simple one of the pillar: the pillar is not empty of itself but is empty of true existence. When the pillar and its own essence become separated, the cause of the two types of omniscience also becomes separated and isolated.

The Two Truths Are the Foundation

After studying the text and reading about the two truths, we might start to feel that there is very little difference between the sutra and the tantra. Mipham Rinpoche clarifies this at the end of the chapter. He says that there is a great difference between the sutra and the tantra, but he also points out that the teachings of both the sutra and the tantra rely upon the foundation of the two truths. So, their foundations are the same, in a sense. Generally speaking, we are able to attain the ultimate result of indivisible wisdom based on the valid cognition of the two truths.

Mipham Rinpoche gives an example of how rubbing two pieces of wood together gives rise to fire. In the analogy, one of the pieces of wood is the basis and the other is rubbed on top of it. If we think about each piece of wood as being one of the two truths, then as soon as the fire blazes, the wood completely burns up. Using this analogy for both sutra and tantra, it is based on the strength of the valid cognition of the two truths that all contrivance—existence, nonexistence, and so on—is burned away and gives rise to indivisible wisdom.

Transforming Ordinary Mind into Wisdom Using Method

If the two truths, or appearance and emptiness, are isolated, it is illogical for indivisible wisdom to arise. How could something isolated give rise to something inseparable? Inseparable wisdom has to do with transforming the essence of ordinary mind into wisdom based on method.

Descriptions such as "meditative equipoise" or "indivisible wisdom" can only be described from the point of view of the post-equipoise period. This is the only time that we can differentiate between the expanse of wisdom and ordinary conceptual experience. When we abide in the nature of all phenomena, however it is, resting in just that, there are no characteristics present, such as color, form, and so on. If any of those characteristics were present, we should recognize that we were not resting in actual meditation. Indivisible wisdom can only be experienced during actual meditation.

Our meditation is mostly conceptual in the beginning. In other words, our meditation is within the sphere of the superior intellect that arises from ordinary mind. Another way to say this is that we are not actually abiding; we are working with conceptual ways to practice meditation. Slowly, over time, we learn more methods and techniques. Because it is conceptual, our practice remains within the sphere of activity of the superior intellect.

This is good for beginning practitioners, since working with conceptual objects enables the perception of duality to dissolve over a long period of time. Some people ask, "When you experience indivisible wisdom directly, will the aggregates, sense bases, objects of perception, and so on, appear as they do ordinarily?" No, they will be completely purified.

If ordinary appearances are purified, then we might wonder if what we will see is the empty void, where emptiness is separate from appearance. The answer to that question is also no. The appearance seen by a buddha is beyond the empty void. The empty void has the characteristic of being obstructed, and that obstruction must be destroyed or cut through. Indivisible wisdom is beyond obstructions to be cut through. When these obstructions are not present, this is called the *setting of duality*.

The wisdom of the buddhas, which is beyond duality, is also beyond the extreme of appearance. It is actually indivisible wisdom. If no appearances are present, this is the definition of the empty void—but that is not what is being conveyed here. It is actually that the impure aspect of appearances has been purified. This is not the same as *nothingness* or an absence of appearance. Indivisible wisdom is also described as *thoroughly supreme emptiness*. If this were not the case, realization of the dharmakaya would not be possible and would cause illogical effects, such as the cessation of karma or cause and effect in the conventional realm.

Differences Between Sutra and Tantra

Mipham Rinpoche gives three defining characteristics of the tantras: they are clear, extensive, and the meaning contained within them is perfectly pure and unmistaken.

When we work with the path of sutra, method and wisdom act as reference points for each other. In other words, we gradually move along the path of sutra based on the two reference points of method and wisdom.

The approach of the tantra is completely different. When we think about method and wisdom, or appearance and emptiness, we do not think about them in relation to each other. They are primordially inseparable, their nature is unborn, and they are the vast expanse of wisdom. In this case, we do not need to alternate or rely on one or the other as a reference. That approach would imply that obstructions are present and must be destroyed. Rather, from the tantric view, we talk about the state of equality. If samsara and nirvana are in a state of equality, then samsara is not taken as the obstruction to be destroyed. Rather, if we think back to topic six, samsara itself is of the nature of great purity. *Samsara and nirvana are of the nature of great purity and equality.*

Another way to understand the difference between sutra and tantra is the way that we work with meditation itself. In the path of sutra, we receive teachings on the two truths and indivisible wisdom. Then we engage in analytical valid cognition and a period of examination. We take up inference as the basis for meditation. Using this as the foundation, a practitioner slowly progresses on the path.

For example, I could sit in front of you and teach about the two truths. You would think about it and think, "Oh, I think that meditation is like this!" Once you gain inner certainty about what meditation is, then you just practice.

A completely different approach is taken in the tantra, and more specifically, the Secret Mantrayana. In the tantric style of Buddhist practice, yogis are directly introduced to inseparable, primordial wisdom through recognition based on individually self-cognizant wisdom. That introduction is done through so-called "forceful means," which means that when the student has deep devotion in the lama and the lama introduces the nature of mind, the lama energetically wakes the student up. Instantaneously, the practitioner can have the experience of the wisdom of great bliss. It is a manifest, direct experience rather than the mere thinking, "Oh, I think meditation is like this." Because experience is the basis for training in meditation, it is beyond inference. That is a major difference between the approaches of meditation taken by the sutra and the tantra.

Since we are studying the path of Secret Mantrayana, most of us probably think that the way that the Indestructible Vehicle works is superior. It is quite wonderful, but it requires that the lama and the student not only both be fully qualified but that they have an uncommon connection. Also, for that direct introduction to take place, the student has to have strong devotion.

If you wonder how to practice a path that has fewer obstacles, I would advise first taking up the path of sutra. For example, when you study Madhyamaka and the two truths and then take up the teachings of the Secret Mantrayana, you become free of all the darkness of doubt regarding the path, the view, and what meditation is. Fewer obstacles arise on this path. While it is possible to take up the path of tantra without taking up the path of sutra, the chance of us actually completing the path and attaining realization are much higher if we take up the path of sutra as well.

We light the beacon of certainty within us based on this kind of practice.

Finally, we could also differentiate sutra and tantra based on consciousness and wisdom. We could say that on the path of sutra, one takes up consciousness and works with superior intellect arisen from ordinary mind to slowly purify and work with the consciousness to bring about the realization of wisdom. Whereas in the tantric path and especially the path of Dzogchen, we directly take up wisdom itself as the path, rather than consciousness.

The Ultimate Nature

Mipham Rinpoche includes several things in this chapter that we need to know as Secret Mantrayana practitioners. The first is about the

Tibetan word *neluk* (Tib. *gnas lugs*), which is often translated into English as the *ultimate nature.*

Both Mipham Rinpoche and Khenpo Kunpal's commentary point out the many different ways that this particular word is used. In the sutra, it is used to describe ideas like the nature of the cause of Madhyamaka and the result of Madhyamaka. It is used when describing the ultimate nature of the aggregates, sense bases, and sources of perception as emptiness.

Mipham Rinpoche points out that even when we talk about the ultimate nature of something, we need to understand to what level the term "ultimate nature" is being taken. The phrase "ultimate nature" is pervasive throughout all Buddhist teachings, but the phrase does not mean the same thing in every text or at every level of teaching; it depends on the context. For example, if we really go into defining the ultimate nature from the point of view of the Secret Mantrayana, we learn that it is not the nonaffirming negative. It is inseparable appearance and emptiness.

On the other hand, when we talk about the ultimate nature in the sutra and Madhyamaka teachings, it remains within the sphere of superior intellect arisen from ordinary mind. It does not go beyond the intellectual level. Since it is confined to superior intellect, it can never reach the definition of the ultimate nature that is being put forth in the Secret Mantrayana.

When we talk about the ultimate nature in Dzogchen, we are specifically referring to the mind's primordial nature endowed with the three inseparable characteristics of a clear nature, empty essence, and omnipresent compassion. If there were any separation between them—if we could count them as one or many or put them into any conceptual sphere—then again, this would fall into the sphere of superior intellect and it would not rise to the level of Dzogchen.

Even within the Secret Mantrayana tradition, *ultimate nature* is used in different contexts; it is used in generation stage practice, perfection stage, and the union of generation and perfection stage. We need to understand what ultimate nature means within the context of each teaching. This is similar to the way our understanding of Madhyamaka becomes more profound the more precise that we are in our analysis.

If we think back over this text, we can reflect upon the ways that the different philosophies described the ultimate nature, especially in the context of the nonaffirming negative and indivisible wisdom. These phrases both describe the ultimate nature as viewed by two different schools, but they have incredibly different meanings. If we read a text that describes the ultimate nature as being synonymous with the non-affirming negative, we should think that the definition of the ultimate nature is something completely different than what is being conveyed by the Secret Mantrayana. Followers of Longchenpa describe the ulti-mate nature as indivisible wisdom. It can never be the nonaffirming negative.

CHAPTER ELEVEN

Concluding the Text

M IPHAM RINPOCHE concludes his text with a summary that begins with rejoicing, gives commentary on the mantra of Manjushri, and finally gives a summary of the meaning of the entire text.

Rejoicing

Mipham Rinpoche concludes his text by beginning with rejoicing. He describes the many benefits of studying this text, especially since it answers these seven incredibly difficult questions and helps us to realize their meaning.

Seven questions were posed at the beginning of the text based on an encounter on the road between a wanderer and a sage. If we think back, we remember that both the wanderer who asks the questions and the sage who answers were acting out an internal dialogue between Mipham Rinpoche and his own mind. The sage is described as having an impartial, honest mind. The wanderer knows that there is a profound meaning to be understood, but sees many contradictions in the path. As a result, his mind is agitated by many questions and doubts. The sage answers the wanderer's questions based on having realization of profound emptiness and taking into account the complete meaning of the sutras and tantras. Now, after hearing the explanations given on the seven topics, the wanderer says that his mind has become completely free of all the darkness of doubt. He rejoices based on his honest respect and devotion for the sage and the authentic Dharma.

The wanderer says that before he heard the answers, he was like a frog in the well that only believed in what he had heard himself. This is a reference to practitioners who are prejudiced and focused on the teachings of their own lineage and find fault with all others with an attitude of jealousy or competitiveness. Like the frog in the well, the wanderer had never seen the ocean, but after hearing the answers to the seven questions, he can now see the entire expanse of the ocean around him. This is cause for great rejoicing, since all of his prejudice was destroyed.

Mipham Rinpoche probably did not really feel these things as he wrote the text, but he sets an example for us, because we ordinary beings tend to denigrate the teachings of others. We will often focus on one kind of teaching but not another, saying, "This is a Nyingma teaching," or "This is a Kagyu teaching." Mipham Rinpoche says this attitude accumulates negative karma that will one day cause us to abandon the Dharma.

The Importance of Studying this Text

Additionally, Khenpo Kunpal's commentary emphasizes that we should study *The Beacon of Certainty*. It presents the ideas of the indivisible mind of Longchenpa and Rongzom Pandita. There are many great texts within the Nyingma tradition, for example, Longchenpa's *Seven Treasuries*, as well as the texts that are the cycle of three: *Rest for the Mind*, *Self-Liberation*, and *Dispelling Darkness*. Khenpo Kunpal says that it would be a great mistake to put this text aside to study these other texts that some might consider to be more profound.

It also says that if we are taught the meaning of *The Beacon of Certainty*, and study it carefully, if we are also endowed with excellent faculties of faith and intelligence, we will absolutely attain certainty. When we attain certainty, we will destroy the *maras* of obstacles.

If we do not gain certainty as practitioners, then doubt will always invade the mind. Certainty enables us to cut through our doubts. The commentary also states that for Dharma practitioners who make the instructions and the meaning of this text important and take it up as the basis of their practice, their practice will be unequaled by other practitioners.

Additionally, Mipham Rinpoche says that any practitioner who has studied *The Beacon of Certainty*, and takes its meaning to heart, should be respected and relied upon as a teacher. Even if that one looks like a thief or beggar, he or she meets the definition of a supreme lama because he or she is endowed with supreme certainty free of all doubt. When Mipham Rinpoche talks about supreme certainty, we must remember that he is not talking about intellectual certainty, nor is he is talking about mere experiential certainty. He is talking about irreversible certainty combined with the ability to abide in meditative equipoise.

Even if a being appears to be a supreme lama, if he or she does not know the meaning of texts such as this one, he or she should not be the supreme teacher of your reliance.

Manjushri's Mantra

The essence of all Dharma is the nature of suchness or the nature of things just as they are. Mipham Rinpoche says that the nature of suchness completely condenses into the six syllables *AH RA PA TSA NA DHIH*. He goes on to explain why the entire meaning of Atiyoga Dzogchen condenses into these syllables.

As background, there are several reasons why Mipham Rinpoche would choose this mantra, the mantra of Manjushri. The first is because Mipham Rinpoche is ultimately indivisible from the essence of Manjushri. But even from a relative perspective, he was the type of realized practitioner who saw Manjushri and even had opportunities to ask questions and have Manjushri answer them directly. For this reason, based on his own realization and his connection with Manjushri, Mipham Rinpoche tells us that the entire meaning of Dharma or the ultimate state condenses into this mantra. This mantra is taken up by practitioners in Tibet in order to increase their supreme intelligence or to increase their ability to understand the meaning of the profound teachings. Practitioners in the shedra at monastic colleges will take up this mantra, for example, as well as children as they go to school. Also, this mantra is often done as guru yoga. Practitioners will visualize Mipham Rinpoche as the object of their guru yoga, and they will use this mantra in the way that we Nyingmapas practice guru yoga with Padmasambhava.

Mipham Rinpoche gives a short explanation of the meaning of each syllable. Also, he says that by using these six syllables, one will realize the entire meaning of sutra and tantra, and the meaning of all profound and vast teachings.

The first syllable, *AH*, is symbolic of the unborn nature of all phenomena. *AH* symbolizes the path of trekchöd and todgyal. Because it symbolizes the unborn nature, it is the door to the realization of all phenomena as unborn. That is why I often instruct students that when a strong conceptual thought or afflictive emotion arises, use the syllable *AH* to release it. Using the syllable *AH* enables us to develop new experience in meditation. In summary, we could say that *AH* is the method for the realization of the unborn nature, and it is a symbolic method for pointing out the mind's nature.

For a Dzogchen yogi, the syllable *AH* is said to be supreme among all syllables and letters. This is true in many languages, and especially the Tibetan language, where the first syllable that children speak is often the syllable *AH*. For example, in Tibetan, the word for mother and father is Apa and Ama, and that is similar in many languages. So *AH* is even the first syllable vocalized by a Tibetan child. In any case, using the syllable *AH* during meditation practices is profound, useful, and potent.

RA is symbolic of stainlessness. From the point of view of establishing our own benefit, the stains are our own obscurations, for example, desire or other afflictive emotions. These obscurations are completely purified by the syllable *RA*. When we abide in or rest on top of the mind's own nature, all afflicted emotions self-liberate based upon the various styles of self-liberation. But without relying upon the recitation of the six syllables as Mipham Rinpoche presents them, we do not know how to recite or work with the method of connecting with the essence of the ultimate nature.

The syllable *PA* is symbolic of the appearance of the ultimate nature. When we abide in meditative equipoise, free of all modes of grasping, we know that, as was said by the great master Sakya Trakpa Gyaltsen, "If any grasping is present at all, then it is not the view." But we also know that abiding in the view is not like sleeping. It is not just a blank or void experience. If so, then this would not be the door to the appearance of the ultimate nature. We say it is the symbolic door to directly seeing the union of clarity and emptiness.

In general, if you recite these syllables slowly, vocalizing each one as you are working on resting or practicing, it will create the condition for the symbolic meaning of each syllable to arise. This is called ultimate recitation. You will actually have a different energetic experience of each syllable. You could try this. If the ultimate nature were devoid of appearance, then it could not be the ultimate nature as we discuss it in the teachings of Dzogchen. It would be the mere ultimate, it would be the empty void, but it would not be the actual ultimate nature. We talked a lot about qualifying the word for the term "ultimate nature" in topic seven. If appearance were missing from the actual experience of resting, then *PA* would be missing from this series of syllables and so the series of syllables would also not be complete.

The syllable *TSA* is symbolic of that which is undying, unmoving, or unchanging. The literal translation is that *TSA* is the door to the "undying nature of suchness." We begin by working with the valid cognition of the two truths. Based on that, we abide in the experience of meditation. That experience can be described as not only unchanging but beyond death or any movement, beyond any arising or passing away. Because we are habituated to see everything as arising and passing away in our conventional life, we have the habitual tendency to perceive things as such. This syllable is symbolic of the fact that actually, ultimately, the nature of phenomena is unchanging and beyond arising and passing.

The syllable *NA* is symbolic of knowing that the nature of suchness is beyond words and names. This is because if something were the object of sounds and concepts, it would not be Dzogchen; Dzogchen is beyond these. However, without words, there would be no method to introduce beings to the teachings of the Secret Mantrayana.

Syllables, these words and names, are absolutely necessary for us as ordinary beings on the path. This is the purpose of our tradition, as Vajrayana Buddhists, of respecting texts, respecting things that have written words on them—not only Tibetan texts, but those in the English language—for without them we would have no method for understanding Vajrayana. We would not be able to learn anything about Dzogchen or any other Dharma teachings. It is not that the texts themselves have conceptual thoughts, it is not that it bothers the text when you step over it, or that you put it on the floor, but you are not showing respect for the method that you rely upon to attain realization. This does not just apply to texts but to anything that we use to support your Dharma practice. We should treat all of these things with respect, as they provide direct support for realization.

The final syllable, *DHIH*, is the essence or the heart of Manjushri. It is his heart syllable. It is symbolic of directly realizing profound wisdom. We should know that it speaks to the realization of the nature of suchness itself—for example, the teachings as presented in the vehicle of the *Prajnaparamita* or the Secret Mantrayana, whether one takes a position or no position, and how to understand the teachings free of any contradiction. These are all related to our ability to directly see the nature of suchness itself.

The Final Summary

Mipham Rinpoche presents a final summary in the conclusory section, where each of the questions and answers is summarized into one sentence. A summary of these is as follows:

- The first question and answer is the way to practice the actual meditation of indivisible appearance and emptiness.
- The second question and answer profoundly shows what is and what is not the sphere of activity of the shravakas and pratyekabuddhas. It also shows that meditation on inseparable appearance and emptiness is an uncommon defining quality of the Secret Mantrayana.
- The third question and answer is the way to meditate on the union of appearance and emptiness just as it is. This includes working with both analytical and directly abiding meditation.
- The fourth question and answer is the way to then generate that style of meditation in one's own mind continuum, by taking the teachings from the third topic and trying to apply them.
- The fifth question and answer is the way that the two truths will appear to someone who has profound realization.
- The sixth question and answer is how phenomena display as the state of equality when one experiences realization.

- The seventh question and answer shows how to teach profound advice on the view to others in accordance with one's own realization.

Mipham Rinpoche goes on to say that the Buddha's teachings are inconceivably vast. It is hard to study everything, but he believes that if we study the seven topics as they are presented within this text, we will attain certainty that is free from all the darkness of doubt and find the marvelous path of the supreme vehicle.

Sarva Mangalam! May auspiciousness prevail!

Index

About the Author

ANYEN RINPOCHE was born in Amdo, Tibet, and his Dharma lineage can be traced back directly to the renowned Dzogchen master Patrul Rinpoche. After many years of extensive study and solitary retreat, he earned the degree of *khenpo* (master teacher) and became the head scholar of his monastic university. He has taught extensively in Tibet and China and now mentors students throughout Southeast Asia, Japan, and North America. He is the author of *Momentary Buddhahood* and *Dying with Confidence*, and lives in Denver, Colorado, where he established the Orgyen Khamdroling Dharma Center.

About the Translator

ALLISON GRABOSKI (Allison Choying Zangmo) is a student of Anyen Rinpoche and his root master, Tsara Dharmakirti Rinpoche. She has been studying Tibetan language and Buddhism under Anyen Rinpoche's personal guidance for the past twelve years. She is Anyen Rinpoche's personal translator for both Dharma talks and textual translations. She lives in Denver, Colorado.

About Wisdom Publications

WISDOM PUBLICATIONS is dedicated to offering works relating to and inspired by Buddhist traditions.

To learn more about us or to explore our other books, please visit our website at www.wisdompubs.org.

You can subscribe to our e-newsletter or request our print catalog online, or by writing to:

Wisdom Publications
199 Elm Street
Somerville, Massachusetts 02144 USA

You can also contact us at 617-776-7416, or info@wisdompubs.org.

Wisdom is a nonprofit, charitable 501(c)(3) organization and donations in support of our mission are tax deductible.

Wisdom Publications is affiliated with the Foundation for the Preservation of the Mahayana Tradition (FPMT).